During its campaign against France in 1940, the German army massacred several thousand black POWs belonging to units drafted in France's West African colonies. This book documents these war crimes for the first time on the basis of extensive research in French and German archives. A massive Nazi propaganda offensive approved by Hitler, reviving traditional images of black soldiers as mutilating savages, formed the background for the massacres. The book shows, however, that the treatment of black French POWs was highly inconsistent and that abuses were often triggered by certain combat situations. It connects the massacres of black French soldiers to the debates on the Nazification of the German army during World War II and places them in the context of the treatment of nonwhite "illegitimate combatants" in colonial wars.

Hitler's African Victims

The German Army Massacres of Black French Soldiers in 1940

During its campaign against France in 1940, the German army massacred several thousand black POWs belonging to units drafted in France's West African colonies. This book documents these war crimes for the first time on the basis of extensive research in French and German archives. A massive Nazi propaganda offensive approved by Hitler, reviving traditional images of black soldiers as multilating savages, formed the background for the massacres. The book shows, however, that the treatment of black French POWs was highly inconsistent and that abuses were often triggered by certain combat situations. It connects the massacres of black French soldiers to the debates on the Nazification of the German army during World War II and places them in the context of the treatment of nonwhite "illegitimate combatants" in colonial wars.

Raffael Scheck is Associate Professor for Modern European History at Colby College, where he has been teaching since 1994. He received his Ph.D. from Brandeis University in 1993 and his *Habilitation* from the University of Basel in 2003. He is the author of two other books, *Alfred von Tirpitz and German Right-Wing Politics, 1914–1930* (1998), and *Mothers of the Nation: Right-Wing Women in Weimar Germany* (2004). Professor Scheck has published numerous articles on German right-wing politics, Swiss funding for Hitler, and the history of childhood. His new project explores the experience of African prisoners in German POW camps during World War II.

*Dedicated to the victims,
to the French physicians and officers who tried to save the lives
of black soldiers, and to those Germans who helped to prevent
a massacre*

Hitler's African Victims

The German Army Massacres of Black French Soldiers in 1940

RAFFAEL SCHECK

Colby College

CAMBRIDGE UNIVERSITY PRESS
Cambridge, New York, Melbourne, Madrid, Cape Town, Singapore, São Paulo

Cambridge University Press
40 West 20th Street, New York, NY 10011-4211, USA

www.cambridge.org
Information on this title: www.cambridge.org/9780521857994

First published 2006

Printed in the United States of America

A catalog record for this publication is available from the British Library.

Library of Congress Cataloging in Publication Data

Scheck, Raffael, 1960–
Hitler's African victims : the German Army massacres of Black French soldiers
in 1940 / Raffael Scheck.
p. cm.
Includes bibliographical references and index.
ISBN-13 978-0-521-85799-4 (hardback)
ISBN 0-521-85799-6 (hardback)
1. World War, 1939–1945 – Atrocities – France   2. World War, 1939–1945
Prisoners and prisons, German.   3. Blacks – Nazi persecution – France.
4. Prisoners of war – Germany – History – 20th century.   5. Prisoners of war –
Africa, West – History – 20th century.   I. Title.
D804.G3S35   2006
940.54'7243'08996–dc22   2005018176

ISBN-13   978-0-521-85799-4 hardback
ISBN-10   0-521-85799-6 hardback

Contents

v

List of Figures

Preface

The idea for this project goes back to my time in graduate school. When I was preparing for my general examinations, I read in a French textbook on the Vichy period that a massacre of black soldiers had taken place outside of Lyon in 1940. No detail and no footnote were provided, and I did not pursue the matter further. After having written two books on German right-wing politics, however, I was looking for a new project and became interested in finding out more about the incident near Lyon and potentially other massacres of black soldiers. At the German Studies Association conference in 2001, I asked the eminent World War II scholar Gerhard Weinberg whether it was worth starting the project, and he very much encouraged me to do so. Since then, many scholars have given me advice and helped my project in a variety of ways: James L. Webb, Martin Thomas, Myron Echenberg, Nancy Lawler, Paul Gaujac, Antoine Champeau, André Siamundele, Alexander Rossino, Jürgen Förster, and James Quinn (in chronological order). Gerhard Weinberg provided helpful criticism of the project, as did another (anonymous) reviewer for Ohio University Press. Myron Echenberg and Nancy Lawler published the most instructive books related to my subject, and they both answered some special questions for me. I want to thank particularly my friend and colleague James L. Webb, who teaches African and world history at Colby College and shared his great expertise on French West Africa. His interest in my project has been as precious to me as his advice. The University of Basel allowed me to present my ideas on my topic as part of my inaugural lecture in January 2004. Paul Gaujac, former director of the military archives in Vincennes, amicably shared his rich insights about French military history. Two anonymous readers for Cambridge University Press offered much-valued suggestions for improving the manuscript. To my dismay, they discovered that my English contains not only the Germanisms that are to be expected from a German expressing himself in English but also Gallicisms that have crept from my research into my writing. Cathy Stankard and the copy editor at Cambridge University Press, Sara Black, gave the manuscript a close look and provided helpful corrections and suggestions. I also want to thank Gillian Berchowitz, senior editor at Ohio University Press, for soliciting extremely insightful reviews for my manuscript, offering me a contract in record time, and, especially, for understanding why I did not sign it. My children, Anselm and Adelia, deserve thanks for letting me participate in their amazing development and for taking my mind off the sad matters covered in this book, and my wife, Lori, has been a wonderful and most supportive partner. Melodies from our duets for violin and cello often resounded pleasantly in my head while I was writing this book.

I have been fortunate to work at an institution that values and supports not only my passion for teaching but also my dedication to research. This book would not have been possible without the support from the Social Science Division at Colby College, which gave me a travel grant for this project every year from 2001 to 2004. Moreover, Colby's Interlibrary Loan department under the leadership of Kathy Corridan was helpful beyond the call of duty. They provided me with more than two hundred books and articles for this project. Jackie Tanner from computer services gave me advice on how to draw the map.

The staffs of the French military archives in Vincennes and of its German counterpart, the Bundesarchiv-Militärarchiv in Freiburg im Breisgau, were admirably helpful. Their expertise and flexibility greatly facilitated my research. The staff of the CHETOM at the Musée des troupes de marine in Fréjus made me feel as if I were part of a large family. Colonel Antoine Champeau shared with me his great insights into French historiography of the Second World War, let me borrow a pile of books that I would otherwise have found only with great difficulty, and was a most generous host. Annie Domenech was always helpful by providing me with documents and giving me rides, which saved me from endless walks across the countryside on the scorching streets of an extraordinarily hot Provençal summer in an area with erratic public transportation. The departmental and communal archives I contacted in France were almost all extremely helpful and generous, belying the negative rumors about work in French archives that I had heard from colleagues. Some of these archives sent me copies of all the materials from their holdings pertinent to my subject. Véronique Blanchard at the town hall of Clamecy and Déborah Lutignier at the Société scientifique et artistique de Clamecy searched out important documents and gave me helpful advice. Janette Colas, a former member of the *Résistance*, met with me and shared some of the documents in her private collection. Miriam Lavie from the archives of the department Nièvre helped me get most of the photos. I am particularly indebted to Mr. Francis Alphonse, the mayor of Aubigny (near Amiens), who wrote me a long letter about the battles in his village and sent me copies from manuscripts and photos of the cemetery that contains the graves of black soldiers killed there at the end of May 1940. The German Military Research Institute in Potsdam patiently answered my inquiries about the positioning of German troops in May and June 1940. Finally, I thank the editors of the *Journal of Modern History* and of the *German Studies Review* for allowing me to use material from articles I published in their journals.

It is possible that more references to black soldiers could be found in the German records. On the advice of colleagues who warned me not to search for a needle in a haystack, I did not venture into the extensive collections of private letters from German soldiers (*Feldpostbriefe*); however, I did find some informative letters in the German military archives that were collected right after the campaign and, in some cases, after the war, as a contribution to a future history of a unit. Nonetheless, I am confident that the rich sources I examined offer a representative image of the attitudes of German officers and soldiers toward black soldiers in 1940. Given that explicit references to executions are extremely rare in the German documents, it is unlikely that the sources I did not consider contain much information about specific massacres. In France, it is possible that some local archives hold more materials about German crimes against African soldiers, but I have explored the most promising places. In any case, additional local information would hardly contradict my general points and conclusions.

Abbreviations

AK	Armeekorps (army corps)
BA-MA	Bundesarchiv-Militärarchiv (German military archives)
CHETOM	Centre d'histoire et d'études des troupes d'outre-mer (historical center for research on overseas troops)
DIC	Division d'infanterie coloniale (colonial infantry division)
ID	Infanterie-Division (infantry division)
NCO	noncommissioned officer
POWs	prisoners of war
PzD	Panzer-Division (tank division)
RIC	Régiment d'infanterie coloniale (colonial infantry regiment)
RICMS	Régiment d'infanterie coloniale mixte sénégalais (mixed Senegalese [West African] colonial infantry regiment)
RTS	Régiment de tirailleurs sénégalais (Senegalese [West African] infantry regiment)
SD	Sicherheitsdienst (security division of the SS)
SHAT	Service historique de l'Armée de terre (French army archives)
SS	Schutzstaffel (protection squad)

Introduction

On 4 December 1945, the president of an association of former French POWs in the Jura Mountains sent a letter to the prefect of the department Oise, about fifty kilometers north of Paris, indicating that he had found a witness of a massacre that had occurred there on 10 June 1940. The witness was Gaston Bousson, a former leader of the French resistance movement in the Jura and thus a person with excellent credentials. As a soldier in 1940, Bousson had observed two German officers overseeing the shooting of sixty-four black prisoners in front of a ditch. He claimed to remember the name of the village where this had happened and offered to travel to the Oise to help the local police search for the mass grave.

The prefect swiftly contacted the local police and the national service for war crimes research and ordered an investigation. A few days later a police inspector found a witness who had seen the shooting of ten black POWs in front of a mass grave in a tiny village near Saint-Just-en-Chaussée, and Bousson was invited to visit the department to help the investigation. When he arrived on 3 January 1946, the police and a representative of the service for war crimes research drove him through the area. They visited the place identified by the other witness and found a grave of thirty-six soldiers from West Africa a few kilometers from there,

1

in the backyard of the farm belonging to the mayor of the village Erquinvillers. According to local residents, these black soldiers had been "cowardly murdered" by the Germans after capture. Bousson, however, did not recognize any of these places. The name of the village he remembered did not exist in the department. The investigators brought him to some places with phonetically similar names, but Bousson was unable to orient himself and to find the site of the massacre he remembered. The police concluded that his memories were too vague to help their investigation. The representative of the service for war crimes research argued that it would be impossible to find out who exactly was responsible for the massacres and did not pursue the matter further.[1]

The scattered pieces of evidence revealed by this short investigation refer to a cluster of massacres that happened in this area on 9 and 10 June 1940. The victims were black soldiers from the 4th Colonial Infantry Division (DIC) based in Toulouse. These soldiers, called Tirailleurs Sénégalais, were part of the force that the French government had mobilized in French West Africa, a vast colony stretching from Mauritania and Senegal to Niger, according to a conscription law of 1919. Altogether, over 100,000 soldiers of the French army in 1939–40 were recruited in French West Africa (including some volunteers), of which approximately three quarters served in France, while the rest performed guard duty in France's colonies. While thousands of Tirailleurs Sénégalais were still in transit to the front or in training in southern France at the time of the armistice, it is estimated that sixty-three thousand of these troops stood in the

---

[1] J. Boichot to Prefect of Oise, 4 December 1945; Prefect of Oise to M. Dumenil, 7 December 1945; M. Dumenil to Prefect of Oise, 17 December 1945; Colonel Laboureur to Prefect of Oise, 4 January 1946; Prefect of Oise to J. Boichot, 7 and 19 December 1945 and 8 January 1946, all in Archives départementales de l'Oise, 33 W 8259.

frontlines against the German Wehrmacht in May and June 1940 and that approximately forty thousand experienced combat, of which ten thousand were killed and thousands more were missing in action.[2] Some Tirailleurs Sénégalais belonged to black regiments (RTS) and some to mixed units (RICMS). The officer corps of these regiments was predominantly white, although there were a few respected and well-known black commanders. Typically, a colonial infantry division combined RTS or RICMS units with some all-white regiments. The 4th DIC, for example, included the 16th and 24th RTS as well as the 2nd Colonial Infantry Regiment (RIC), which consisted of white soldiers and volunteers from other French colonies.[3]

How many black POWs were murdered on 9 and 10 June in the department Oise is unclear (the estimates in archival sources range from 150 to 600), but it is certain that these massacres were by no means unique. Whereas German troops, with some notable exceptions, treated white French and British POWs according to the Geneva Convention on Prisoners of War (1929), they dealt with the black Africans in a way that anticipated the horrors of the racialized warfare associated with the later German campaigns in the Balkans and the Soviet Union. The Germans often separated the black prisoners from the whites, North Africans, and soldiers from other colonies and subjected them to abuse and

[2] Myron Echenberg, *Colonial Conscripts: The Tirailleurs Sénégalais in French West Africa, 1857–1960* (Portsmouth, New Hampshire, and London: Heinemann and James Currey, 1991), 88; Ministère de la Défense, ed., *Les Tirailleurs sénégalais dans la campagne de France 10 mai–25 juin 1940, Collection "Mémoire et Citoyenneté" 10* (Paris: Ministère de la défense, 2001). This publication speaks of 17,000 casualties among the 40,000 troops in combat.

[3] Ch. Deschênes, "Les troupes coloniales dans la bataille de France (mai–juin 1940)," *L'Ancre d'Or*, no. 255 (1990): 30–1. Some Tirailleurs Sénégalais also belonged to West African infantry battalions and colonial artillery units.

neglect. On many occasions, black prisoners of war were shot – sometimes up to several hundred at a time. In some battles, moreover, the Germans gave no quarter to Tirailleurs Sénégalais, thus contributing to their unusually high casualty rate. Most of these incidents happened during the German offensive launched on 5 June against the French defenses along the Somme River and during the pursuit of the retreating French forces in the following two-and-a-half weeks. The abuse and killing of black POWs continued on the way to the POW camps and in the camps themselves, although the situation improved after August 1940 when permanent camps were built and when Germany renewed its interest in acquiring African colonies.

There were several investigations of the massacres against black POWs after the war, such as the one conducted in the Oise, but none of them led to a trial. Until the liberation of France in the summer and fall of 1944, the German occupation regime would have discouraged a judicial inquiry, and most potential French witnesses were in German POW camps and could not have been interrogated.[4] After the liberation, special tribunals were created for the prosecution of German war crimes, but most of them focused on more recent events, particularly the crimes committed during the fighting in France after the Allied invasion on 6 June 1944. On the basis of the French Law of 15 September 1948, which held all members of a German unit responsible for an atrocity unless they could prove *not* to have participated in it, several German soldiers and commanders were taken to court for crimes committed after 1940, but these trials were hampered

---

[4] The war crimes sections of the French and German national archives have no materials relating to a trial: Françoise Adnès (Archives Nationales de France) to author, 31 July 2003, and Melanie Wehr (Bundesarchiv Ludwigsburg) to author, 28 January 2004. For an argument regarding the difficulties of prosecuting crimes from the 1940 campaign, see Francis Rey, "Violations du droit international commises par les allemands en France dans la guerre de 1939," *Revue générale de droit international public* 49, no. 2 (1945–46): 7.

by controversies over the legality of punishing people for being unable to prove their innocence. In any case, the trials revealed how difficult it was to identify and track down potential perpetrators. Many witnesses and suspected perpetrators had been killed or were held in POW camps, where they could be difficult to find (particularly in the Soviet Union, which had the majority of German POWs and did not release much information about them).[5]

Still, it is hard to avoid the impression that the German crimes against French civilians and white members of the Free French forces were considered more important than the massacres of black POWs in 1940. The French efforts to investigate these massacres usually entailed little commitment. On the events in the region of Erquinvillers, for example, significant documentation had accumulated in the French official records by 1945, mostly in reports submitted by white French officers from the units that were destroyed there on the night of 9 to 10 June 1940. Had the service on war crimes research pursued access to this documentation in 1946, it might have been able, with the help of local witnesses and German documents captured by the Allies, to fill the gaps in Bousson's account and to gather enough evidence for a trial. Instead, the material languished in files of the French military archives that were closed to the public until the 1980s.[6]

---

5 Yves Frédéric Jaffré, *Les tribunaux d'exception, 1940–1962* (Paris: Nouvelles Editions Latines, 1963), 223–8.

6 Another example of a half-hearted inquiry is the investigation into the murder of the black Captain Charles N'Tchérérér (53rd RICMS). The French director of military justice in Paris had received a tip that N'Tchérérér, who was murdered in Airaines (Somme) on 7 June 1940, might have been one of the victims of the massacres near Lyon (hundreds of kilometers away from Airaines) on 19 and 20 June. It would not have been that difficult for a high military justice official to determine N'Tchérérér's unit and to find out where it actually did fight. See Archives départementales du Rhône, Lyon 3808 W 908 (Tchérérér).

What motivated the German atrocities against black soldiers from the French army? In their study *Crimes of Obedience*, Herbert Kelman and Lee Hamilton discuss the concept of "sanctioned massacres," defined as "acts of indiscriminate, ruthless, and often systematic mass violence, carried out by military or paramilitary personnel while engaged in officially sanctioned campaigns, the victims of which are defenseless and unresisting civilians, including old men, women, and children."[7] Obviously, civilians were not victimized by Wehrmacht atrocities against blacks in 1940, but soldiers who have surrendered and been disarmed are just as helpless as civilians. Therefore some of the observations that Kelman and Hamilton derive from sanctioned massacres committed by the U.S. Army in Vietnam also apply to the executions of black POWS in 1940.

The first criterion for a sanctioned massacre is authorization.[8] It needs to be evident that violence against defenseless groups is, even if not ordered, *permitted* or *encouraged* by the authorities in charge. Although some perpetrators may be sadists, such predisposition is not necessary for massacres to occur on a larger scale if soldiers believe that the authorities condone excessive violence. As will be shown, the German commanders in 1940 had no orders to shoot black POWs, but they considered killing them a legitimate choice under certain circumstances, even though they knew that this contradicted the Geneva Convention. The men carrying out mass executions[9] usually acted on the orders

---

7 Herbert C. Kelman and V. Lee Hamilton, *Crimes of Obedience: Toward a Social Psychology of Authority and Responsibility* (New Haven: Yale University Press, 1989), 12. For a confirming approach, see James Waller, *Becoming Evil: How Ordinary People Commit Genocide and Mass Killing* (Oxford and New York: Oxford University Press, 2002).

8 Kelman and Hamilton, *Crimes of Obedience*, 17.

9 An anonymous reviewer asked me to substitute "murder" or "killing" for "execution," because "execution" implies that some legal procedure, no matter

of their officers, and when they committed individual acts of violence against black POWs, they could justify their behavior with reference to the massacres ordered by officers. Violence against black POWs was never prosecuted by the Nazi authorities. The only known legal case concerns a soldier of a Waffen-SS unit who *refused* to shoot a wounded black POW. The soldier was acquitted of criminal charges by an SS court but expelled from the SS.[10]

A second criterion is routinization. Although moral scruples may be present when soldiers carry out a sanctioned massacre the first time, such scruples tend to vanish as the killing is repeated. Christopher Browning persuasively documented this process in a German reserve police battalion involved in the execution of Jews in Poland in 1942–43. Some men who had at first been revolted by their orders turned into hardened, ruthless killers with the help of lavish amounts of alcohol. In the words of social psychologist Ervin Straub, they practiced "learning by doing."[11] In the Western campaign of 1940, the time span between the first and last executions of black POWs was relatively short (less than one month), but some units were repeatedly involved in massacres and thus likely to have experienced routinization.

how distorted, took place. I did not find this nuance relevant enough to adopt the suggestion. Most massacres of black soldiers probably occurred without any legal procedure, but they were a legitimate act of reprisal in the minds of many German officers. The decisive point is that all massacres were illegal. Whether a feigned legal procedure occurred or not seems secondary to me. I therefore use "execution," "massacre," and "murder" (as well as the related verbs) interchangeably.

[10] Robert W. Kesting, "Blacks Under the Swastika: A Research Note," *Journal of Negro History* 83 (1998): 95.

[11] Christopher R. Browning, *Ordinary Men: Reserve Police Battalion 101 and the Final Solution in Poland* (New York: Harper Row, 1992); Ervin Staub, *The Roots of Evil: The Origins of Genocide and Other Group Violence* (Cambridge and New York: Cambridge University Press, 1989), xi.

Moreover, we have to consider that the German army had already committed crimes against civilians and POWs in Poland in September 1939. While shooting civilian hostages and POWs the previous fall, a significant number of German soldiers fighting in France had gathered experience in mass executions. This must have made it easier for them to shoot black POWs.[12]

The last criterion for a sanctioned massacre is dehumanization. Soldiers are more willing to engage in systematic killing if they can strip their victims of human status, denying them an individual identity. Dehumanization occurs more readily if directed against groups who have experienced a long history of discrimination and hatred.[13] As will be shown, German public discourse had stigmatized black men in arms from the colonial wars of the early 1900s right up to the Western campaign of 1940. They were depicted as cruel savages and animals – as illegitimate combatants not worthy of the legal protection granted to white soldiers.

While Kelman and Hamilton focus on the massacres of civilians, John Dower has analyzed the Pacific theater of the Second World War as a "race war," a conflict in which racial stereotypes transformed individual enemies into a mass of dehumanized beings to whom moral principles did not apply. This view served to justify unspeakable cruelties against POWs and enemy civilians on both sides. Dower takes a cynical view by claiming that "atrocities follow war as the jackal follows the wounded beast." The fallacy, he argues, lies not in ill-grounded rumors of enemy atrocities but in suggesting that such behavior is peculiar to the other side.[14] Although symmetry of race hatred – and atrocities

[12] Alexander Rossino, *Hitler Strikes Poland: Blitzkrieg, Ideology, and Atrocity* (Lawrence: University of Kansas Press, 2003).
[13] Kelman and Hamilton, *Crimes of Obedience*, 15 and 19.
[14] John Dower, *War Without Mercy: Race and Power in the Pacific War* (New York: Pantheon Books, 1986), 12.

legitimized by it – does not apply to the encounters of Germans and black Africans in 1940, Dower's concept of race war is useful when looking at German perceptions of the black French soldiers.

The German Wehrmacht did conduct a race war against black Africans in the Western campaign of 1940, which, as far as white soldiers were concerned, seems to have followed more conventional patterns of confrontation. The operational diaries of German divisions specifically recorded the presence of black troops on the other side of the front, in some cases warning against their "mischievous" way of fighting.[15] Members of German units involved in massacres carried with them the full baggage of racial prejudice that had built up over the past forty years and was heightened by a massive Nazi propaganda offensive during the campaign in France. They saw black soldiers as bestial, savage, and perfidious, and they described them in animalistic terms.

Germany's race war in 1940 primarily targeted blacks in the French army. The Tirailleurs Sénégalais, who formed the largest contingent of France's colonial troops, also included the vast majority of black troops in 1940. There were a few black soldiers from French Equatorial Africa, but recruiting efforts were much less organized there than in French West Africa. A group of black soldiers also came from small French Somalia, and some blacks were present in North African, Caribbean, and Madagascarian units. Soldiers from these units also became victims of German massacres in 1940. The Germans showed more respect toward North Africans with their generally lighter skin color, often hoping that these soldiers would desert and help Germany. During the battle near Erquinvillers, for example, Moroccan prisoners were ordered to gather with the white soldiers, not with the blacks

[15] BA-MA, RH 26–4, vol. 16, page 1.

who were shot.[16] But there was some ambiguity. Not all Germans making selections for a massacre were able or willing to distinguish between North Africans and blacks. Even a small number of white French officers in charge of black soldiers were murdered.

That the German army conducted a race war against black Africans is not surprising given that it served a state whose ideology posited a hierarchy of races and whose police apparatus ruthlessly persecuted members of "lower" races. In the German campaign against Poland in 1939, some aspects of a race war had already become apparent. The Poles were considered to belong to a lower race than the Germans (in blatant denial of the widespread mixing between Slavic and Germanic populations that had taken place over more than a thousand years), and atrocities against Polish POWs did happen. The worst offenses in Poland, however, were carried out by the SS, not by the Wehrmacht, which on several occasions intervened against the abuses committed by the SS.[17] During the German campaigns in Yugoslavia and the Soviet Union, aspects of race war became predominant even in the Wehrmacht, which actively collaborated with the SS and whose leadership approved orders leading to an atrocious treatment of POWs. A powerful racist propaganda helped to justify the classification of the Soviet enemy and of Jewish civilians as subhumans.[18] As we will see, the massacres of

---

[16] Long, CHETOM 15 H 144, dossier 24ème RTS.

[17] Rossino, *Hitler Strikes Poland*, 103–9.

[18] Omer Bartov, *Hitler's Army* (Oxford and New York: Oxford University Press, 1992); Christian Gerlach, "Verbrechen deutscher Fronttruppen in Weißrußland 1941–1944. Eine Annäherung," in *Wehrmacht und Vernichtungspolitik. Militär im nationalsozialistischen System*, ed. Karl Heinrich Pohl (Göttingen: Vandenhoek & Ruprecht, 1999); Christian Streit, *Keine Kameraden. Die Wehrmacht und die sowjetischen Kriegsgefangenen 1941–1945* (Stuttgart: Deutsche Verlags-Anstalt, 1978); Christian Streit, "Die Behandlung der verwundeten sowjetischen Kriegsgefangenen," in *Vernichtungskrieg. Verbrechen der Wehrmacht 1941–1944*, eds. Hannes Heer and Klaus Naumann (Hamburg: Hamburger Edition, 1995); Jürgen Förster, "Operation Barbarossa as a War of Conquest

black soldiers in 1940 form a missing link between the limited Wehrmacht atrocities in Poland and the full-fledged race war it later conducted in the Balkans and the Soviet Union.

The most prolific archival sources for the massacres of black POWs in 1940 are the records of the French army in Vincennes (SHAT). Although incomplete, they contain precious material from West African units involved in the campaign, including the operational journals of some units. These journals provide information about the nature of combat preceding the massacres and about the massacres themselves, but some of them end at the moment when the unit was surrounded or destroyed. This is unfortunate because massacres tended to happen just then. The best source of information on massacres, also in Vincennes, are the reports that the collaborationist Vichy government asked French officers to file on their experiences during combat, captivity, and escape or liberation from POW camps.[19] These reports, written shortly after the campaign, also shed light on the thinking of the Germans who ordered the massacres. White French officers in charge of Tirailleurs Sénégalais often recounted dialogues they had had with German officers right after capture. These dialogues could be amiable: The German officer, speaking fluent French, might offer drinks and cigarettes to a French officer, compliment him on the performance of his unit, and only casually express his astonishment that the French army had so many non-Europeans in its ranks. In other cases, an argument might break out over the use of colonial soldiers by the French. In the most dramatic circumstances, a French officer might desperately try to convince a German commander not to carry out a massacre, and the German commander might

and Annihilation," in *Germany and the Second World War. Volume IV: The Attack on the Soviet Union,* ed. Militärgeschichtliches Forschungsamt (Oxford: Clarendon Press, 1998).

[19] The notes in this book will list the last name of the witness followed by the folder in the SHAT that contains the report.

threaten to execute the captured officer together with the black soldiers.

In addition, a special research center on the history of France's overseas forces in Fréjus (CHETOM) holds a variety of documents on the Tirailleurs Sénégalais including some postwar inquiries and testimonies. Some local archives in France also contain important materials. Sometimes the building of a military cemetery, a monument, or a memorial site relating to a battle or a massacre triggered research by local citizens into the circumstances of Tirailleur deaths in 1940. This led in some cases to the gathering of eyewitness reports and other sources.

In Germany, the most important – though also incomplete – archival holdings are the Wehrmacht records in the German military archives in Freiburg im Breisgau. They contain orders, war diaries, personal journals, memoirs, and many other sources from the army corps commands down to single divisions and regiments. Although the German documents almost never explicitly mention massacres, they provide information on the nature of combat through German eyes, the context of the massacres, and the German perceptions of black soldiers. Newspapers, magazines, and wartime publications on the campaign, available in various libraries, add background to this information.

Literature on the German executions of black Africans in 1940 is scarce, and no focused treatment of the topic has been published so far. General works about the campaign of 1940 and the defeat of France often do not even mention the black Africans in the French army. Laudable exceptions are the works of Jean-Pierre Azéma and Roger Bruge.[20] Two books on African

---

[20] Jean-Pierre Azéma, *From Munich to the Liberation, 1938–1944*, trans. Janet Lloyd (Cambridge: Cambridge University Press, 1984), 39–40; Jean-Pierre Azéma, "Le choc armé et les débandades," in *La France des années noires. Tome 1. De*

soldiers in the service of France treat some incidents in more detail but do not consider German archival sources. The first, Nancy Lawler's *Soldiers of Misfortune: Ivoirien Tirailleurs of World War II*, is based on interviews with veterans from the northern provinces of Ivory Coast. The second, Myron Echenberg's *Colonial Conscripts: The Tirailleurs Sénégalais in French West Africa, 1857–1960*, presents a survey of the recruitment and deployment of the Tirailleurs Sénégalais. Lawler, who complemented her interviews with research in the French military archives, shows the intensely confusing and brutal experience of many black Africans in combat and as prisoners, but her focus is on memory and not on explaining why the executions happened. Echenberg refers to Lawler's materials and makes perceptive comments on the fighting of 1940, but his book is a long-range history of French military recruitment in West Africa and thus has a broader focus than the executions of black Africans in 1940.[21] David Killingray's essay on "Africans and African Americans in Enemy Hands" draws interesting comparisons between the treatment of black Africans and African Americans as POWs of the Axis powers but adds little to the information provided by Lawler and Echenberg.[22] The unpublished master's thesis by

la défaite à Vichy, eds. Jean-Pierre Azéma and François Bédarida (Paris: Seuil, 2000), 102 and 111; Roger Bruge, *Juin 1940: Le mois maudit* (Paris: Fayard, 1980), 117–18; Roger Bruge, *Les combattants du 18 juin: Le sang versé*, vol. 1 (Paris: Fayard, 1982).

[21] Nancy Ellen Lawler, *Soldiers of Misfortune: Ivoirien Tirailleurs of World War II* (Athens, Ohio: Ohio University Press, 1992); Echenberg, *Colonial Conscripts*. Echenberg used material from Lawler's dissertation (1988), which was also used later in her book. See also Myron Echenberg, "Morts pour la France; the African Soldier in France during the Second World War," *Journal of African History* 26, no. 4 (1985). This is an earlier version of the relevant chapter in *Colonial Conscripts*.

[22] David Killingray, "Africans and African Americans in Enemy Hands," in *Prisoners of War and Their Captors in World War II*, eds. Bob Moore and Kent Fedorowich (Oxford and Washington, D.C.: Berg, 1996).

Julien Fargettas, "Le massacre des soldats du 25ème Régiment de Tirailleurs Sénégalais," presents an excellent discussion of one massacre, but it is limited by the author's exclusive use of French-language materials.[23] In Germany, Peter Martin has published pioneering works on the history of blacks in the German lands, some of which cover the fate of black POWs in Nazi camps and briefly mention a few of the 1940 massacres, though without recourse to French documents.[24] Some information can also be found in biographies of the poet and first president of Senegal, Léopold Sédar Senghor, who was a Tirailleur in 1940. Senghor was almost killed with men of his unit after being captured near La Charité-sur-Loire on 20 June 1940. As in some other cases, the intervention of a white French officer induced the Germans not to carry out the massacre.[25] Some works on antiblack feeling during the Nazi period mention the massacres of black

---

[23] Julien Fargettas, "Le massacre des soldats du 25ème Régiment de Tirailleurs Sénégalais Région lyonnaise – 19 et 20 juin 1940" (Mémoire de maîtrise, Université de Saint-Etienne, 2000). For a summary, see Julien Fargettas, "Les tirailleurs sénégalais dans la campagne de mai–juin 1940," in *Les troupes de marine dans l'Armée de terre. Un siècle d'histoire*, ed. Centre d'études d'histoire de la défense (Panazol: Charles-Lavauzelle, 2001).

[24] The most important works are Peter Martin, "'Schwarze Pest.' Traditionen einer Diffamierung," *Mittelweg 36* 4, no. 3 (1995); Peter Martin, "'...auf jeden Fall zu erschießen.' Schwarze Kriegsgefangene in den Lagern der Nazis," *Mittelweg 36* 8, no. 5 (1999); Peter Martin, *Schwarze Teufel, edle Mohren* (Hamburg: Junius, 1993); Peter Martin and Christine Alonzo, eds., *Zwischen Charleston und Stechschritt: Schwarze im Nationalsozialismus* (Hamburg: Dölling und Galitz, 2004).

[25] Janet G. Vaillant, *Black, French, and African: A Life of Léopold Sédar Senghor* (Cambridge: Harvard University Press, 1990), 166–7; Jacques L. Hymans, *Léopold Sédar Senghor: An Intellectual Biography* (Edinburgh: Edinburgh University Press, 1971), 109; János Riesz, "Léopold Sédar Senghor in deutscher Kriegsgefangenschaft," in *Zwischen Charleston und Stechschritt. Schwarze im Nationalsozialismus*, eds. Peter Martin and Christine Alonzo (Hamburg: Dölling and Galitz, 2004).

soldiers, but they derive their information from the titles mentioned previously.[26]

[26] Clarence Lusane, *Hitler's Black Victims: The Historical Experiences of Afro-Germans, European Blacks, Africans, and African Americans in the Nazi Era* (New York: Routledge, 2002); Robert W. Kesting, "Forgotten Victims: Blacks in the Holocaust," *Journal of Negro History* 77 (1992); Kesting, "Blacks Under the Swastika"; Robert W. Kesting, "The Black Experience During the Holocaust," in *The Holocaust and History: The Known, the Unknown, the Disputed, and the Reexamined,* eds. Michael Berenbaum and Abraham J. Peck (Bloomington and Indianapolis: Indiana University Press, 1998).

FIGURE 1. Map of main sites of massacres mentioned in the text (places in italics).

1

The Fate of Black French Soldiers in 1940

FROM THE "PHONY WAR" TO THE "SICKLE CUT"

On 3 September 1939, France declared war on Germany in response to the German invasion of Poland. The French army mobilized quickly in the following days. Several colonial divisions, including many Tirailleurs Sénégalais, left their camps in the south of France and moved into positions on the Maginot Line, the defensive system on the German border, and along the Franco-Belgian frontier. Other units were mobilized in French West Africa and transported to France in the following months. Wishing for a better career and hoping that military service would win them French citizenship, young West Africans generally complied with the draft or even joined the French army voluntarily. Approximately 63,300 West Africans are estimated to have fought in France in 1940. They belonged to eight RTS units and contributed to eight mixed regiments (RICMS) as well as some smaller units.[1]

[1] "Troupes Coloniales en 1939–1940: La mobilisation et la période d'attente," *L'Ancre d'Or Bazeilles*, no. 256 (1990): 35; Ministère de la Défense, ed., *Les Tirailleurs sénégalais dans la campagne de France 10 mai–25 juin 1940*; Echenberg, *Colonial Conscripts*, 88; Catherine Akpo-Vaché, *L'AOF et la seconde guerre mondiale* (Paris: Karthala, 1996), 21–3.

The French army, committed to defense, saw little combat at first, and a period began that was soon dubbed the "phony war" in English and *drôle de guerre* in French. On 9 September 1939, nonetheless, some French units including the 6th RICMS and 16th RTS crossed the border and occupied several German villages south of Pirmasens in the Palatinate.[2] Given German propaganda detailing the alleged outrages of black French occupation troops in the Rhineland after World War I, this incursion might have been expected to create an outcry in Germany. Yet the German population in the border areas had been evacuated. Moreover, the French units only stayed until October, when the majority of the German army began leaving defeated Poland and taking positions in western Germany.

During the following six months, the western front remained quiet, as repeated German attack orders were revoked because of unfavorable weather. In November, following a practice established during the First World War, the French army returned the Tirailleurs Sénégalais to their bases in the warmer south of France to avoid exposing them to diseases prevalent in the harsh winter climate of the north. In the southern camps, the French High Command expanded the existing units and built up new ones with recruits arriving from West Africa. In April 1940, many West Africans were sent to the borders again, while others remained in the camps for further training.[3]

On 10 May 1940, the Germans unleashed their offensive against the Netherlands, Belgium, Luxembourg, and France. The French High Command, expecting the main German attack to come through central Belgium, moved its strongest forces into Belgium to form a defensive front together with

---

[2] CHETOM 15 H 141 and 15 H 145; Claude Paillat, *Le désastre de 1940. La guerre éclair* (Paris: Robert Laffont, 1985), 181–2 and 187–8.

[3] "Troupes Coloniales en 1939–1940: La mobilisation et la période d'attente," 30.

the retreating Dutch and Belgian armies. The main German thrust, however, came through the Ardennes forest in the border area of Luxembourg, Belgium, and France. On 13–15 May, the first German forces, having crossed the Ardennes, fought their way across the Meuse River. They established bridgeheads that allowed a massive force, including the bulk of Germany's tanks, to stream across northern France to the English Channel within one week. This "sickle cut" maneuver, which caught the Allied leadership by surprise, encircled the French forces and their British allies in Belgium. By 15 May, with the German bulge west of the Meuse growing rapidly, many French military and political leaders concluded that they had lost the campaign. As a consequence, Maurice Gamelin, the commander-in-chief of the French army, was replaced by General Maxime Weygand on 19 May.[4]

Tirailleurs Sénégalais and other colonial units from North Africa, Madagascar, and Indochina fought in some of the most exposed sectors during this stage of the campaign. One half-brigade of machine gunners from Madagascar put up a heroic defense in and around Monthermé, a French strongpoint on the Meuse River close to the Belgian frontier.[5] Further south, the 1st Colonial Infantry Division including the 6th RICMS and the 12th RTS rushed to counter an expected German move toward the southeast into the back of the Maginot Line. When the German forces turned northwest instead, the 12th RTS attacked German rearguard positions near Beaumont and Stenay (about twenty kilometers south of Sedan) on 18 and 19 May. In one case, members of the 12th RTS launched an attack under terrifying screams, using hand grenades and *coupe-coupes*, the

---

[4] For a detailed and up-to-date description of the campaign, see Julian Jackson, *The Fall of France: The Nazi Invasion of 1940* (Oxford and New York: Oxford University Press, 2003).

[5] Maurice Rives and Robert Dietrich, *Héros méconnus 1914–1918, 1939–1945* (Paris: Association Frères d'Armes, 1990), 150–1.

forty-centimeter-long knives that were the customary close-combat weapon of the Tirailleurs Sénégalais. German soldiers, who had begun to infiltrate the French positions, became scared and surrendered.[6]

During these battles along the Meuse, the Germans for the first time took large numbers of French prisoners. German soldiers and frontline reporters often expressed astonishment at seeing among them so many people of different races. A diary entry of a soldier from the 9th Infantry Division on 19 May reads: "The transports of prisoners coming toward us are growing bigger and bigger. There are flat faces of Negroes, Algerians with nostalgic almond eyes, Belgians with blond hair and the pert tassel on their hats, Frenchmen in all hair and skin colors."[7] Often this astonishment was underpinned with contempt for states that, unlike Nazi Germany, did not value racial homogeneity. The war diary of one battalion from the German 32nd Infantry Division, for example, recorded: "In droves, they walk toward us with white rags and raised hands: white, brown, and black 'bearers of culture' of the French...nation."[8] In another instance, a war reporter writing for the *Völkischer Beobachter* commented on the allegedly indistinct "African mixture of peoples" among French POWs, while finding some "good heads" among white soldiers in the same group, particularly those with "bold Norman or Breton features."[9] Still, no massacre of West African prisoners was recorded during this phase of the campaign, although German

6 Rives and Dietrich, *Héros méconnus*, 155–6; Louis Dartigues, *Des coloniaux au combat: La 1re D.I.C. en 1939–40* (Bordeaux: Amicale des anciens de la 1re D.I.C. 1939–1940, 1971), 86–7. See also CHETOM 15 H 141, dossier 1.

7 "Frankreich 1940. Tagebuchblätter und Berichte aus dem II/I.R. 36," BA-MA, RH 37/6420. This report is from a soldier belonging to Infantry Regiment 36 (part of the 9th Infantry Division), which later committed some of the crimes near Erquinvillers.

8 BA-MA, RH 26–32, vol. 11 (Anlagen zum KTB Nr. 2. Gefechtsberichte), p. 101.

9 Wolfgang Mansfeld, "Die Straße zur Front," *Völkischer Beobachter* 53, no. 146, 25 May 1940, p. 1.

propaganda claimed that the 12[10] RTS had mutilated German prisoners near Beaumont.[10] Captain Mathias of the 5th RICMS, captured south of Sedan on 24 May, observed how one white and one black soldier were shot in their hiding place because they did not surrender in time, but he claimed that the Germans treated all prisoners very well. Typically, captured officers were separated from the soldiers as stipulated by the Geneva Convention, but the soldiers were not divided by race as happened later during the campaign.[11]

The first recorded massacre of black soldiers occurred on 24 May in Aubigny, a village on the southern shore of the Somme River. While most of the German forces moving toward the English Channel remained north of the Somme, some units were ordered to establish bridgeheads on its southern shore in preparation for a later offensive toward Paris and the center of France. The French High Command tried to eliminate them, and several West African units were involved in these attacks.[12] One of the bridgeheads comprised Aubigny and Fouilloy, two villages a few kilometers east of Amiens. The 16th and 24th RTS, belonging to the 4th DIC, received orders to attack this bridgehead on 23 May. The 16th RTS moved to take Fouilloy and the 24th RTS to take Aubigny. Extremely hard fighting ensued. Whereas the

---

[10] Rives and Dietrich, *Héros méconnus*, 156. Barcellini and Wieviorka mention a plaque in Laxou near Nancy for eleven soldiers from Madagascar allegedly executed by the Germans in May 1940. The date must be an error, however, because German troops did not appear in that area before 17 June 1940. Serge Barcellini and Annette Wieviorka, *Passant – souviens-toi – Les lieux du souvenir de la Seconde Guerre mondiale en France* (Paris: Plon, 1995), 62. The town government of Laxou has no information about this incident: Brigitte Carpentier (Mairie de Laxou) to author, 1 October 2003.

[11] Mathias, SHAT 34 N 1070. For the lack of separation by race, see, for example, the records of the Madagascarian machine-gunners fighting near Monthermé: Laivorona, Ranarison, SHAT 34 N 1104.

[12] Pierre Rocolle, *La guerre de 1940: La défaite, 10 mai–25 juin* (Paris: Armand Colin, 1990), 229.

attack on Fouilloy failed, the 24th RTS accomplished a major feat of arms by reconquering Aubigny, though at a casualty rate of 30 to 40 percent. The next day, however, the German 13th Infantry Division counterattacked with air support and pushed the French out of the village again. It proved impossible for the French to take with them all of their wounded. When Lieutenant Hollecker, a physician from the 24th RTS, learned that fifty wounded Africans had been left behind, he decided to join them but was held back by his commander because of the dangers involved in approaching the village. Later, Hollecker found out from eyewitnesses that these soldiers had been murdered by the Germans.[13] On 26 and 27 May, during another French attempt to dislocate the German troops in Aubigny and Fouilloy, several wounded West Africans were killed by the Germans in front of the French medical aid personnel who were preparing to carry them away on stretchers.[14]

What caused the massacres of Aubigny is not clear. A memoir of veterans from the SS Totenkopf Division, which had passed nearby but not participated in the fighting, argues that isolated French soldiers had used illegal dum-dum ammunition.[15] Although this was an accusation frequently made by German soldiers during the campaign and echoed in German propaganda, it was denied by the German Army Command. Unfortunately, the war diary for this period of the German 13th Infantry Division, which fought in Aubigny, is lost, and the few other documents preserved by the German archives give no indication of motivation. A history of the 24th RTS written by veterans says that

---

[13] "Les attaques vers la Somme," CHETOM 15 H 144, dossier 7; Hollecker, SHAT 34 N 1097.

[14] Froissard-Broissia, SHAT 34 N 1095; "Les attaques vers la Somme," CHETOM 15 H 144, dossier 7.

[15] Wolfgang Vopersal, *Soldaten, Kämpfer, Kameraden. Marsch und Kämpfe der SS-Totenkopf-Division*, 5 vols., vol. 1 (Bielefeld: Selbstverlag der Truppenkameradschaft der 3. SS-Panzer-Division e. V., 1983), 136.

the Germans were angered by their heavy losses, but it does not reveal how this information was obtained.[16]

Over the following days, the front remained stable along the Somme although the French continued to attack the bridgeheads. The Germans meanwhile concentrated on eliminating the pocket around Dunkirk, where the Allied forces cut off in Belgium gathered for evacuation. Most West African troops, however, were stationed along the defensive line that the French High Command was preparing from the mouth of the Somme River to the Maginot Line. While the French hastily sought to fortify their position, dubbed the "Weygand Line" after their new commander-in-chief, the Germans prepared to attack on the lower Somme and later in the other sectors as well. Tank and infantry divisions streamed south as the pocket around Dunkirk contracted and finally ceased to exist on 4 June. Whereas the Germans had been roughly even in numbers to their opponents in May, they now enjoyed a clear superiority, and not even Weygand himself expected France to hold out for long.

THE BATTLES ON THE SOMME

On 5 June, at dawn, the Germans attacked on the Somme, making use of their bridgeheads and a few river crossings the French had neglected to destroy. Heavy shelling and several waves of bombers terrorized the defenders, and a massive force including tank divisions sought to dislocate them in the following hours. Fighting was heaviest on the southern shore of the Somme midway between Amiens and Abbeville, in and near the villages Hangest-sur-Somme and Airaines. Two colonial units, the 44th and 53rd RICMS, mounted heroic resistance against

---

[16] Jean-François and Raymond Mouragues, "Les tirailleurs du 24ème R.T.S. dans la tourmente de 1940," manuscript in the possession of the Mairie d'Aubigny.

overwhelming forces, including Erwin Rommel's 7th Panzer Division. Some pockets of French resistance in and near Airaines surrendered only on 7 June, at a time when German tank units were already fighting fifty kilometers further south.

During the combat around Airaines, the French used a new method of defense, the "hedgehog" tactic, which was applied in most sectors of the new front by the French and the few remaining British forces. Instead of trying to keep a continuous frontline at all cost and to contain quickly enemy forces that had broken through, the defenders now let superior German units pass and then attacked the Germans from the rear and the side from prepared strongholds in villages, castles, and forests. Most frontline French units had received the order to hold "*sans esprit de recul*" – without thought of withdrawing.[17] The Germans thus ran into unexpected resistance from hidden strongholds in areas they thought were under their control. This often led to bitter close combat, as the Germans tried to "cleanse" the hedgehog positions. The French tactic did succeed in slowing down the German advance in several places, but the armored counteroffensives, for which the hedgehogs were meant to buy time, rarely materialized.

The 44th and 53rd RICMS, which formed the backbone of French defenses in this area, belonged to the 5th DIC. Stationed in the Vosges Mountains near the Swiss border at the beginning of the German attack in the west, the 5th DIC was moved to the lower Somme in the last week of May. It took its positions in the region of Airaines only during the night of 4 to 5 June, at a time when German vanguards were already infiltrating the French advance posts south of the Somme. When a massive artillery and air force bombardment began in the early morning hours of 5 June, some groups of Tirailleurs Sénégalais, from

---

[17] Jackson, *The Fall of France*, 179; Alistair Horne, *To Lose a Battle: France 1940* (London: Macmillan, 1969), 489; John Williams, *The Ides of May: The Defeat of France, May–June 1940* (London: Constable, 1968), 276–7.

the 44th RICMS in particular, panicked and fled. The 44th RICMS had been drafted only recently in the Ivory Coast and lacked combat experience. In most places, however, French commanders stopped and regrouped the fugitives.[18] After the initial panic, the Tirailleurs Sénégalais fought heroically.

The Germans crossing the Somme on 5 June were surprised by the resistance they encountered. An exceptionally bitter combat ensued, and the Germans suffered heavy casualties as they fought their way from house to house in burning villages, swarmed through forests used as hideouts by dispersed Tirailleurs Sénégalais, and stormed ruined castles converted into defensive positions. An account from the German 6th Infantry Division exemplifies the fear and rage triggered during close combat with black soldiers west of Amiens on 5 June: "In one house Private Apke wants to search the basement with his pistol in his hand when a Negro jumps on him out of the dark and hits him three times with his bayonet. Apke, having received only a light neck wound, drops the pistol and takes the gun from the black man in a wrestling match. He rams the bayonet through the black man's chest. The wounded man screams and grabs Apke, trying to bite through his throat. Apke liberates himself from the huge Negro only with great difficulty. Still reeling and wounded from this fight, he calls his comrades. A hand grenade finishes off the Negro."[19]

From the beginning of their offensive on the Somme, the German troops vented their anger on the black soldiers and sometimes also on the white officers commanding them. After trying to defend a road near the Somme River, Second Lieutenant Joseph Latour of the 44th RICMS had to surrender

[18] Binet, Campos-Hugueney, Chaminot, Fortunade, and de Lapasse, SHAT 34 N 1079; see also Brugnet, Pilet, Vuchot, and "Récit succinct des opérations auxquelles le 2ème Bataillon a pris part pendant la période du 19 mai au 24 juin 1940," SHAT 34 N 1081.

[19] "Gefecht an der Somme am 5.6.1940," BA-MA, RH 26–6, vol. 108.

with some other white officers and a group of Tirailleurs Sénégalais on 5 June. He reported: "The enemy then appears, furious, beside himself, ready to finish us off all together. An extremely energetic intervention by a German officer prevents the troops from executing the European officers, but there was no indigenous man alive any more after a few moments."[20] In Hangest-sur-Somme, some captured Tirailleurs and a French second lieutenant were shot by Germans in black uniforms, most likely members of Rommel's 7th Panzer Division (the personnel of German tanks and armored carriers wore black uniforms).[21] During "cleansing operations" of forests near the villages Saint Pierre-à-Gouy and Cavillon, German soldiers showed no mercy toward dispersed Tirailleurs Sénégalais. At least fifty Africans belonging to the 44th RICMS were chased down and summarily executed after capture on 5 June.[22] A French captain who had defended a castle with Tirailleurs commented that the Germans seemed possessed by an "indescribable rage." When he surrendered on the evening of that day, he was handled roughly; his glasses were ripped away and smashed.[23] Another French officer commanding black soldiers witnessed more contradictory attitudes. When he surrendered in Condé-Folie on the morning of 6 June, a German captain, speaking fluent French, congratulated him on his skillful defense that had inflicted heavy casualties on the attacking battalion. Later, however, a German lieutenant threatened to shoot him because he had commanded black troops. In the end, the German battalion commander intervened and saved his life.[24]

By the evening of 6 June, the Germans had conquered most French positions in the area, but some groups of Tirailleurs

[20] Latour, SHAT 34 N 1079.
[21] Campos-Hugueney and Chaminaut, SHAT 34 N 1079.
[22] Fortunade, SHAT 34 N 1079.
[23] Brugnet, SHAT 34 N 1081.
[24] Cros, SHAT 34 N 1081.

Sénégalais still held out. When they were overcome, many more were massacred. A few kilometers to the south of the Somme, between Le Mesge and Riencourt, a French officer observed some German soldiers undressing black prisoners and killing them with captured *coupe-coupes* on 7 June. A German officer declared that from noon on no more black prisoners would be taken because black troops had shot at dispersed Germans, even though such shooting was not a war crime.[25] In Airaines, a village at the intersection of two important roads, a group of Tirailleurs under the command of Lieutenant Colonel Polidori and the black Captain Charles N'Tchoréré from the 53rd RICMS withstood several German attacks on 6 and 7 June. Neither the Allies nor even many Germans were aware that the place was still in French hands. On 7 June, Canadian and British bombers attacked the village two times, and German military vehicles repeatedly tried to drive through it only to face French artillery fire. Finally, on the evening of 7 June, the Germans stormed Airaines and captured most of its defenders. After surrendering, N'Tchoréré was shot in the neck by a German soldier when he ignored orders to join the black footsoldiers and insisted on being grouped together with the white officers. Some of the French prisoners and also several Germans, who had been held captive by the 53rd RICMS in the church of Airaines, protested against this murder.[26] An unknown number of his men, perhaps fifty, were shot in the village Le Quesnoy-sur-Airaines, a few kilometers to the east of Airaines, on 8 June. As a justification for the massacre, a German officer showed Second Lieutenant Jean Guibbert the corpses of three German soldiers who he said had been beheaded by Tirailleurs

[25] Pottier, SHAT 34 N 1097.
[26] Erwan Bergot, *La Coloniale, du Rif au Tschad, 1925–1980* (Paris: Presses de la Cité, 1982), 78. See also Louis Bigmann, *Le capitaine Charles N'Tchoréré. Un officier gabonais dans la tourmente de la deuxième guerre mondiale* (Dakar and Libreville: NEA and Lion, 1983), 107–22.

Sénégalais in the morning.[27] Lieutenant Colonel Polidori was interrogated by German General Staff officers who threatened him with disciplinary action because his Tirailleurs had allegedly fought like savages.[28] The German units involved in the operations against Airaines and nearby villages came from the 2nd and 46th Infantry Division and possibly also from the 6th and 27th Infantry Division (Rommel's 7th Panzer Division had already advanced much farther).[29] For its spirited defense of Airaines, the 53rd RICMS received a collective medal, and two monuments were erected in Airaines after the war, one dedicated to the unit as a whole and one specifically to N'Tchoréré.[30] The 53rd RICMS paid heavily for these honors, however. It was virtually annihilated in Airaines, suffering close to 90 percent casualties.[31]

THE DESTRUCTION OF THE 4TH COLONIAL INFANTRY DIVISION IN THE OISE

The 4th DIC had experienced the first recorded massacres of Tirailleurs Sénégalais in and near Aubigny at the end of May.

[27] Guibbert, SHAT 34 N 1081. Fargettas mentions altogether 112 corpses of Tirailleurs Sénégalais in two burial sites in the area of Airaines, but it is not clear how many of these soldiers were killed in combat and how many were massacred after capture. Moreover, the burial sites may include victims from massacres in neighboring villages. Julien Fargettas, "Der andere Feldzug von 1940: Das Massaker an den schwarzen Soldaten," in *Zwischen Charleston und Stechschritt. Schwarze im Nationalsozialismus*, eds. Peter Martin and Christine Alonzo (Hamburg: Dölling and Galitz, 2004), 567.

[28] Polidori, CHETOM 15 H 145.

[29] Bergot ascribes the murder of N'Tchoréré to an SS soldier, but there were no SS troops in the immediate vicinity. Bergot, *La Coloniale, du Rif au Tschad*, 78. Fargettas attributes the massacre of Airaines to the 7th Panzer Division. Fargettas, "Der andere Feldzug von 1940," 568.

[30] Echenberg, *Colonial Conscripts*, 166–8. Barcellini and Wieviorka, *Passant – souviens-toi*, 63.

[31] SHAT 34 N 1081. See also André Laboulet, *Les combats d'Airaines et environs. Juin 1940* (Abbéville: Lafosse, 1972), 7–10; Rives and Dietrich, *Héros méconnus*, 168–9.

The division had hardly recovered from the heavy fighting in this area when it had to defend its positions against superior German forces on 5 June. It held out valiantly at first but after two days had to fight a retreat to the south. On the night of 8 to 9 June, fast-moving German units (the 9ᵗʰ and 10ᵗʰ Panzer Divisions) outflanked and surrounded most of the 4ᵗʰ DIC in a group of villages between the small towns Saint-Just-en-Chaussée and Estrées-Saint-Denis, some forty kilometers south of the Somme. The slower-moving German 9ᵗʰ Infantry Division, which had pursued the 4ᵗʰ DIC out of the Amiens bridgehead, began attacking the pocket from the north on the next day.

What then happened is recorded in numerous reports of French officers. The commander of the 24ᵗʰ RTS, Amadée Fabre, witnessed widespread abuse of black POWs. After forming small groups of black soldiers with white officers for a breakthrough attempt to the south on 9 June, Fabre realized that 250 to 300 Tirailleurs were left behind without officers in Angivillers, a village four kilometers north of Erquinvillers. Declaring that the Germans took no black prisoners, he prepared the Tirailleurs for the defense of the village to the last man. After ten minutes, however, they were overrun by the Germans. Fabre reported: "After capturing us, the Germans treated the Senegalese with unprecedented brutality. They stabbed them with their bayonets and beat them with belt buckles. Finally a German officer ordered the abuses to be stopped, and the prisoners were led toward an assembly point along the railroad Angivillers-Ravenel."[32] When Fabre protested against the maltreatment of black POWs, a German colonel replied: "They are just savages." According to Fabre, the prisoners did not receive food and water for several days, and many died of thirst under the eyes of their guards.[33]

[32] Fabre, SHAT 34 N 5 1097.
[33] Ibid.

In Léglantiers, a neighboring village, Lieutenant Hollecker, the physician from the 24th RTS who had recorded the shooting of fifty wounded Africans in Aubigny, cared for twelve wounded Tirailleurs in the basement of a house during the night of 9 to 10 June. Hollecker, who spoke fluent German, hoped to save them by surrendering to the Germans. When he heard cries and shots, which he ascribed to nearby executions of Tirailleurs, he left the basement and called on a group of ten German soldiers. He identified himself as a physician and asked the soldiers to come and rescue his wounded men, whom he had disarmed according to the conventions on warfare. When the group arrived in front of the house sheltering the wounded, however, one of the soldiers asked whether there were blacks inside. Upon hearing that all the wounded were blacks, the soldier proceeded to the air vent of the basement, tore off the cover, and prepared to throw down his hand grenade. Hollecker nearly jumped on the soldier and appealed to his humane sentiments. One German who professed to have been a missionary came to Hollecker's aid. This was enough to prevent the massacre, and the group of German soldiers helped Hollecker to carry the wounded out of the basement and to a safer place.[34]

Meanwhile, groups of West Africans and dispersed white soldiers and officers tried to break through the defensive line the Germans had established in the south. In Erquinvillers, many were captured by the Germans after short combat. After separating white and black soldiers, the Germans set up machine guns and began shooting the blacks. Those who tried to escape were also killed. When Lucien Carrat, an officer from the 16th RTS, protested, German officers answered that some Tirailleurs had tried to escape by wounding German guards with their *coupe-coupes*. Carrat's demand to see proof of the crime was denied, and he was told that "an inferior race does not deserve

---

[34] Hollecker, SHAT 34 N 1097.

to do battle with such a civilized race as the Germans." Carrat claims that he put an end to the killings by officially apologizing for the outrages committed by his soldiers against the Germans – although he did not believe that these outrages had actually happened.[35]

In a forest not far from Erquinvillers, Lieutenant Michaël Dhoste was captured with a few other white officers and a group of Tirailleurs during the night. He recorded: "Immediately the Germans separated us from the indigenous people, who were led in the opposite direction. A little later, we heard rapid salvoes from an automatic weapon coming from the direction where they had disappeared." That same night, Dhoste saw a German soldier shooting a wounded black corporal into the head twice.[36] Some nearby white French officers were threatened with machine pistols and had to sit down in front of a small hill, while almost fifty black soldiers were led away and shot with machine pistols. The officers later saw the corpses when they boarded trucks bringing them to POW camps.[37] In the same area, a German officer shot several wounded blacks lying on a road and exclaimed to the white French officers, "You will tell this in France!"[38] Outside of Saint-Just-en-Chaussée, the West African Sergeant Mamadou Aliou witnessed the shooting of ten Tirailleurs Sénégalais on 10 June, which was probably the execution that the police inspector mentioned in response to Bousson's testimony in December 1945. Aliou himself was spared for unknown reasons.[39]

After failing to cross the German line near Erquinvillers, a group of some forty Tirailleurs Sénégalais and an unknown

[35] Carrat, SHAT 34 N 1095.
[36] Dhoste, SHAT 34 N 5 1097.
[37] Bénézet, SHAT 34 N 5 1097.
[38] "Le massacre des Sénégalais de la 4ème DIC," CHETOM 15 H 144.
[39] Aliou, CHETOM 15 H 144. Aliou was dismissed from a German POW camp on 20 December 1940 and completed his report in Perpignan (Southern France) in January 1942.

number of white soldiers and officers hid in a forest nine kilometers southeast of Erquinvillers, hoping to break through during the following night. These soldiers were captured, however, when the Germans surrounded the forest on the evening of 10 June after having discovered and shot a French officer on a scouting mission outside the forest. Stepping in front of the group of prisoners, a German officer pointed at a *coupe-coupe* and exclaimed, "*That* is your war, you bastards."[40] The Tirailleurs were shot immediately. The white soldiers and officers were kept in a farm for the night. The next morning, these prisoners, with the exception of eight officers, were driven to an assembly point in Saint-Just-en-Chaussée. The eight officers were led to a remote place in the forest and shot through the head, apparently because they had protested the killings of black soldiers. One of the officers was an Alsatian; before being led away to the execution site, he declared in German that he was proud of having commanded Tirailleurs Sénégalais.[41] Local citizens exhumed and identified the officers in June 1941 and gave them a regular burial in the cemetery of the nearby village Cressonsacq.[42]

How many Tirailleurs Sénégalais of the 4th DIC were murdered after surrendering on 9 and 10 June remains unclear because it was difficult to determine who was killed in combat and who was shot after being captured. Conservative estimates indicated that at least 150 black soldiers were killed right after capture; some witnesses spoke of five hundred to six hundred, but they probably included soldiers killed in combat.[43] Taking

---

[40] "Déclaration faite par le Sergeant Long," CHETOM 15 H 144.

[41] "Le massacre des Sénégalais de la 4ème DIC," CHETOM 15 H 144.

[42] "La mort du commandant Bouquet et de ses officiers," CHETOM 15 H 144.

[43] CHETOM 15 H 144. One of the documents in this folder estimates that around one thousand French soldiers were killed in the pocket between Saint-Just-en-Chaussée and Estrées-Saint-Denis, among them some six hundred Tirailleurs Sénégalais. This number seems to include combat deaths and victims of massacres.

into account that some reports may describe the same killing, it can be estimated that the shootings of 150 to 200 captured Tirailleurs Sénégalais have left an archival trace. But the documents are incomplete. The records of the 16th RTS, for example, are much thinner for this battle than are the records of the 24th RTS.

MASSACRES IN THE PURSUIT OF FRENCH FORCES

After the German breakthroughs on the Somme, the French defensive position quickly unraveled. There could be no doubt anymore that the campaign was lost. On 10 June, the French government left Paris for the south. On the same day, Italy declared war on France and Britain. On 14 June, German troops – including the 9th Infantry Division implicated in the massacres near Erquinvillers – occupied undefended Paris. New German offensives were unleashed in the northeast against the French positions in the Meuse and Moselle regions as well as the Maginot Line. While these offensives encountered much resistance, the German advance farther west ran into few obstacles and proceeded at a breathtaking pace. On the evening of 17 June, as the Germans had reached the Loire River and were rushing toward Lyon, Marshal Philippe Pétain, the new prime minister of France, inquired about the terms of an armistice. Although there were some famous cases of last-ditch resistance even after this date, many French soldiers, demoralized by the military setbacks and immobilized by the huge crowds of civilian refugees, began to surrender without a fight. Civilians often tried to prevent further resistance in order to save their homes and villages from destruction. Yet even in this last phase of the campaign, massacres of black soldiers occurred.

In the northeast, where the Germans faced the stiffest resistance, black prisoners from the first battalion of the 12th RTS, many of them severely wounded, were shot in a forest near Brillon (south of Bar-le-Duc) on the night of 15 to 16 June by members of the 6th Panzer Division. The Germans had sent emissaries asking the French commander to surrender, but he had instead opened fire and mounted a last-ditch resistance effort.[44] Possibly some survivors from this battle were part of a group of one hundred POWs from the 12th RTS, mostly blacks, who were shot in a barn near Neufchateau (southeast of Brillon) on 19 June.[45] Further south, in the upper Meuse valley, units of the 14th RTS had prepared defensive positions in and near Bourmont, a picturesque small town lying at the crease of a mountain. Not having received a withdrawal order from the French High Command, these units decided to hold their positions to the last man. On 18 and 19 June, two German infantry regiments stormed the town, suffering heavy casualties. Witnesses then observed German soldiers shooting captured black soldiers behind the local castle. Some of the prisoners were beaten with rifle butts. At least thirty black POWs were killed. Local witnesses later testified that a Tirailleur had beheaded a German soldier with his *coupe-coupe* and that they saw one dead German soldier who had his ears cut off.[46]

Further west, the Tirailleurs Sénégalais in the French forces withdrawing toward the Loire and Lyon became the victims of massacres, too. In the department Eure-et-Loir, near Maintenon and Chartres, the 26th RTS was destroyed on 16 June by the German 18th Army during heavy fighting. Remnants of the unit were pursued and captured the following day fifteen kilometers

---

[44] Rives and Dietrich, *Héros méconnus*, 179–81; Dartigues, *Des coloniaux au combat*, 125–7. See also BA-MA, RH 27–6, vol. 1 (Kriegstagebuch), Anlage I 9.

[45] Delrive and Guériaud, SHAT 34 N 1071.

[46] Société historique et archéologique de Bourmont, ed., *Témoignages recueillis à l'occasion du cinquantenaire de la bataille de Bourmont 18–19–20 juin 1940* (Neufchateau: Imprimerie du Progrès, 1990), 14 and 17. Montangerand and Voillemin, SHAT 34 N 1093; "Sépultures militaires," Archives départementales Haute-Marne, 15 W 74. See also Dartigues, *Des coloniaux au combat*, 131–44.

south of Chartres. Several massacres of black POWs are reported, involving between fifty and one hundred wounded Tirailleurs.[47] Many white French officers were threatened with executions, too. When Lieutenant Georges Parisot surrendered, a German officer exclaimed that his unit had found a *coupe-coupe* and protested against the use of this weapon and France's deployment of black soldiers. During this lecture, a soldier held up a revolver in front of Parisot's face.[48] Lieutenant Christian-Marie Rendinger experienced severe intimidation after he was captured with thirty officers on 16 June near Chartres: "I have to report that the German battalion that had taken us prisoner, after initially treating us correctly, prepared a joke revealing very bad taste in the afternoon. My comrades and I, we had to stand in front of a wall opposite a group of armed soldiers and listen to the accusations of Germans who complained of having been mistreated by our officers and claimed that some of their comrades had become the victims of cruelties carried out by our Tirailleurs Sénégalais. The German officer who directed this comedy spoke seriously of having us shot."[49] Another French officer from this group, Captain Paul Chouanière, was led away for an interrogation. When he was asked by a German officer, "Why do you wage war with savages, with Negroes?" he answered that the blacks fought for France because they were grateful for the civilization France had brought them (a standard French justification for the use of black African soldiers in both world wars). A German general, who had followed the interrogation with the help of a translator, went into a fit over the word "civilization." The general, "red with anger," explained that a wounded German officer had been killed and mutilated by Tirailleurs Sénégalais the night before. As a reprisal, he would shoot all the prisoners including

47 Taillefer-Grimaldi, SHAT 34 N 1099; Rives and Dietrich, *Héros méconnus*, 187.
48 Parisot, SHAT 34 N 1099.
49 Rendinger, SHAT 34 N 1099.

the officers. He sent Chouanière back to the French officers and shouted that he had no interest in the fate of an officer who commanded Negroes. A little later, however, the general announced to Chouanière: "Unfortunately I do not have the right to shoot you. But you will hear from me."[50]

Lieutenant Jean Coutures, captured outside of Chartres at night, witnessed German soldiers shooting Tirailleurs Sénégalais who panicked and ran away when the Germans launched illumination rockets. When Coutures was captured moments later, a German sergeant, speaking French, threatened to shoot him in retaliation for alleged Tirailleur cruelties: "Your dirty Negroes are savages who take no prisoners and mutilate German soldiers before killing them." Coutures was not shot, but when he was led to a POW camp, he saw many corpses of Tirailleurs and found out that almost all the black soldiers in his unit had been shot – either in combat or after capture. Only Rendinger's group of fifty Tirailleurs survived, perhaps because they had surrendered without a fight.[51]

Further massacres happened in the days following the destruction of the 26th RTS on various sectors of the front. Outside of Clamecy, a town halfway between Paris and Lyon, forty-one African POWs were shot in an improvised POW camp on 18 June, among them some North Africans. An African prisoner had attacked an SS officer, starting to beat or, according to some reports, bite him. In retaliation, the guards lined up twenty randomly chosen African prisoners for execution together with the guilty man. When twenty other Africans selected to dig the graves for this group refused to do so, they were shot, too. After the execution, the guards cut off the fingers of the dead POWs carrying golden rings. One prisoner survived the execution. When a few days later a black soldier (whether he was the survivor of the

[50] Chouanière, SHAT 34 N 1099.
[51] Coutures, SHAT 34 N 1099.

execution or a straggler is uncertain) begged for food at a nearby farm, somebody betrayed him. He was shot by the Germans.[52]

On 19 June, a German unit captured a large group of retreating French soldiers in Sillé-le-Guillaume, a small town west of Le Mans. Afterward, German soldiers separated fourteen black members of a small colonial artillery unit from the other prisoners. They then led the blacks to a railroad bridge outside of the town and shot them there.[53] A motive for this massacre is not known. The colonial artillery unit to which the victims belonged had only arrived at the front at a time when the French army was in full retreat. They had not been in combat.

At this time, a cluster of massacres was occurring northwest of Lyon. There, the Regiment *Großdeutschland* (attached to the 10th Panzer Division during this period) and the SS Totenkopf Division, already infamous for its murder of one hundred British POWs in Le Paradis in late May, ran into unexpected resistance from several well-entrenched battalions of the 25th RTS.[54] This unit had only recently been constituted and had not yet

---

[52] Janette Colas, "A propos des 43 Tirailleurs," Archives Communales de Clamecy; Fiche 1940, juin 18, in Archives départementales de la Nièvre, 50 J 9. See also Pierre Pannetier, "Le quarante-quatrième tirailleur," *Bulletin de la Société Scientifique et Artistique de Clamecy* (2000): 74–9.

[53] For a list of the killed soldiers, see Archives départementales de la Sarthe, 2 R 88. For documents on the burial of the executed soldiers, see Archives communales de Sillé-le-Guillaume, 4 H 99 (accessible only in 2007), 4 H 106, and 4 H 107. The SHAT holds two unpublished manuscripts with detailed descriptions of this massacre: André Hu, "Information sur le massacre des soldats sénégalais à Sillé-le-Guillaume le 19 juin 1940," and André Hu and Frank Tourel, "Les Tirailleurs Sénégalais à Sillé-le-Guillaume."

[54] For the massacre of the British POWs, see Charles W. Sydnor Jr., *Soldiers of Destruction: The SS Death's Head Division, 1933–1945* (Princeton: Princeton University Press, 1977), 106–9, and George H. Stein, *The Waffen SS: Hitler's Elite Guard at War* (Ithaca: Cornell University Press, 1966), 76–8. For the (unlikely) claim that British troops had previously killed German POWs from the SS, see Nicholas Harman, *Dunkirk: The Necessary Myth* (New York: Simon & Schuster, 1980), 88–90 and 97–9, and Angus Calder, *The Myth of the Blitz* (London: J. Cape, 1991), 94.

seen combat. Its commanders knew that Pétain had called for an armistice and that Lyon could not be defended. The 10ᵗʰ German Panzer Division stood on the other bank of the Saône and was already negotiating a peaceful surrender of the city. The French High Command had even declared Lyon an open city and ordered the 25ᵗʰ RTS to withdraw to the south. Yet, some officers of the regiment, after consulting with their soldiers, decided to make a heroic last stand on the northwestern approaches to the city. Having prepared defensive positions in the monastery of Montluzin, the nearby villages of Chasselay and Lentilly, and in other places near important road intersections, the Tirailleurs opened fire on the approaching enemy.[55] The Germans, surprised by the resistance, launched several costly counterattacks. The commander of the 10ᵗʰ Panzer Division even sent some of his tanks to help.[56]

After storming the French positions at the monastery of Montluzin on 19 June, the Germans killed the surviving black defenders as well as some of their white officers.[57] In Lentilly, thirteen captured Tirailleurs Sénégalais were shot with machine guns.[58] In Chasselay, a village two kilometers from Montluzin, a

---

[55] For a detailed study of this massacre, see Fargettas, "Le massacre des soldats du 25ème Régiment de Tirailleurs Sénégalais Région lyonnaise – 19 et 20 juin 1940."

[56] "Kriegstagebuch," 10. Panzer-Division, BA-MA, RH 27–10, vol. 9.

[57] Letolle and Pangaud, SHAT 34 N 5. Françoise Meifredy and Robert Hervet, *Missions sans frontières* (Paris: Editions France-Empire, 1966). "Les combats de Montluzin," *L'Ancre d'Or*, no. 96 (1968). The postwar histories of the involved German units mention these combats but, predictably, are silent on the massacres: Albert Schick, *Die 10. Panzer-Division 1939–1943* (Köln: Pohle, 1993), 228–32. Vopersal, *Soldaten, Kämpfer, Kameraden*, 246–9. Helmut Spaeter, *Die Geschichte des Panzerkorps Großdeutschland* (Duisburg-Ruhrort: Selbstverlag, 1958), 184–5. Wolf Durian, *Infanterie-Regiment Großdeutschland greift an. Die Geschichte eines Sieges* (Berlin: Scherl Verlag, 1942).

[58] Jean Marchiani, "Tata Sénégalais de Chasselay," in Archives départementales du Rhône, 437 W 173; Colonel Bouriand, "Additif au Rapport No 1155(OP du 28 juin," SHAT 34 N 1098.

group of Tirailleurs held out in a castle until the next day. Having run out of ammunition, they surrendered on the afternoon of 20 June. The Germans then led eight white officers and sixty to seventy Tirailleurs Sénégalais down the road to Chères, the next village. Near a field where two tanks were parked, the officers had to lie down. Meanwhile, the Germans ordered the Tirailleurs to assemble with raised hands in the field with the tanks and ordered them to start running, as if attempting to escape. The two tanks then fired their machine guns and cannons at the fleeing black soldiers while driving over the wounded and dead.[59] Close to fifty Tirailleurs were murdered in what an observer described as a Dantesque "vision of horror."[60] A German soldier deliberately wounded the white French commander with a pistol shot, but the other officers were not hurt. In the days that followed, some surviving Tirailleurs were found in the houses of Chasselay and the surrounding fields and orchards. Françoise Meifredy, an energetic woman working for the *Amitiés Africaines*, a support organization for African soldiers, searched the area for survivors and drove black soldiers, many of them seriously wounded, to Lyon saving them from internment as POWs and possibly from

---

59 The text at the memorial site in Chasselay (visited on 22 July 2004) claims that these tanks belonged to the 3rd or 4th Panzer Division. However, the Infantry Regiment Großdeutschland, one of whose units was almost certainly responsible, had its own stock of tanks [see the notes in BA-MA, RH 37 (6392)]. The tanks could also have belonged to the reinforcements sent by the 10th Panzer Division or to the SS Totenkopf Division, which had some formerly Czecho-Slovak tanks.

60 Meifredy, Archives départementales de Lyon, 3808 W 879 (Chasselay). Some sources claim that the tanks deliberately ran back and forth over the bodies, but witnesses closer to the events state that the tanks drove over the bodies while in pursuit of the fleeing Tirailleurs without apparent intention to crush them. For testimonies, see Archives départementales de Lyon, folders 3808 W 879 (Chasselay) and 437 W 173. The most detailed and reliable witness reports are by Marcel Requier, one of the surviving officers, and by Raymond Murard, a resident of Chasselay who helped bury the corpses the next day.

being shot.[61] Fifteen Tirailleurs are known to have survived, most of them wounded. Altogether, around one hundred black and about a dozen white prisoners (mostly officers in charge of the blacks) were murdered in the villages northwest of Lyon.

The black soldiers killed during these massacres were not the only victims of these battles. Some German units fighting the Tirailleurs Sénégalais obviously decided that no quarter would be given to them. This becomes clear in the records of the SS Totenkopf Division, which came from the west and clashed with the French strongholds near Lentilly, a few kilometers west of Montluzin. The division's war diaries list almost exclusively white French prisoners. A report regarding one of the fights concludes: "The IIIrd company took twenty-four prisoners (whites); twenty-six Negroes died." Similarly, the report states after another clash with black soldiers: "Result: twenty-five prisoners (Frenchmen). Fallen: forty-four Negroes."[62]

After the bloodshed near Lyon, not much fighting occurred. On 22 June, agreement was reached on an armistice, which took effect three days later. The collaborationist government under Marshal Pétain, which had taken residence in the spa town Vichy, ordered the Tirailleurs Sénégalais who had avoided capture by the Germans to march south and demobilized the majority of them. The same happened to the small contingent of Tirailleurs Sénégalais fighting on the border with Italy. Some black soldiers, as well as some dismissed black POWs, were later integrated into units that the Pétain government sent to guard France's North African colonies.[63] Other West Africans were gathered in transit camps in anticipation of repatriation. Given the poor

---

[61] "Le groupe de subdivisions de Lyon en alerte et en campagne à la IIème armée 10 mai–24 juin 1940," SHAT 34 N 5; Meifredy and Hervet, *Missions sans frontières*, 16–32.

[62] "Betreff: Kurzer Bericht. 21.6.1940. Von SS-Hauptsturmführer und Kompaniechef Kuntz," in BA-MA, RS 3–3, vol. 7.

[63] Killingray, "Africans and African Americans in Enemy Hands," 190.

communications between mainland France and French West Africa, however, the repatriation of demobilized Tirailleurs and dismissed POWs proceeded slowly. Many of them had to remain in camps in mainland France until the liberation of the country in 1944. Even after the liberation, shipping shortages and administrative chaos made repatriation a slow and frustrating process.[64]

AFTER THE BATTLES

The German hatred and fear of Tirailleurs Sénégalais continued after the battles. Frequently, the Germans seized or destroyed the military nametags of Tirailleurs, thus preventing the identification of the corpses.[65] Special orders were issued prohibiting the burial of Tirailleurs or the decoration of their graves. In Fouilloy, for example, the local German commander published the following proclamation on 19 August 1940: "The commander hears that the towns take good care of the graves of French soldiers on their territory. This is obviously a national duty, but it applies only to French and Allied soldiers from Europe, who fought courageously in the defense of their fatherland. The black troops, however, fought in the manner of savages and abused, even killed, German prisoners who were unlucky enough to fall into their hands. That is why the German Army Command does not like, and expressly prohibits, the decoration of the graves of black soldiers; they have to be left in the place and state just as they are now."[66]

Similar orders were given in other regions of France, but the French population often ignored them or asked the German

---

[64] Echenberg, *Colonial Conscripts*, 98 and 103–4; Lawler, *Soldiers of Misfortune*, 110 and Chapter 8.

[65] Fargettas, "Le massacre des soldats du 25ème Régiment de Tirailleurs Sénégalais Région lyonnaise – 19 et 20 juin 1940," vol. 2, 99–100, 114–15.

[66] Standortkommandatur Marcelcave, Einheit 13113 B, CHETOM 15 H 144.

occupation authorities to grant exceptions. After the execution in Clamecy, for example, the corpses of the Africans were left in the open to rot; townspeople, disturbed by the stench and out-raged about this policy, finally obtained permission to bury them at the site of the execution five days later.[67] When Jean Coutures of the 26th RTS returned to the area near Chartres in late Novem-ber 1940, he found that the Germans had refused to bury the dead Tirailleurs after the battle. Some corpses had been buried after ten days by civilians returning from their flight to the south; other corpses were still decomposing in the fields. Coutures was told that a group of eight to ten armed Tirailleurs Sénégalais had hidden in a forest for twenty days after the battle. Farmers had supplied them with food, but some locals had betrayed them to the Germans. The German authorities, however, were apparently so afraid of the Tirailleurs that they did not try to capture them. Finally, the Tirailleurs left for the unoccupied zone in the south of France.[68]

In one case, German officials tried to blame Tirailleurs Sénégalais for the death of French civilians during a German bombardment. Jean Moulin, the prefect of the department Eure-et-Loir, was pressured to sign a declaration confirming this lie on 17 June. Moulin refused to do so even under torture and was released only after he tried to kill himself. He later became a resistance leader in occupied France and was arrested and mur-dered by the German secret police in 1943.[69]

Frequent abuses of black prisoners happened on their marches to transitional POW camps after the battles and in those

---

[67] Colas, "A propos des 43 Tirailleurs," Archives communales de Clamecy; Pannetier, "Le quarante-quatrième tirailleur," 76.

[68] Coutures, SHAT 34 N 1099.

[69] See Moulin's report, as cited in Pierre Péan, *Vies et morts de Jean Moulin* (Paris: Fayard, 1998), 232–43. For the circumstances, see Jean-Jacques François, *La guerre de 1939-1940 en Eure-et-Loir* ([Mainvilliers]: Ed. La Parcheminière, n. d.), vol. 4, 65–84.

camps. Many white soldiers observed Tirailleurs Sénégalais being brutalized or shot by their guards. Lieutenant Taillefer-Grimaldi, a regimental physician of the 26th RTS, witnessed guards using bayonets to poke three Tirailleurs at the end of a marching column of POWs. When one of the Tirailleurs jumped to the side because of the sudden pain, he was shot. Obviously, trigger-happy guards interpreted every rapid move of a black soldier as an escape attempt.[70] In La Machine, not far from Nevers, three Tirailleurs Sénégalais were shot on 24 June for unknown reasons.[71] Papa Gueyé Fall, a black officer and schoolteacher from Dakar captured in Lorraine, recorded in his diary that German guards threw stones at him and would have killed him but for the protection of his white colleagues.[72] On their way to German POW camps, black POWs were often deprived of food and drink. Among the POWs kept in the castle of Le-Quesnoy-sur-Airaines, for example, only white French soldiers and officers received food rations, which they shared with the black prisoners.[73] French physicians also reported that the Germans sometimes denied medical care to wounded Tirailleurs Sénégalais after the battles and on the marches to the camps.[74] Moreover, black POWs often had to sleep in the open air on their way to the camps. The lack of shelter proved particularly inhumane during a period of heavy rainfall in northern France in late June.

Not having expected such a rapid victory over France, the German army was overwhelmed by the large numbers of prisoners it took in May and June 1940. Most French POWs, regardless

---

[70] Taillefer-Grimaldi, SHAT 34 N 1099.

[71] Archives départementales de la Nièvre, 999 W 62/5 and 80 W 159/2.

[72] Fall, SHAT 34 N 1090.

[73] Bonne, SHAT 34 N 1081. For similar observations, see Hans Habe, "The Nazi Plan for Negroes," *The Nation* 152 (1941): 233.

[74] See, for example, Jourdain, SHAT 34 N 1079: "With respect to the indigenous wounded, they [the Germans] were very hard and allowed us to care for them only under great difficulties." See also Bonne, SHAT 34 N 1081.

of skin color, experienced hardship during the first months of their captivity, as food supplies and housing accommodations were inadequate for everybody.[75] The transportation of POWs from the front to the rear happened slowly and under chaotic circumstances, as the roads were clogged with millions of refugees who had been overtaken by German troops on their way south. Not enough German guards and support personnel for the POWs were available. In some cases, the Germans asked huge groups of French POWs to march to camps in the rear without *any* guards (though never, to my knowledge, large numbers of black soldiers). The building of transitional POW camps not too far from the frontline took time and claimed scarce resources.[76]

Despite these difficult circumstances, however, it is clear that black POWs were singled out for particularly bad treatment. The blacks were often separated from their white comrades and led to makeshift camps where tiny food rations, poor sanitary conditions, and the lack of medical aid produced high death rates. Frequent executions of black POWs for minimal offenses were reported from the POW camps at Béthune and Tournai in the north of France in June and July 1940.[77] In Clamecy, two Tirailleurs Sénégalais were shot in a POW camp in July after a razor and a knife had been found on them, which was against camp rules.[78] In Villacourt, a village in Lorraine, a group

[75] Yves Durand, *La captivité: histoire des prisonniers de guerre français, 1939–1945* (Paris: Fédération nationale des combattants et prisonniers de guerre et combattants d'Algérie, de Tunisie et du Maroc, 1982), 44–7. See also Simon Paul MacKenzie, "The Treatment of Prisoners of War in World War II." *The Journal of Modern History* 66, no. 3 (1994), 497.

[76] On the bad food supply and prevalence of diseases in the camps located in France during the summer of 1940, see Meifredy and Hervet, *Missions sans frontières*, 38–45. For a similar image, see the reports of Red Cross representatives in France: "Mission en France, Frédéric Barbey et Marcel Junod, oct.–nov. 1940," Archives du Comité international de la Croix-Rouge, B, G 3/21b.

[77] Pilet, SHAT 34 N 1081.

[78] Archives communales de la ville de Clamecy, 4 H 55–56 and 1 M 49.

of between forty and eighty Africans, including some North Africans, were shot in retaliation for a sniper attack on German soldiers shortly before the armistice took effect. The remainder of the African POWs were kept in a fenced area set up like a zoo in the middle of the camp and received no food or drink for long periods of time. Contacts with these prisoners were forbidden, and a German soldier who befriended one of them was sent to prison for two weeks.[79] Sergeant Dang-Mao Nguyen, a member of a Vietnamese half-battalion held with a large group of French colonial POWs in Hanover and later in camps within the German-occupied zone of France, summarized his experiences by saying that "the Germans always beat us, particularly the blacks, who were very poorly regarded."[80] Sometimes German soldiers and reporters added insult to injury by photographing or filming captured black soldiers. The blacks were presented as exotic curiosities in the weekly newsreels and in documentaries about the campaign, as in *Sieg im Westen*, where black prisoners had to perform a strange dance shown toward the end of the film. Books published shortly after the campaign juxtaposed unflattering photos of black soldiers with photos of well-groomed German soldiers. Witnesses and surviving photos indicate that some German soldiers and guards took pride in posing with black POWs for a picture.[81]

---

79 The Austrian writer Hans Habe published two slightly different accounts of these incidents in 1941. In his book, Habe claimed that forty "Negroes and Arabs" were shot. In an article, however, he spoke of eighty victims. Habe is also inconsistent regarding the date of the incident (22 June in the book; 25 June in the article). Hans Habe, *A Thousand Shall Fall* (New York: Harcourt, Brace and Company, 1941), 234–7; Habe, "The Nazi Plan for Negroes," 233.

80 Nguyen, SHAT 34 N 1105.

81 *Der Sieg im Westen. Ein Film des Oberkommandos des Heeres* (1940), released as a video cassette by International Historic Films in 1985. For another example of the use of black soldiers in a documentary film, see Echenberg, *Colonial Conscripts*, 96. Hans Habe commented on the urge of German soldiers to take photos of black prisoners: "The Nazi Plan for Negroes," 233. For the

Most POWs from the French colonies were held within the German-occupied zone of France because Hitler did not wish to keep members of such different races on German territory. Some were sent to Germany initially, but most were returned to camps in France during the summer and fall of 1940.[82] Regardless of where they were held, however, the situation of black POWs took a turn for the better later in the summer of 1940. Permanent camps offering better housing and sanitation were completed, and the diet and treatment of the black POWs improved. In accordance with the Geneva Convention, Muslims, the predominant religious group among the West Africans, received rooms reserved for prayer. Moreover, whereas some black POWs worked in the mines in northern France, the majority were sent to work on farms or in forests. The West Africans found it easier than other POWs to get this more attractive work because they were less likely to run away than white French and North African POWs.[83]

Representatives from the International Committee of the Red Cross drew a positive picture in their reports on the POW camps in France from 1941 on. After visiting twenty main camps and fifteen branch camps, which held over a quarter of all colonial POWs and more than half of the Tirailleurs Sénégalais, a Red

---

juxtaposition of pictures, see *Der Feldzug in Frankreich. 10. Mai–23. Juni 1940*, and *Mit dem Generalkommando XXXX. A.K. vom Rhein zum Atlantik*, at the library of the Bundesarchiv-Militärarchiv.

[82] Armelle Mabon and Martine Cuttier, "La singulière captivité des prisonniers de guerre africains (1939–1945)," in *Les prisonniers de guerre dans l'histoire. Contacts entre peuples et cultures*, eds. Sylvie Caucanas, Rémy Cazals, and Pascal Payen (Carcassonne and Toulouse: Les Audois and Editions Privat, 2003); Durand, *La captivité*, 58–60; Georges Scapini, *Mission sans gloire* (Paris: Editions Morgan, 1960), 27 and 335. See also "Mission en France, Frédéric Barbey et Marcel Junod, oct.–nov. 1940," Archives du Comité international de la Croix-Rouge, B, G 3/21b.

[83] Fall, SHAT 34 N 1090; on the Muslim prayer room, see Auffret, SHAT 34 N 1090.

Cross mission concluded in July 1941 that housing, hygiene, and food supplies were good – the latter due in no small measure to supplemental deliveries by charitable organizations such as the Red Cross and the *Amitiés Africaines*. The vast majority of prisoners from the colonies worked, and they all received a small daily wage. Muslim prayer services were available. Prisoners sometimes lacked shoes and the ability to exchange letters with their families.[84] But the latter difficulty could not be ascribed to the German authorities alone. Most African prisoners (and their families) were illiterate, the addresses of their family members could be hard to find, and mail service via Geneva to Africa, particularly to French West Africa, was slow and unreliable.[85] The Red Cross reports expressed concern that many African POWs were kept in camps in the north of France where they would be more susceptible to contagious diseases during the winter. The German army responded by transferring some, but by no means all, African POWs to camps in the milder west and warm southwest of France in the fall of 1941.[86]

Testimonies from prisoners tend to confirm the impressions of Red Cross representatives. Roger-Jacques Vergez, a regimental physician from the 12th RTS assigned to a Tirailleur camp in Neufchateau (Lorraine), left detailed notes about the changes in the situation of black POWs. Initially, the camp was in poor condition. Many prisoners had to sleep outside, and the diet was insufficient. At the end of July 1940, however, the inmates

---

[84] CSC, Service des camps, France (Frontstalags), and "Résumé des visites des camps de prisonniers de guerre en France occupée, du 21.5.41 au 27.6.41" (dossier B, G 3/21c, Mission en France, Marti et de Morsier), both in Archives du Comité International de la Croix Rouge.

[85] Comité International de la Croix-rouge, ed., *Rapport du Comité international de la Croix-Rouge sur son activité pendant la seconde guerre mondiale (1er septembre 1939–30 juin 1947): Volume II L'Agence centrale des prisonniers de guerre* (Geneva: CICR, 1948), 225–39.

[86] "Rapport du Docteur J. de Morsier," Archives du Comité International de la Croix Rouge, B, G 3/21d.

were transferred to a camp in the town of Chaumont, where the diet was much better and where many black POWs were allowed to work on farms in the surrounding area. Assignment to this work, called the *corvée*, was coveted by the camp inmates; the relative freedom of movement, extra food, and friendly relations with the farmers made the longer hours one might have to work seem worthwhile.[87] Vergez also took note of the changed behavior of the German guards. They gave food and beer to the black POWs, made sure they received food packages from the Red Cross, and made it easy for sick Tirailleurs to be liberated without formalities. Vergez believed that the black POWs now received better food and treatment than white prisoners.[88] Reports and diaries from French officers in other camps disclose similar observations. On 7 September 1940, for example, Second Lieutenant Emile Philippe noted in the camp of Épinal that the Tirailleurs received preferential treatment; they were given extra bread rations, cigarettes, candy, and chocolate.[89] Tirailleurs in rural regions were better off than those who had to work in the factories and mines of northern France and those who were forced to work illegally in armament factories, but the treatment appears to have improved for all of them.[90]

French officers, and probably the Tirailleurs themselves, quickly understood the political motivation for the wooing of black Africans: The German government had begun to consider establishing a colonial empire in Africa at the expense of the territories still under French control.[91] At the very least, the German

---

[87] POWs in German camps generally seem to have preferred agricultural work for these reasons. See A. J. Barker, *Prisoners of War* (New York: Universe Books, 1975), 100.

[88] Vergez, SHAT 34 N 1090.

[89] Philippe and Fall, SHAT 34 N 1090.

[90] Mabon and Cuttier, "La singulière captivité des prisonniers de guerre africains," 141–2.

[91] Alexandre Kum'a N'dumbé III, "Afrika in der NS-Planung eines großgermanischen Reiches." In *Zwischen Charleston und Stechschritt. Schwarze im*

government hoped to prevent French West Africa from defecting to the Free French movement of General Charles de Gaulle, as French Equatorial Africa had done in July. On 19 September 1940, the British and the Free French launched an attack on Dakar, the capital of French West Africa. Although the attack was repelled and the French West African governor Pierre Boisson reaffirmed his loyalty to the Vichy government under Pétain, it was clear that this giant colony with only tenuous connections to Nazi-dominated Europe might easily slip out of the control of Nazi Germany and the Vichy government.[92] The Germans understood that continuing the inhumane treatment of West Africans would nourish anti-Vichy and anti-German feeling in West Africa and help to destabilize the colony. In September 1940, German officials tried to select West Africans in the POW camps who might be used as collaborators in a future German colonial administration. Papa Gueyé Fall, as a schoolteacher and respected community leader, was asked by an officer of the German counterintelligence service, the *Abwehr*, what he would do for Germany should the Germans create a large African empire. Fall did not respond and escaped from the camp in January 1941.[93] Other testimonies confirm that the black soldiers, while welcoming the extra bread, cigarettes, and chocolate, did not waver in their loyalty to France. As a French officer reported: "Altogether, they remain strongly attached to us."[94]

The French population, in turn, was generally supportive of the black prisoners. The Tirailleurs Sénégalais had received a

---

Nationalsozialismus, eds. Peter Martin and Christine Alonzo (Hamburg: Dölling and Galitz, 2004); Alexandre Kum'a N'dumbé III, *Hitler voulait l'Afrique: Les plans secrets pour une Afrique fasciste, 1933–1945* (Paris: L'Harmattan, 1980).

[92] Akpo-Vaché, *L'AOF et la seconde guerre mondiale*, 32–7, Echenberg, *Colonial Conscripts*, 97.

[93] Fall, SHAT 34 N 1090.

[94] Dutel, SHAT 34 N 1090.

cordial welcome in the beginning of the war, and many French people remained grateful for the contribution they had made to the defense of France at great cost to themselves. Civilians were happy to give them food, and a support network for the West African POWs developed. Many of them were assigned a *marraine* (Godmother), a French woman who sent them letters and food while they were in captivity and sometimes cared for them when they were dismissed. The philanthropist Hélène de Gobineau played an important role in these efforts and documented them in a book published after the war.[95] Quite typical is the fate of an otherwise untypical man: Léopold Sédar Senghor, the Senegalese poet who became the first president of independent Senegal in 1960. Senghor suffered much hardship in several POW camps, but in 1942 he was dismissed on the basis of an illness (and a sympathetic paper from a French doctor). Like many other dismissed Tirailleurs, he went to Paris, where he resumed work as a schoolteacher.[96] For those who could not obtain dismissal, running away became a more viable option as a support network for escaped prisoners developed. With the help of civilians, escapees were able to reach the south of France where they were safe even after the German occupation of the south in November 1942.[97]

Despite the improved treatment by the Germans and the support of the French population, it would be wrong to conclude that the lives of black Africans in German POW camps were easy and safe for the remainder of the war. Every winter, infectious diseases took their toll among the thousands of Tirailleurs

---

[95] Hélène de Gobineau, *Noblesse d'Afrique* (Paris: Fasquelles Editeurs, 1946); Echenberg, *Colonial Conscripts*, 97; Lawler, *Soldiers of Misfortune*, Chapter 8; Mabon and Cuttier, "La singulière captivité des prisonniers de guerre africains," 142–4.

[96] Hymans, *Léopold Sédar Senghor*, 109; Vaillant, *Black, French, and African*, 166–7.

[97] Mabon and Cuttier, "La singulière captivité des prisonniers de guerre africains," 144–6.

Sénégalais who were kept in the north all year round in spite of the Red Cross suggestion to move all of them to the south. Tuberculosis and pneumonia were particularly virulent among these prisoners. That the Germans were willing to dismiss sick Tirailleurs (or healthy ones who could obtain a fake diagnosis from a French doctor) helped only a little. Many dismissed Tirailleurs died of illness before the war ended.

It appears, moreover, that the German interest in the Tirailleurs was short-lived. By the end of 1942, with the U.S. Army assisting the British and Free French in North Africa and the Soviet Union rebounding from its initial setbacks, there could be no question anymore of a German colonial empire in sub-Saharan Africa. Indifference toward the black POWs thus became the rule for the rest of the war. Reacting to their increasing manpower shortage after the attack on the Soviet Union, the Germans, assisted by the Vichy government, recruited several hundred white French officers to guard the black POWs in France, but there is no indication that this led to an improvement in the treatment of the prisoners.[98] Some Tirailleurs Sénégalais still experienced abuse later in the war. German physicians interested in developing drugs against tropical illnesses used black soldiers for medical experiments, while anthropologists measured their skulls and conducted "racial physiological" research on them.[99] There were also a few reports of killings of Tirailleurs

---

[98] Ibid., 146–9.

[99] Kesting, "Blacks Under the Swastika," 93; Kesting, "The Black Experience During the Holocaust," 359; MacKenzie, "The Treatment of Prisoners of War in World War II," 504; Martin, "'... auf jeden Fall zu erschießen,'" 84–6. Françoise Meifredy from *Amitiés Africaines* gathered some information on these experiments and sent it to the Vichy authorities: Meifredy and Hervet, *Missions sans frontières*, 133. For the anthropologists' research, see Margrit Berner, "Rassenforschung an kriegsgefangenen Schwarzen," in *Zwischen Charleston und Stechschritt. Schwarze im Nationalsozialismus*, eds. Peter Martin and Christine Alonzo (Hamburg: Dölling and Galitz, 2004).

Sénégalais who had been transferred to Germany toward the end of the war, but the evidence is sparse.[100]

German prejudices and fears regarding colonial soldiers certainly changed very little. When the Vichy government planned the establishment of a military unit to defend its North African colonies in early 1943 (the *Phalange africaine*), the German Armistice Commission reacted with the utmost suspicion because the proposed unit would have included a half-brigade of Tunisians.[101] After the occupation of the southern zone of France on 8 November 1942, the German authorities repeatedly drafted black troops under Vichy command for forced labor. Tirailleurs from West Africa and Madagascar had to clean up after Allied bombing raids, build defensive positions, and work in mines and chemical factories – probably producing ammunitions. In response to the protests of the Vichy government, the German Armistice Commission argued that it had the right to use these units because they, as remaining parts of the pre-armistice French army, should have been dissolved and repatriated (although the Germans also admitted that their repatriation would have been nearly impossible). Labor of uniformed black soldiers for German defense, the commission argued, would help to dispel the widespread suspicion of regular German soldiers toward black troops.[102]

---

[100] Kesting, "Blacks Under the Swastika," 93; Kesting, "The Black Experience During the Holocaust," 359; Lusane, *Hitler's Black Victims*, 150. One SS commander in charge of black POWs used as forced laborers in Fritzlar (Northern Hesse) was accused after the war of having ordered the execution of one thousand Tirailleurs Sénégalais who had allegedly stolen potatoes. An American investigation remained inconclusive, and the materials came into the hands of French prosecutors, but nothing further seems to have happened: Kesting, "Forgotten Victims," 31.

[101] BA-MA, RW 34, vol. 45.

[102] BA-MA, RW 34, vol. 60.

THE PROBLEMS OF COUNTING THE VICTIMS

Establishing a total count of Tirailleurs Sénégalais murdered by the Germans is an impossible task. The numbers in the French records of black soldiers killed in combat, captured as prisoners, and deceased or killed in POW camps vary greatly. The disastrous events of May and June 1940 were not conducive to record keeping. Local civilians and French officials often tried to count and identify the corpses of black soldiers, but this was made difficult by the German practice in many areas of destroying their military nametags and preventing their burial. Even in places where specific data on the graves of Tirailleurs Sénégalais existed, it was not always possible to determine in retrospect whether a soldier was killed in combat or murdered after capture. Based on the incidents described in French archives and cautious guesses as to the number of soldiers meant by such expressions as "several" and "many" in these sources, we arrive at roughly 1,000 to 1,500 documented killings in the frontline or immediately after the end of a battle (see Table 1).

This number, however, is certainly too low. The records of many Tirailleur Sénégalais units are lost or incomplete. For a regiment of three thousand men, the archives contain at best ten relevant testimonies from officers who wrote primarily to explain the conditions of the French defeat and to recommend fellow officers or soldiers for medals, not to document atrocities. Not always did white officers witness the murder of black POWs because most German units after early June separated white and black prisoners. Moreover, many units lost their operations diaries, which could have furnished more information.[103] Local sources, including the memories of civilians, fill in some gaps, but in many areas (particularly on the Somme) the local population had fled before the onset of the battle. Moreover,

---

[103] Deschênes, "Les troupes coloniales dans la bataille de France."

TABLE 1. *List of Recorded Killings, May–June 1940*

Date	Place	Description of Event	French Unit	German Unit	Number of Victims
24 May	Aubigny	Murder of wounded prisoners	24th RTS	13th ID	50
26–27 May	Near Aubigny and Fouilloy	Killing of wounded Tirailleurs	16th RTS	9th ID; also 87th ID?	"several"
5 June	St. Pierre à Gouy and Cavillon (Somme); near Picquigny and Hangest-sur-Somme	Murder of prisoners, some of them wounded. Germans chase and kill at least 27 blacks in a forest west of St. Pierre and more in the forest west of Picquigny and in the park of Cavillon	44th RICMS	46th ID; in the evening also: 6th ID; possibly also 27th ID as well as 5th and 7th PzD	50
5 June	Hangest-sur-Somme	Killing of prisoners	44th RICMS	7th PzD? (Germans in black uniforms)	"some"
5 June	Near Hangest-sur-Somme?	Killing of black POWs; white POWs are threatened but not shot thanks to the intervention of a German officer	44th RICMS		At least 5
6 June	Domart (Somme)	Killing of one POW too slow to follow the others; brutalization of others en route to POW camps	57th (53rd?) RICMS		1

Date	Location	Description	French unit	German unit	Number
7 June	Le Mesge and Riencourt (Somme)	Germans undress Africans and kill them with *coupe-coupes*; threaten that white French officers would be shot if POWs escaped	44th RICMS	6th or 46th ID	"several"
7 June	Airaines	Murder of N'Tchoréré	53rd RICMS	2nd ID (Inf. Reg. 25)	1
8 June	Near Quesnoy-sur-Airaines	Shooting of all Tirailleurs after capture in Airaines	53rd RICMS and stragglers	Likely 2nd ID (Inf. Reg. 25)	50?
9–10 June	Erquinvillers, Léglantiers, and Angivillers (Oise)	Murder of prisoners, some of them wounded; execution also of eight white officers	24th RTS and 16th RTS	9th ID; Gruppe Kleist (9th and 10th PzD); perhaps also 28th ID, 33rd ID, and 87th ID	At least 50
9–10 June	Angivillers-Ravenel (near Erquinvillers)	Germans abuse black POWs with bayonets and belts; shooting of two POWs; threat to shoot a white officer; black POWs are left unsupplied; many die of thirst	24th RTS	9th ID	50?
10 June	Near Erquinvillers; on the road to Montdidier	Shooting of black POWs who step out of line; the corpses are left unburied on the side of a street	24th RTS and 16th RTS	Inf. Reg. *Großdeutschland*; 9th ID	20? At least 150 total for all incidents near Erquinvillers
10 June	Between Vernon (Seine) and Pacy-sur Eure	Murder of frightened Tirailleur getting out of line	44th RICMS	6th, 27th, or 46th ID	1

(continued)

TABLE 1 (*continued*)

Date	Place	Description of Event	French Unit	German Unit	Number of Victims
14 June	Perthes (Haute-Marne)	Shooting of black prisoners allegedly trying to escape	6th DIC	II. Bat. Of 1st PzD	5
15–16 June (night)	Bois du Chêne (forest near Brillon-en-Barois and Bar-le-Duc)	Killing of wounded prisoners	12th RTS	6th PzD (Kampfgruppe v. Esebeck; Kampfgruppe Koll; Aufkl. Abt. 57)	50?
16 June	Feucherolles	Murder of prisoners, many of them wounded	26th RTS	18th Army; most likely its 1st Cavalry Div.	50?
16 June	Near Maintenon (on the Eure)	Shootings of fleeing black soldiers	26th RTS	18th Army; most likely its 1st Cavalry Div.	50?
16 June	Bréchamps, Maintenon, Nogent-le-Roi	Murder of prisoners	26th RTS	18th Army; most likely its 1st Cavalry Div.	50?
16 June	Nogent-le-Rotrou (near Chartres)	Murder of prisoners, many of them wounded	26th RTS	18th Army; most likely its 1st Cavalry Div.	20?
17 June	North of Nogent-le-Rotrou (near Chartres)	Three Africans are abused by German guards; one of them is shot after making a leap in reaction to a hit with a bayonet	26th RTS	18th Army; most likely its 1st Cavalry Div.	1
17 June (?)	Laxou (near Nancy)	Killing of POWs from Madagascar			11
17–18 June	Balot, Coulmier-le-Sec, Villaines-en-Duesnois (Côte d'Or)	Murder of captured stragglers following a battle near Arthonnay	42nd RIC (2nd batallion)	XXXXI. Panzerkorps (Reinhardt); SS Totenkopf Div.?	50?
18 June	Clamecy (Nièvre)	Murder of prisoners including at least 13 North Africans	4th, 10th, 16th, and 24th RTS	SS Totenkopf Div.?	41

Date	Location	Description	Unit	German unit	Number
19 June	Bourmont and Graffigny (Haute-Marne)	Killing of prisoners	14th RTS	86th ID (Inf. Reg. 167); 10th ID (Inf. Reg. 41)	Over 30
19 June	Loire (near Orléans?)	Killing of stragglers in a forest north of the Loire River	24th RTS		50?
19 June	A barn near Neufchateau	Murder of 100 prisoners (black and white)	12th RTS		80?
19 June	Sillé-le-Guillaume (near Le Mans)	Killing of prisoners	208th RACL	6th, 27th, or 46th ID. Possibly also units of I. or XV. AK	14
19–20 June	Les Chères, Montluzin, Chasselay, Lentilly, Fleurieux, L'Abresle, Lyon	Murders of Tirailleurs and some white officers and soldiers	25th RTS	SS Totenkopf Div.; Inf. Reg. *Großdeutschland*; some tanks of the 10th PzD	ca. 100
20 June	Lantignié (near Villefranche-sur-Saône)	Killing of prisoners			18
After 20 June	Mirecourt-Mattincourt	Shooting of POW having fallen behind	14th RTS		1
21 June	Lyon	Murder of some African prisoners in marching column of POWs; also killing of two Moroccan civilians			20–25
22 June (or later)	Villacourt	Killing of African POWs (including North Africans) in response to French sniper fire			40 or 80
24 June	La Machine (Nièvre)	Killing of prisoners			3

the murder of small groups of Tirailleurs or of individual soldiers, though frequently mentioned in the sources, would just as often not have left any witnesses except for the Germans themselves, whose records almost never explicitly mention executions. It therefore appears safe to say that at least three thousand captured Tirailleurs Sénégalais were murdered in May and June 1940. To this number would have to be added all those Tirailleurs who were hunted down mercilessly without having an opportunity to surrender, as happened for example during the "cleansing" of "hedgehog" positions. The casualties of Tirailleurs Sénégalais in 1940 were extremely high: According to estimates of the French Defense Ministry, seventeen thousand soldiers were killed or missing in action from an estimated total of forty thousand who were engaged in combat with the Germans. This must in part have been an effect of the no-quarter policy adopted by German units in some battles with Tirailleurs Sénégalais.[104]

The margin of error becomes even wider if we consider the mortality of black soldiers from the French army in German POW camps. French wartime inquiries put the number of Tirailleurs Sénégalais who were POWs at the time of the armistice between fifteen thousand and sixteen thousand. Approximately four thousand black soldiers from colonies other than French West Africa would have to be added to this figure.[105] Hélène de Gobineau believed that eight thousand Tirailleurs Sénégalais were still in German camps at the time of the liberation. It is known, however, that the Germans dismissed several thousand Tirailleurs Sénégalais and other black soldiers between 1940 and

---

[104] Ministère de la Défense, ed., *Les Tirailleurs sénégalais dans la campagne de France 10 mai–25 juin 1940.*

[105] Durand, *La captivité*, 59; Mabon and Cuttier, "La singulière captivité des prisonniers de guerre africains," 138. Echenberg mentions 15,000 to 20,000 POWs: *Colonial Conscripts*, 88 and 193, note 40.

1944. De Gobineau claimed that around five thousand of them lived in Paris during the war, and, as a key figure in the relief effort for these former prisoners, she was in a good position to make an accurate estimate.[106] Shortly after the liberation, the French government believed that there were still between five thousand and ten thousand ex-POWs from French West Africa in France.[107] Several groups of black soldiers, however, were not likely to be included in this figure: Some had escaped and crossed the border to neutral Switzerland or joined the French resistance, a number of ex-POWs had been remobilized and sent to North Africa, and some were already repatriated.[108] Discounting these soldiers still leaves us with between one thousand and four thousand POWs not accounted for. But how many of these individuals died in the POW camps or as a consequence of their captivity, and how many died from causes not related to their captivity, is impossible to say. (Dismissed Tirailleurs Sénégalais could have contracted fatal illnesses in the harsh conditions of life in wartime Paris.) Some difficulties in accounting for the fate of Tirailleurs Sénégalais in the campaign and in POW camps come from the fact that archival documents and secondary sources do not always differentiate among colonial soldiers (soldiers from all French colonies, including their white residents), Tirailleurs Sénégalais (soldiers from French West Africa), and other black soldiers (units from French Central Africa, French Somalia, Madagascar, North Africa, and the Caribbean also included a few thousand blacks). Considering the deficiencies of the documentation,

---

[106] Gobineau, *Noblesse d'Afrique*, 99–102.

[107] Echenberg, *Colonial Conscripts*, 98.

[108] Rives and Dietrich, *Héros méconnus*, 289–91. For Tirailleurs Sénégalais in the French resistance, see Maurice Rives, "Die Tirailleurs Sénégalais in der Résistance," in *Zwischen Charleston und Stechschritt. Schwarze im Nationalsozialismus*, eds. Peter Martin and Christine Alonzo (Hamburg: Dölling and Galitz, 2004).

precise data on the mortality of black French soldiers in German POW camps are impossible.[109]

There is no doubt, however, that the Tirailleurs Sénégalais and other black French soldiers were singled out for particularly harsh treatment during the campaign and that many of them died under the difficult conditions in the transitional camps or of diseases contracted in the permanent camps during the following war winters. The majority of deaths among black French POWs probably occurred in the aftermath of the campaign and were caused by deliberate neglect and maltreatment. After August 1940, however, the German army generally respected the Geneva Convention toward African prisoners, and the evidence for intentional neglect and maltreatment is much thinner.

THE QUESTION OF AUTHORIZATION

To better understand how the murder of black POWs came about, it is necessary to examine the structure of typical massacres and probe the legal situation. Many massacres were ordered by an officer of the German army. As happened in Erquinvillers and other places, captured French soldiers were separated according to skin color. The blacks were then led away and shot with machine pistols or machine guns in front of a wall or a ravine. The soldiers participating in these executions faced no question of authorization because they acted on the orders of the officer. Similarly, a massacre such as the killing of the black soldiers near

---

[109] Killingray argues that only half the Tirailleurs Sénégalais survived captivity, but this claim receives no support from the numbers he cites. He adopts the official estimate of 15,000 to 16,000 Tirailleurs Sénégalais as prisoners of the Germans but says a few pages later that 16,000 were released by the end of 1940: Killingray, "Africans and African Americans in Enemy Hands," 181 and 190.

Chasselay must have involved some preparation (the parking of tanks at the corners of the open field, for example) that required the order of an officer. Other murders of black soldiers rested on the group consent of soldiers, though probably with the tacit approval of officers. The soldiers of a unit could, for example, agree not to take any black prisoners when conducting a "cleansing operation" in a forest or a village. Consequently, they would immediately shoot dispersed blacks without giving them the opportunity to surrender. This was as illegal as a massacre but easier to cover up. If officers did not approve this ruthless procedure from the start, they usually sanctioned it retrospectively. In their combat reports, many officers noted that a certain number of white prisoners had been taken during such an operation and that a certain number of blacks had been killed. Although it was suspicious that all the POWs were white and all the killed enemy soldiers black, no officer seems to have started an inquiry.[110]

Sometimes a murder sprang from the initiative of individual soldiers, usually with the tacit approval of officers. In the typical occurrence mentioned previously, a German guard poked a captured Tirailleur Sénégalais with his bayonet and shot the prisoner when he jumped to the side. The guard then walked up to the next officer who had watched the scene and told him laughingly that he had killed the Tirailleur. The officer accepted that the Tirailleur had been shot while trying to escape and thus sanctioned the murder.[111] In the scene recorded by Dr. Hollecker in

---

[110] On 19 June 1940, for example, the command of XIVth Army Corps noted that the SS Totenkopf Division had taken 2,886 white French POWs as well as thirty-four Belgians and twenty-two blacks. Nobody asked why there was such a discrepancy between the number of white and black soldiers, although it was known that the SS Totenkopf Division had been fighting Tirailleurs Sénégalais: BA-MA, RH 24–14, vol. 163 (Kriegstagebuch der Qu. Abt. Gen. Kmdo XIV).

[111] Taillefer-Grimaldi, SHAT 34 N 1099.

Erquinvillers, a soldier intended to throw a hand grenade into the basement harboring wounded Tirailleurs. This soldier did not claim to act on a specific order, but the fact that officers nearby had ordered executions must have served as tacit authorization for him. The question, therefore, is why did German officers feel justified in ordering or condoning massacres of black POWs?

During the 1940 campaign, a German sergeant told a French officer that Hitler had ordered the shooting of all West African POWs.[112] This rumor, which also circulated among the Tirailleurs Sénégalais, was false, however. The Wehrmacht had no general order pertaining to the treatment of black POWs. It is true that Hitler later issued the notorious *Kommissarbefehl* for the shooting of all political commissars from the Red Army and that the German Army Command issued guidelines for Soviet POWs that blatantly contradicted international conventions.[113] Yet nothing comparable existed with respect to black POWs in 1940. Where could the German officers and soldiers in the Western campaign have looked for guidelines on how to treat black prisoners?

The ultimate authority was the Geneva Convention on POWs of 1929. Article 2 of this treaty specifically prohibits acts of violence, insults, and reprisals against POWs. A captured enemy soldier must be removed quickly from the combat zone and

---

[112] "Le massacre des sénégalais de la 4ème D.I.C.," CHETOM 15 H 144.

[113] For a detailed analysis, see Streit, *Keine Kameraden*. See also Jürgen Förster, "The German Army and the Ideological War against the Soviet Union," in *The Policies of Genocide: Jews and Soviet Prisoners of War in Nazi Germany*, ed. Gerhard Hirschfeld (London, Boston, and Sydney: Allen & Unwin, 1986); Jürgen Förster, "'Verbrecherische Befehle,'" in *Kriegsverbrechen im 20. Jahrhundert*, eds. Wolfram Wette and Gerd R. Überschär (Darmstadt: Primus Verlag, 2001); Christian Streit, "Deutsche und sowjetische Kriegsgefangene," in *Kriegsverbrechen im 20. Jahrhundert*, eds. Wolfram Wette and Gerd R. Überschär (Darmstadt: Primus Verlag, 2001), 179.

transferred to a POW camp in the rear. On differences in the treatment of POWs, Article 4 of the convention states: "Difference in treatment among prisoners is lawful only when it is based on the military rank, state of physical or mental health, professional qualifications or sex of those who profit thereby." However, Article 9 calls for racial segregation in the housing of POWs: "Belligerents shall, so far as possible, avoid assembling in a single camp prisoners of different races or nationalities."[114] While it was therefore legal for the German army to establish separate camps for black POWs, it was illegal to treat them differently from white POWs of the same rank. Although a pre-Nazi German government had negotiated and signed the Geneva Convention, Nazi Germany was bound by it and accepted it *de jure* in its campaigns against Western powers (but not in the war against the Soviet Union, which had not signed the Geneva Convention).[115] The German Army Command distributed the text of the convention to all officers in early 1939, and some units received a sheet repeating its basic principles at the start of the German offensive on the Somme (5 June 1940).[116] Moreover, every German soldier's paybook contained a list of ten rules including such provisions as: "No enemy who has surrendered will be killed, including partisans and spies. . . . P.O.W. [sic] will not be ill-treated or insulted." The last rule, however, conflicted with the Geneva Convention's interdiction of reprisals by stating: "Reprisals are only

---

[114] "Convention between the United States of America and other powers relating to prisoners of war," The Avalon Project at Yale Law School: *http://www.yale.edu/lawweb/avalon/lawofwar/geneva02.htm* (last visited 9 February 2004).

[115] MacKenzie, "The Treatment of Prisoners of War in World War II," 490.

[116] "Merkblatt zum Gefangenenwesen," BA-MA, RH 26–12, vol. 12 (Anlagen zum KTB Nr. 2, Bd. V, 5.6.–8.6.1940). For the brochure on the Geneva Convention, distributed by the Wehrmacht, see BA-MA, RHD 4/38, vol. 2.

permissible on order of higher Commands."[117] Some officers
tried to inform themselves about the legal situation as did, for
example, the general who threatened to shoot the white officers
of the 26th RTS but then concluded that he had no right to do so.
He did not, however, utter any concern about killing the black
prisoners.[118]

Other normative documents available to German soldiers in
1940 concerned the civilian population of enemy countries.
Mindful of the charge of German atrocities against unarmed
men, women, and children in Belgium and northern France
in 1914, the Wehrmacht took great care to ensure that its soldiers behaved impeccably toward enemy civilians. Crimes against
the civilian population were strictly prosecuted. A soldier from
the 2nd Infantry Division, for example, was sentenced to death
for having raped a French woman while drunk.[119] Interestingly,
the death sentence was announced on 6 June, just as parts of
this unit were murdering black POWs near Airaines.[120] Civilians
forfeited their protection only if they threatened or attacked
German soldiers. An order handed out to members of the 11th
Infantry Division, for example, stated with respect to "franc-
tireurs [*Freischärler*] and alike": "If inhabitants are found with
a weapon in their hand, they have to be court-martialled."[121]
This happened rarely, however. French civilians widely praised
the *korrekt* behavior of the German troops in 1940. As one

---

[117] Russell Lord of Liverpool, *The Scourge of the Swastika: A Short History of Nazi War Crimes* (New York: Philosophical Library, 1954), 253–4.

[118] Chouanière, SHAT 34 N 1099.

[119] "Divisionstagesbefehl Nr. 38/40 (6.6.1940)," in BA-MA, RH 26–2, vol. 4.

[120] For other examples of strict prosecution of soldiers' crimes against civil-
ians, see Alfred-Maurice de Zayas, *The Wehrmacht War Crimes Bureau 1939–45* (Lincoln: University of Nebraska Press, 1990), 19.

[121] "Tagesbefehl Nr. 9" 9.4.1940, in BA-MA, RH 26–11/3 Anlagen zu KTB Nr. 2, vol. 1.

French officer recorded in Cambrai in early 1941: "The attitude of the occupiers of 1940 was so different from the attitude of their predecessors of 1914 that those people who had experienced both occupations said that they did not recognize the Germans."[122]

Very few German official communications mention black soldiers specifically. One example is a message from the commander of the 4th Infantry Division, positioned some fifty kilometers east of Amiens on the eve of the German attack on the Somme. This message informed the division that it was facing colonial units including black Africans and warned about the "mischievous character of these troops." The officers should instruct their men about the "way of fighting and the character" of these forces, but the document says nothing about the treatment of black POWs.[123] More specific was an order by Colonel Walther Nehring, chief of staff of the Guderian Panzer group, stating: "It has been found that *French colonial soldiers* have mutilated the German wounded in the most bestial fashion. Toward native soldiers, all mildness would be misplaced. Sending these prisoners towards the rear *without* a guard has to be avoided by all means. They must be treated with the greatest rigor."[124] The Nehring order has been cited as an invitation to massacre, but it was issued only on 21 June, when almost all massacres had already occurred and hostilities had for the most part ended. Moreover, it does not justify violence against black POWs but merely calls for strict surveillance, which was often not applied to white French prisoners. By requiring that black soldiers be sent to the rear with a guard, the order implies that black POWs

---

[122] Taillefer-Grimaldi, SHAT 34 N 1099. See also Philippe Burrin, *La France à l'heure allemande: 1940–1944* (Paris: Seuil, 1995), 28–9.

[123] BA-MA, RH 26–4, vol. 16, page 1.

[124] For a copy of this order, see BA-MA, RH 27–2, vol. 45.

should be transferred to POW camps, not shot on the spot.[125] Other orders issued by Nehring and other German staff officers at this time reveal that minimizing the chaos caused by the masses of French POWs falling into German hands at the end of the campaign was their main concern.[126]

The practice of not giving quarter to black soldiers, although illegal, was certainly facilitated by the fact that the legal provisions for surrender could be difficult to apply in close combat. Whereas the commander of a compact unit might communicate his wish to surrender by radio or by raising a white flag, it was much harder for a single soldier involved in close combat to make clear his intention to surrender. According to the Geneva Convention, he had to throw away his weapons and raise his hands. But memoirs of former POWs from all countries involved in World War II confirm that surrendering could be dangerous, particularly for dispersed soldiers after close combat.[127] Would the enemy recognize the intention to surrender? Would he respect it? The psychological dynamics of battle fever could make it difficult for soldiers in killing mode during the heat of battle to stop and treat enemies willing to surrender with decency: "After a long and bloody fight, it is possible to visualize circumstances when men will kill rather than take pity on an enemy who decides to surrender when it suits him to do so. In the heat of battle there is not much opportunity for sentiments of pity, and the sight of the dead and dying may weaken a soldier's sense of fairness. Refusal to grant quarter in such circumstances is understandable, even if it is not justifiable."[128] International observers, who had the right to examine POW camps, were usually unable to

---

[125] See Rives and Dietrich, *Héros méconnus*, 166; Bruge, *Juin 1940*, 118. For a correct interpretation, see Fargettas, "Les tirailleurs sénégalais dans la campagne de mai–juin 1940," 147–8.

[126] See, for example, Nehring's order of 22 June 1940: BA-MA, RH 27–1, vol. 16.

[127] Barker, *Prisoners of War*, 27–8, 35, 43.

[128] Ibid., 27–8.

help surrendering soldiers because they were not admitted to the battlefield.[129]

There is no doubt that the Germans who abused and executed black POWs were acting illegally both by international and German standards. Although executions of POWs as a reprisal for violations of the other side had occurred during the First World War, sometimes in combat between Germans and Tirailleurs Sénégalais, such actions were illegal according to the Geneva Convention.[130] Moreover, many of the alleged outrages of the Tirailleurs Sénégalais did not even constitute war crimes. To fire at dispersed enemy soldiers was entirely legal, as was the use of *coupe-coupes* in close combat. How then did German officers defend the killing of black prisoners?

GERMAN JUSTIFICATIONS

German officers ordering the killings of black POWs clearly considered the West Africans illegitimate combatants and therefore not protected by the Geneva Convention. The question of who is a legitimate combatant has bedeviled the international codes of war since their inception. When Francis Lieber, a law professor at Columbia University and former Prussian officer, devised a code for the conduct of the American Civil War in 1863, the widespread assumption was that it applied only to white "gentlemen" and could be ignored in combat with nonwhite peoples. The Confederate armies in the Civil War repeatedly abused and killed black soldiers fighting for the Union.[131] When American armies fought Indians, Mexicans, and Filipinos, they committed

---

[129] MacKenzie, "The Treatment of Prisoners of War in World War II," 518.

[130] See Joe Lunn, *Memoirs of the Maelstrom: A Senegalese Oral History of the First World War* (Portsmouth, New Hampshire: Heinemann, 1999), 136.

[131] See the essays in Gregory J. W. Urwin, ed., *Black Flag over Dixie: Racial Atrocities and Reprisals in the Civil War* (Carbondale: Southern Illinois University Press, 2004).

indiscriminate slaughter including the murder of women and children. As generals and government lawyers argued, standards of decency were misplaced, even fatal, in fighting "savages." Indians, Mexicans, and Filipinos were considered barbarians who themselves knew no restraint in war and therefore could be abused with impunity. The fact that some attacks by Indians and Filipinos had violated the Lieber Code served as a justification for unrestrained revenge without distinction between combatants and civilians.[132] This logic also characterized the behavior of many European powers in colonial wars, as shown for example by the German army's reaction to the Herero and Nama uprisings in Southwest Africa. The tendency in these wars was to launch a blanket accusation that the enemy consisted of "savages" who conducted war in a perfidious manner. The standards of warfare shared by non-European peoples, of course, often differed from European norms, and therefore incidents occurred that violated European codes. But these incidents were then generalized and used as a justification for crimes ranging from local massacre to genocide. In the Second World War, too, decent treatment of POWs in part depended on whether the captured enemy was seen as "possessing the same essentially human nature as his captor."[133] Many members of the Wehrmacht, however, denied black prisoners this status.

Often the German definition of the blacks as illegitimate combatants rested merely on the racist assertion that they were "savages" who should not be used in a war between "civilized" European nations. As we have seen, a German officer told Adjutant-Major Lucien Carrat of the 16th RTS that "an inferior

---

[132] Peter Maguire, *Law and War: An American Story* (New York: Columbia University Press, 2000), Chapters 1 and 2.
[133] MacKenzie, "The Treatment of Prisoners of War in World War II," 490 and 518.

race does not deserve to do battle with such a civilized race as the Germans," while Colonel Amadée Fabre, commander of the 24th RTS, was told: "They are just savages."[134] On the lower Somme, Jean Guérin, regimental physician of the 53rd RICMS, overheard several German officers expressing their contempt toward the black soldiers by calling them "beasts."[135]

The German sources confirm the observations of racial bias recorded by French officers. For example, the commander of the 16th Infantry Division, Major General Hans Hube, distributed a pamphlet to the men of his unit specifying how they should respond to French officers asking about the German treatment of black POWs: "The deployment of black and colored troops against the German army contradicts the conception of the white race's master role toward the colored peoples. We perceive it as a shame and dishonor, all the more so because our division has had to wage the hardest fights against Negroes. The frequently posed question whether we kill Negroes and colored people has to be answered as follows: 'The German soldier shoots his opponent only during combat. Shooting of captured soldiers who are not guilty of crimes against the laws of war contradicts the German soldierly mentality and is out of the question. However, we think that those people who have led the blacks and colored people into war against the German soldiers deserve to be shot.' If the captured officer apologizes and claims to be of the same opinion, we have to answer: 'Every people has the government it merits, and every soldier the leadership that he deserves.'"[136]

---

[134] Carrat, SHAT 34 N 1095; Fabre, SHAT 34 N 1097.
[135] Guérin, SHAT 34 N 1081.
[136] "Richtlinien für das Verhalten gegenüber Gefangenen," BA-MA, RH 26–16, vol. 19 (Kriegstagebuch Ia), approximately 21 June 1940 (the margins of the document including the date are burned).

Such blatant racism also appears in the war diaries of some German soldiers. One member of Infantry Regiment 36, for example, was deeply troubled by the racial diversity of French troops in contrast to the alleged homogeneity of Germans. When he saw a group of German soldiers pass, he noted: "They are all so blond; they all have such clear eyes! I have to swallow hard not to allow my anger to burst out against this damned racial chaos against which our army has to fight."[137] Another soldier confided to his diary his deeply alienating impressions of black soldiers in a POW camp that he visited on 22 June: "I notice a young pitch-black twenty-one year old Sudanese. He has black lips and slit eyes – a dangerous beast of prey. Around his neck I notice leather strings. I ask him what they mean, but he does not speak a word of French. I find out that this is an amulet. . . . We leave it alone because he is afraid that we will take it. Turning to the captured Frenchmen, I say to one of them: the composition of the French army is rather colorful. Then this man replies in dead earnest: Oh God, you also have Bavarians among you."[138] The diarist, a member of the 27th Infantry Division based in Bavaria, obviously was stunned by the French soldier's indifference to racial categories evident in his comparison of Africans with Bavarians. A similar experience was recorded by the commander of Rifle Regiment 69 from the 10th Panzer Division when he negotiated the surrender of a group of French colonial soldiers north of Lyon on 19 June: "I stumbled upon a strange scene: a battalion of black soldiers with the most diverse headgear. Some soldiers had faces similar to human faces; many others, however, resembled wild animals rather than humans. Their skin color ranged

---

[137] In "Frankreich 1940. Tagebuchblätter und Berichte aus dem II/I.R. 36," BA-MA, RH 37/6420 (entry 9 June 1940).
[138] "Gefreiter Rehm: Einige kleine Notizen aus meinem Tagebuch," BA-MA, RH 37/1341 (Erlebnisberichte), entry of 22 June 1940.

from orange-yellow to ebony black. A wild mixture – for our conceptions an impossibility. This impossibility was commanded by a white French officer. The commander of the battalion was well-groomed, well-dressed, wore a monocle and was a knight of the Legion of Honor." Clearly, the German officer could not understand how a prestigious French commander, somebody he could consider his equal, was in charge of this exotic group. His estrangement only increased when his unit inadvertently fired a warning shot, whereupon some black soldiers "began dancing around me, showing their teeth, always ready to jump on me and finish me off. But I calmed down the wild guys who were running wild."[139]

These examples demonstrate that many German commanders and soldiers, committed to a concept of white racial superiority, objected on principle to the presence of black soldiers on European battlefields. Although this objection did not always refer to any actual behavior of the black troops, the charge that blacks were fighting in a perfidious way and with illegitimate methods was never very far. German battle reports on combat with black troops often accused the blacks of shooting at dispersed Germans, of shooting from hideouts, of using their *coupe-coupes*, and of mutilating POWs or dead Germans. Of these practices, which were not all unique to black troops, only the mutilation of POWs or dead soldiers was illegal. But whatever black troops did was frequently seen as "perfidious," "cunning," and "treacherous" by German troops. Typical of this is a combat description from the 21st Infantry Division fighting in the Argonne region in mid-June: "A fierce combat starts in the forest. The opposing Frenchmen, mostly blacks, are resisting tenaciously and fighting cunningly and insidiously. Soldiers who shoot from trees

---

[139] "Von Stonne – Calais," BA-MA, RH 37/1910 (Erlebnisberichte Schützen-regiment 69).

[*Baumschützen*] fire on our supply units and often continue to fight with long bush knives even after they are wounded. They are a most unwelcome addition."[140]

Of particular concern to the Germans was the *coupe-coupe*, the long knife that the Tirailleurs Sénégalais traditionally carried and with which they charged and fought in close combat, especially after having exhausted their ammunition. German war diaries often took note of the *coupe-coupes* of captured Tirailleurs. Many Germans automatically assumed that the blacks were using their *coupe-coupes* for illegitimate purposes such as the mutilation of German prisoners or corpses. The mere finding of a *coupe-coupe* could inspire the desire for revenge and even spark a massacre, as becomes clear from the report of Georges Parisot, a lieutenant of the 26th RTS: "I am alone in a courtyard; five minutes later the first German arrives and puts his revolver under my nose. I protest vehemently. Other Germans arrive. They are mad because they have found a *coupe-coupe*, and they protest against this weapon and our use of blacks."[141] Near Erquinvillers, a German officer showed a *coupe-coupe* to a French commander and exclaimed: "*That* is your war, you bastards."[142] When members of Infantry Regiment 36 discovered *coupe-coupes* in an abandoned French position in Moreuil north of Erquinvillers, one of them noted in his diary: "We will remember the knives of Moreuil very well! A nation that needs to boost its dwindling population with such people is close enough to the abyss."[143]

German soldiers also believed that black POWs were prone to hiding their *coupe-coupes* so that they could suddenly kill their

---

[140] "Die 21. Infanterie-Division im Westfeldzug. Vom Rhein an die Saône!" BA-MA, RH 26–21, vol. 6, pp. 35–6 (entry 14 June 1940).

[141] Parisot, SHAT 34 N 1099.

[142] Long, CHETOM 15 H 144.

[143] "Frankreich 1940. Tagebuchblätter und Berichte aus dem II/I.R. 36," BA-MA, RH 37/6420 (entry on 9 June 1940).

guards and escape.[144] This fear probably helped trigger the order of Walther Nehring, discussed previously, to guard black POWs with special strictness. On some occasions, black prisoners did escape with the help of their *coupe-coupes*, perhaps because the Germans, when disarming prisoners, at first paid attention only to their firearms and overlooked the *coupe-coupe*, which the Tirailleurs Sénégalais traditionally carried in an inconspicuous sheath on their trousers.[145] The Germans' fear of the *coupe-coupe*, however, was often so great that the slightest movement by a Tirailleur Sénégalais could trigger violence.

The obsession with *coupe-coupes* was, according to historian Sandra Maß, a reaction to the trauma of physical fragmentation from World War I, projected specifically on the black soldiers fighting for France during that war and used as part of France's occupation troops in the Rhineland thereafter. In a similar vein, historian Jean-Yves Le Naour observes that the person-to-person violence, as symbolized by the mutilation charge, often provoked more outrage than the much greater impersonal violence of modern weapons. He therefore argues that the notion of the savage black soldier wielding his *coupe-coupe* served as a coping mechanism for soldiers and civilians terrorized by modern warfare.[146] We will examine the veracity of the mutilation charges later, but the important fact is that, in many cases, the very presence of black soldiers in the French army as well as the fact that they used *coupe-coupes* inspired the Germans to cast them as illegitimate combatants and thus as soldiers not protected by the

---

[144] Chatelard, SHAT 34 N 1081.

[145] Such an incident happened, for example, in late May 1940 with prisoners from the 12th RTS in Argonne: Dartigues, *Des coloniaux au combat*, 90.

[146] Sandra Maß, "Das Trauma des weißen Mannes. Afrikanische Kolonialsoldaten in propagandistischen Texten, 1914–1923," *L'Homme. Zeitschrift für feministische Geschichtswissenschaft* 12, no. 1 (2001); Jean-Yves Le Naour, *La honte noire. L'Allemagne et les troupes coloniales françaises 1914–1945* (Paris: Hachette Littérature, 2003), 27.

Geneva Convention. Not infrequently, they were placed in the context of franc-tireurs, who could be court-martialled and shot by German officers. Authorization for the massacres of 1940 thus did not emanate from legal documents or specific orders; it came from racial prejudice. It is to the origins of this prejudice that we now need to turn.

FIGURE 2. Capitaine Charles N'Tchoréré, one of the commanders during the defense of Airaines. He was murdered on 7 June 1940 after he disobeyed an order to leave a group of captured officers and join the rank and file. Some German officers were outraged by the fact that the French army not only drafted black soldiers but also promoted a few of them to officer. Musée des troupes de marine, Fréjus.

FIGURE 3. German soldiers watch black prisoners at a makeshift gathering point set up with barbed wire in front of the cathedral of Clamecy (Nièvre). Some prisoners would later be murdered in nearby camps. Archives départementales de la Nièvre, Fonds Edouard Bélile.

FIGURE 4. Captured black soldiers marching to a
POW camp. In many cases, guards attacked and
killed black prisoners on these marches and
prevented them from getting water and food.
Archives départementales de la Nièvre, Fonds
Edouard Bélile.

FIGURE 5. Black prisoners digging a trench. Perhaps this picture shows the
preparations for the shooting of forty-one African POWs in Clamecy on 18 June
1940. Archives départementales de la Nièvre, Fonds Edouard Bélile.

FIGURE 6. Prisoners doing work on a farm. Black POWs were more likely to get permission for work on farms outside the POW camps because they were less likely to escape. Relations with the farmers could be cordial. These prisoners often received extra food and pay. Archives départementales de la Nièvre, Fonds Edouard Bélile.

FIGURE 7. POWs with their guards on a farm. Archives départementales de la Nièvre, Fonds Edouard Bélile.

FIGURE 8. Prisoners, probably North Africans, on their march to work. Archives départementales de la Nièvre, Fonds Edouard Bélile.

FIGURE 9. German soldiers posing with an African prisoner. The stick in his hand and the sign around his neck ("police") indicate that the black man was an auxiliary guard. The soldier on the right seems to mockingly suggest a Napoleonic pose to the African. Archives départementales de la Nièvre, Fonds Edouard Bélile.

FIGURE 10. German guard posing with a West African (left) and probably North African prisoner (right). Germans often looked at the Africans with a certain curiosity and amusement. Archives départementales de la Nièvre, Fonds Edouard Bélile.

FIGURE 11. North African prisoners taking a break. Archives départementales de la Nièvre, Fonds Edouard Bélile.

FIGURES 12, 13, AND 14. Recruitment posters for the French colonial troops. Although France had introduced a conscription system in French West Africa after World War I, it also relied on volunteers from West Africa and other colonies. Musée des troupes de marine, Fréjus. Limited rights.

2

The Origin and Evolution of the Prejudice

THE COLONIAL WARS

Although discourses on Africans had a long tradition in Germany
as in other European countries, Germany's experience as a colonial power from 1884 to 1918 formed the background for most of
the perceptions and prejudices relevant for the events of 1940.[1]
Most revealing was the public discussion of instances of combat
between German army units and black African insurgents. During a series of colonial uprisings in 1904–7, German army units
fought the rebels with methods that were considered unusually
harsh even in the rough context of colonial counterinsurgency
wars. Under scrutiny from critics in parliament and the press,
the army spread atrocity stories about the rebels that were widely
publicized in the right-wing press. Both the publication of atrocity stories about armed black men as well as the ruthlessness of
the German army's repression are significant in the light of the
atrocities of 1940.

[1] Russell Berman, *Enlightenment or Empire: Colonial Discourse in German Culture*
(Lincoln: University of Nebraska Press, 1998); Martin, *Schwarze Teufel, edle
Mohren*; Sara Friedrichsmeyer, Sara Lennox, and Susanne Zantop, eds., *The
Imperialist Imagination: German Colonialism and Its Legacy* (Ann Arbor: Univer-
sity of Michigan Press, 1998). On prevalent images of sub-Saharan Africans in
Germany, see Jutta Bückendorf, *"Schwarz-weiß-rot über Ostafrika!" Deutsche Kolo-
nialpläne und afrikanische Realität* (Münster: Lit Verlag, 1997), 263–7.

81

In January of 1904, the Herero people started a revolt in German Southwest Africa (today's Namibia). The repression of this revolt quickly became a question of prestige for the German army, particularly after the Emperor began taking a personal interest in the war and charged Alfred von Schlieffen, the Chief of the General Staff, with the direction of operations. Because the German army experienced a series of setbacks until the summer of 1904, the local commander faced massive pressure to put down the uprising by whatever means he deemed necessary. Lieutenant-General Lothar von Trotha, according to one historian "a veritable butcher in uniform," conducted a counterinsurgency campaign aiming not only to beat the Hereros militarily but also to destroy the entire people. Trotha's conduct of the campaign at first enjoyed the unconditional support of the General Staff and the Emperor.[2] In the German press loyal to the government, stories of atrocities allegedly committed by Hereros spread quickly. The Herero were accused of mutilating wounded German soldiers by cutting off ears, noses, or other body parts; of castrating German settlers; and of raping, slaughtering, and disemboweling women.[3] On the basis of these largely fallacious atrocity stories, Trotha ordered that all Herero tribesmen in German-controlled territory be shot and that women

---

[2] Horst Drechsler, *Let Us Die Fighting: The Struggle of the Herero and Nama against German Imperialism (1884–1915),* trans. Bernd Zöllner (London: Zed Press, 1980), 147; Helmut Bley, *South-West Africa under German Rule, 1894–1914,* trans. Hugh Ridley (Evanston: Northwestern University Press, 1971), 150; Woodruff D. Smith, *The German Colonial Empire* (Chapel Hill: University of North Carolina Press, 1978), 63–5. For a detailed history of the war, see Jon Bridgman, *The Revolt of the Hereros* (Berkeley: University of California Press, 1981).

[3] Drechsler, *Let Us Die Fighting,* 146; Helmut Walser Smith, "The Talk of Genocide, the Rhetoric of Miscegenation: Notes on Debates in the German Reichstag Concerning Southwest Africa, 1904–1914," in *The Imperialist Imagination: German Colonialism and Its Legacy,* eds. Sara Friedrichsmeyer, Sara Lennox, and Susanne Zantop (Ann Arbor: Michigan University Press, 1998), 112–13.

and children be expelled to the desert. German military leaders considered this war a race war between blacks and whites that could only be decided by the destruction of the one or the other. The campaign led to the death of between sixty thousand and sixty-five thousand Hereros (75–80 percent of the population).[4]

More atrocity stories about butchered German women and children circulated later in 1904 when the Nama, a Hottentot people living in southern Namibia, started their uprising. This time, even the army had to admit that the stories were invented and that the Nama had on some occasions protected German women and children.[5] Still, the repression of the Nama uprising was almost as severe as the war on the Hereros; about ten thousand Nama, roughly half of the population, are believed to have died in the course of the war. Many Hereros and Namas who survived the initial onslaught of the German army perished of malnutrition and disease in concentration camps or as forced laborers.[6]

In 1905, the Maji-Maji uprising, a vast rebellion triggered largely by colonial abuses, broke out in German East Africa. The lingering crisis over German colonial policy that the army had hoped to end through rapid and ruthless repression in Southwest Africa thus threatened to get out of control. In East Africa, the German army used large numbers of askaris, African

---

[4] Bridgman, *The Revolt of the Hereros*, 126–31; Bley, *South-West Africa under German Rule*, 163–5; Jon Bridgman and Leslie J. Worley, "Genocide of the Hereros," in *Genocide in the Twentieth Century: Critical Essays and Eyewitness Accounts*, eds. Samuel Totten, William S. Parsons, and Israel W. Charny (New York and London: Garland, 1995); Gesine Krüger, *Kriegsbewältigung und Geschichtsbewusstsein: Realität, Deutung und Verarbeitung des deutschen Kolonialkriegs in Namibia 1904 bis 1907* (Göttingen: Vandenhoeck & Ruprecht, 1999). Krüger offers cautious remarks on the accuracy of numbers but does not dispute the enormity of the Herero death toll.

[5] Drechsler, *Let Us Die Fighting*, 184–5.

[6] Smith, "The Talk of Genocide, the Rhetoric of Miscegenation," 111.

mercenaries, to suppress the Maji-Maji uprising with great harshness. Thousands of captured rebels were shot, and the scorched earth policy adopted by the German army brought devastation to large areas. At least seventy-five thousand Africans were killed in these operations.[7]

These gruesome policies, initiated and carried out by the German army, triggered resistance from the civilian colonial authorities, some of the white settlers, Reich Chancellor Bernhard von Bülow, and a large segment of the German public. The methods of the German army in Southwest Africa became the subject of critical inquiries by the Social Democrats and the Center Party in the national parliament (*Reichstag*), and the government moderated its policies toward Africans after 1907.[8] Still, the public debate in these years established images of black people that were important for the encounters of Germans with black soldiers in the future. Conservatives denied that the Hereros and Namas were human at all. Conservative Party deputy Ludwig zu Reventlow, for example, claimed that they were "blood thirsty beasts in the form of humans."[9] Liberals took a middle position by arguing that the Hereros were perhaps human but could not be civilized and therefore should be enclosed in reservations, as were Native Americans.[10] The Social Democrats defended the humanity of black Africans and attacked the army's practices as "bestial," but even they believed that the Hereros and Namas were uncivilized and "barbaric."

7 Smith, *The German Colonial Empire*, 106–7; Michael Adas, *Prophets of Rebellion: Millenarian Protest Movements against the European Colonial Order* (Chapel Hill and London: University of North Carolina Press, 1979), 25–34; John Iliffe, *Tanganyika under German Rule, 1905–1912* (London: Cambridge University Press, 1969), 9–29; Walter Nuhn, *Flammen über Deutschost: Der Maji-Maji-Aufstand in Deutsch-Ostafrika 1905–1906* (Bonn: Bernhard & Graefe, 1998).

8 Smith, *The German Colonial Empire*, 192–209.

9 Smith, "The Talk of Genocide, the Rhetoric of Miscegenation," 112.

10 Ibid., 114–15.

Germany's colonial experience therefore was instrumental in establishing notions of black men as brutal and illegitimate warriors. In public debate, the image of the mutilating black soldier and of the wild rapist was widely advertised by conservatives – though against much criticism from Social Democrats and Center Party members. The spread of these images in public discourse was probably more important than the actual memory of German military men. The army units deployed in the colonies were never very large (at most fifteen thousand in Southwest Africa in 1904–07), and few Germans involved in the counterinsurgency operations are likely to have served in 1940.

THE FEAR OF FRANC-TIREURS

In addition to the negative stereotype of the black man in arms established during the colonial wars, we have to consider the German army's obsession with illegitimate warfare, particularly its fear of franc-tireurs (armed civilians, isolated soldiers, or illegal paramilitary groups). This obsession harkened back to the Franco-German War of 1870–71. When the German armies invaded France in 1870, French irregular units and civilians, calling themselves franc-tireurs, began attacking German soldiers and communications. The Prussian General Staff saw these largely inefficient attacks as a form of terrorism and reacted with reprisals. Recollections of the franc-tireur war influenced the institutional memory of the German army and the training at its officer schools in the following decades.[11] As a consequence,

---

[11] John Horne and Alan Kramer, *German Atrocities, 1914: A History of Denial* (New Haven and London: Yale University Press, 2001), 140–5; Fernand Thiébaud Schneider, "Der Krieg in französischer Sicht," in *Entscheidung 1870. Der deutsch-französische Krieg,* eds. Wolfgang von Groote and Ursula von Gersdorff (Stuttgart: Deutsche Verlags-Anstalt, 1970); Dennis Showalter, *The Wars of German Unification* (London: Arnold, 2004), 318–24.

the Germans expected large-scale irregular resistance when they invaded Belgium and northern France in 1914. This expectation, fanned by the excitement and rumors that characterized the first weeks of the war, soon intensified to paranoid levels and led to the execution of thousands of innocent Belgian and French civilians accused of being franc-tireurs from August to October 1914. In most cases, the German casualties blamed on franc-tireurs had been caused by friendly fire or the fire of distant regular soldiers.[12]

Although German army leaders never publicly admitted the scale of their delusion in 1914, it was obvious to many that they had gone too far. The "reprisals" stopped almost completely after October 1914, and in 1940, German army units, as we have seen, were under strict orders to behave impeccably toward the civilian population. Still, the German Army Command upheld the fiction that a franc-tireur war had taken place in 1914 against which it had carried out legitimate reprisals.[13] As perpetrator or witness, a large part of the German army was involved in the atrocities in Belgium and northern France (only small forces were at first mobilized in the east against Russia). The paranoia about a franc-tireur war, as well as the atrocities committed in reaction to it, must have belonged to the shared memory of many officers in 1940.

There is an intriguing connection between the German atrocities in 1914 and colonial warfare. As John Horne and Alan Kramer argue, "the treatment of Africans in colonial wars probably influenced German military doctrine on how to deal with civilian resistance" in 1914.[14] In the First World War, Germans and Belgians accused each other of using methods associated

---

[12] Lothar Wieland, *Belgien 1914. Die Frage des belgischen "Franctireurkrieges" und die deutsche öffentliche Meinung 1914–1936* (Frankfurt am Main: Peter Lang, 1984), 1–38; Horne and Kramer, *German Atrocities, 1914.*

[13] Horne and Kramer, *German Atrocities, 1914,* 402–5.

[14] Horne and Kramer, *German Atrocities, 1914,* 223; Wieland, *Belgien 1914,* 21.

with colonial wars. One Belgian civilian, for example, argued that a German officer formerly stationed in the German colony Cameroon "treated us as Negroes." On the other side, a German newspaper in August 1914 stated that Germans had been the victims of cruelties seen only "in combat with Negroes" in Southwest Africa. A German general, moreover, argued that Belgian civilians had committed atrocities "such as are found otherwise only among the hordes of inferior races" and concluded: "The Belgians rank with the Hereros well below the level of the Hottentots!"[15] Interestingly, the same atrocity stories circulated in both cases: In 1914, German soldiers claimed that Belgian civilians had gouged out the eyes of their wounded comrades, poisoned them, and mutilated them. Perhaps the alleged implication of women in the Belgian resistance also evoked (or reflected) memories of the struggle against the Hereros, whose women had cheered the men into battle and were accused of having committed atrocities themselves. In any case, like the African insurgent of 1904–7, the franc-tireur was seen as treacherous, cunning, and brutal.[16] He (or she) was an often invisible enemy not unlike the Tirailleur Sénégalais in the close combat situations of June 1940. Black rebels and franc-tireurs were both considered illegitimate combatants, as were, later on, black soldiers fighting in Europe. As we have seen, German officers in 1940 had orders to court-martial franc-tireurs.[17] Moreover, they often associated the resistance of dispersed black soldiers with franc-tireur warfare. The massacre of at least forty Africans in Villacourt on 22 June, for example, was motivated by claims that

[15] Horne and Kramer, *German Atrocities, 1914*, 35, 135, 156.

[16] Ibid., 14, 95, 111.

[17] The German guidebook for the conduct of war, issued by the General Staff in 1902, justified terror in response to irregular warfare. Manfred Messerschmidt, "Völkerrecht und 'Kriegsnotwendigkeit' in der deutschen militärischen Tradition seit den Einigungskriegen," *German Studies Review* 6, no. 2 (1983): 241, 243.

an African franc-tireur (in reality a dispersed soldier) had shot at some Germans.[18]

THE DEBATE ON THE USE OF BLACK TROOPS IN
EUROPEAN WARS

Given the depiction of insurgent Africans as mutilating and rap-ing savages during the colonial wars, it comes as no surprise that the deployment of African troops in European theaters of war was highly controversial. All colonial powers had, however, drafted native soldiers and workers in their efforts to expand, control, and defend their colonies. Using African troops against other Africans never was a contentious issue. In fact, it was a necessity, and African mercenaries played a crucial role in the buildup of European empires.[19] Even the Germans had used African mercenaries from as far away as Somalia, the askaris, in their repression of the Maji-Maji uprising in 1905, and the pro-tection force in German East Africa consisted predominantly of askaris.[20] The idea of stationing and deploying African soldiers in Europe, however, provoked much resistance. At the center of controversy was France, which used colonial troops (predomi-nantly North Africans) in the Crimean War (1853–6), the Italian campaign against Austria (1859), and the Franco-German War (1870–1).[21] In the years preceding World War I, the low birthrate in France and the resulting military disadvantage strengthened arguments for a bigger colonial army that could help to cancel out Germany's numerical superiority. Under the leadership of

---

[18] Habe, *A Thousand Shall Fall,* 234–37.

[19] Bruce Vandervort, *Wars of Imperial Conquest in Africa, 1830–1914* (Bloom-ington: Indiana University Press, 1998).

[20] Smith, *The German Colonial Empire,* 106–7.

[21] Hugues de la Barre de Nanteuil, "L'Armée d'Afrique dans les campagnes du Second Empire (1854–1871)," in *L'Armée d'Afrique (1830–1962),* ed. Robert Huré (Paris: Charles-Lavauzelle, 1977).

General Charles Mangin, who published a book called *La force noire* in 1910, plans were drafted for a large-scale recruitment of troops in French West Africa, of which a significant part was meant to serve in Europe.

While advertising their idea, Mangin and his associates claimed that some of the West African populations belonged to particularly vigorous and courageous races (*races guerrières*) that would be ideally suited to assault warfare. Allegedly, these groups had an unusual ability to cope with fear and were obedient and loyal. Led firmly by (white) officers, these warriors could be fierce storm troopers whose appearance on the battlefield would spread panic among the Germans.[22] Similar arguments for using colonial units in European wars also existed in Britain, which did not have the draft and therefore relied heavily on its Indian army. But for geographic reasons, preparing colonial units for a land war in Europe seemed less pressing to Britain than to France. Italy had ambitious plans for drafting armies in its African colonies and realized a small part of them in World War I, while Spain drafted soldiers from Spanish Morocco. But none of these countries launched a colonial recruiting program as ambitious as the French and was as committed to deploying colonial troops in the defense of the mainland.[23]

[22] Echenberg, *Colonial Conscripts*, 14–15. Christian Koller, *"Von Wilden aller Rassen niedergemetzelt"*. *Die Diskussion um die Verwendung von Kolonialtruppen in Europa zwischen Rassismus, Kolonial- und Militärpolitik (1914–1930)* (Stuttgart: Franz Steiner, 2001), 30–9; Marc Michel, "Colonisation et défense nationale. Le Général Mangin et la force noire," *Guerres mondiales et conflits contemporains* 37, no. 145 (1987). This argument fit well with the mood of cultural pessimism, which was widespread in Europe throughout the early decades of the twentieth century. The West African warrior appeared as an unspoiled counterimage to the European weakened by an industrialized civilization. See János Riesz, "L'Afrique dans les lettres allemandes entre les deux guerres (1919–1939)," in *Rencontres franco-allemandes sur l'Afrique. Lettres, sciences humaines et sociales*, eds. Hélène D'Almeida-Topor and János Riesz (Paris: L'Harmattan, 1992), 104–6.

[23] Koller, *"Von Wilden aller Rassen niedergemetzelt,"* 79–81, 185–6, 342.

Given that Germany was France's most likely opponent in land warfare, the planned deployment of large French colonial units in Europe elicited the strongest response there. Germany had no colonial troops to use in Europe and every interest in preventing the strengthening of the French army through deployment of African soldiers in Europe. German critics tried to delegitimize Mangin's program with four core arguments that were also advanced in other colonial powers, including France, where Mangin always faced opposition.[24] The first argument was that such a deployment would undermine the notion of white supremacy and thus weaken a cornerstone of European colonialism. Africans, living at close quarters with white people in Europe and fighting against the armies of other white people, might lose their respect for the white man. Veterans returning to the colonies might then join the anticolonial resistance and make their military expertise available to the struggle for independence. In a pamphlet published in 1940, for example, Rudolf Dammert echoed many earlier arguments: "The European colonizing peoples have always justified their colonial possessions and their rule by mandate with reference to the cultural superiority of the white race over the natural peoples. Therefore it was the worst act of betrayal of the white race to arm colored natives of colonial territories against peoples of the white race and to lead them to struggle against them."[25] This argument was frequently used by Germans in an appeal to the solidarity of white

---

[24] For a detailed discussion of the arguments about the *force noire* in France, see Charles John Balesi, *From Adversaries to Comrades-in-Arms: West Africans and the French Military 1885–1918* (Waltham: Crossroads Press, 1979), 58–60, 67–76. A summary of some arguments is provided by Peter Bernard Clarke, *West Africans at War, 1914–18/1939–45: Colonial Propaganda and Its Cultural Aftermath* (London: Ethnographica, 1986), 6–8.

[25] Rudoph Dammert, *Der Verrat an Europa: Die Greueltaten der farbigen Truppen Frankreichs im Weltkrieg* (Stuttgart: Deutsche Verlags-Anstalt, 1940), 8.

colonizing powers, but it also had strong adherents in Britain and France.

Second, the critics argued that the use of colonial troops in Europe was an offense to the cultural norms of Europeans. This argument was particularly virulent when employed against black soldiers from sub-Saharan Africa, who were believed to come from the lowest ranks of civilization. The animalized image of these soldiers implied that a European power using them in Europe would be doing the same as letting loose wild animals against a "civilized" enemy and thus would violate the codes of conduct for wars between nation states. The underlying assumption was that black Africans were savages who could not be expected to adhere to civilized norms and who should therefore not be used in a war between civilized nations. As international laws of war were being codified from the 1890s to 1907, this line of thought inspired efforts to make illegal the deployment of colonial subjects in Europe, but to no avail. The prevailing opinion among European legal experts was that colonial troops could be deployed in Europe as long as they were led by Europeans and as long as they respected the international conventions on warfare.[26]

Third, many critics denied that colonial soldiers would be fit to participate in European warfare. If not already decimated by the effects of the foreign climate, colonial troops might panic when coming under artillery and machine gun fire or, as was claimed later, aerial bombardment. This argument, which was most prominent in France, did not necessarily dispute the legitimacy of deploying colonial soldiers in Europe but rejected the utility and wisdom of such a deployment. In the First World War, the French army introduced a concession to its medical aspect by instituting the practice of *hivernage*: Black troops

[26] Koller, *"Von Wilden aller Rassen niedergemetzelt,"* 53–63.

were transferred to the south of France or North Africa from November to March to protect them from the infectious diseases widespread in the harsher climate of the north.[27] The concern about the suitability of non-European soldiers for mechanized warfare, however, never died down. Even in 1940, French officers worried that their colonial troops would not hold out under the bombardment of German artillery and dive-bombers.[28]

Fourth, critics sought to undermine the legitimacy of using colonial troops in Europe by arguing that they would be used as cannon fodder for their army. This argument had the advantage of not being racist, at least not on the surface, and it suggested a well-meaning attitude toward the colonial soldiers, who could be depicted as having been seduced or blackmailed by their colonial masters to fight for a foreign cause. The cannon fodder thesis appeared in Nazi propaganda and in newspaper reporting on the 1940 campaign in the United States.[29] Although the cannon fodder thesis may have helped many Germans overcome their rage against Tirailleurs Sénégalais in POW camps once better treatment became the norm, it hardly helped to protect the Tirailleurs from execution during the campaign. If German soldiers saw Tirailleurs Sénégalais as savage beasts, it mattered little whether these "beasts" had been set on them by somebody else or had attacked without any instigation. When the SS newspaper *Das Schwarze Korps*, which had repeatedly employed the cannon fodder thesis, reported alleged war crimes by black troops in its issue of 6 June 1940, it concluded: "We feel no hatred against the snake that chokes us; but we crush it."[30]

---

[27] Balesi questions the necessity of this measure on purely physical grounds: Balesi, *From Adversaries to Comrades-in-Arms*, 100–7.

[28] Binet and Lapasse, SHAT 34 N 1079; "Les attaques vers la Somme," CHETOM 15 H 144.

[29] C. L. R. James, George Breitman, and Edgar Keemer, *Fighting Racism in World War II* (New York: Monad Press, 1980), 86.

[30] "Die Garde der Zivilisation," *Das Schwarze Korps* 23, no. 23, 6 June 1940, p. 8.

Interestingly, the rhetoric in support of using West African troops in Europe often shared the same racist notions that the opponents used.[31] When advertising the fighting virtues of West African recruits, Mangin and his supporters tended to stress the ferocity of West African warriors so much that they played into the hands of those critics who saw black Africans as savages. When colonial units arrived in France at the outbreak of the First World War, crowds gathered and called on the Africans to cut off the heads of the Germans.[32] The efforts to prove the feasibility of using Africans in mechanized warfare thus were grist for the mill of those critics who claimed that the Africans would not respect the conventions of warfare. The French proponents of colonial troops in Europe responded to this criticism by claiming that France had "civilized" these warriors. Mangin and his successors cast the West African soldier as a big child: innocent, good-natured, and somewhat naïve; he had been educated by the French without losing his allegedly inborn courage and viability in war. It was only fair that he should sacrifice his blood to defend the country that had brought him civilization.[33]

THE DEPLOYMENT OF TIRAILLEURS SÉNÉGALAIS IN THE FIRST WORLD WAR

In the First World War, France's use of colonial troops on the Western front, the Gallipoli peninsula, and Macedonia made the

---

[31] This aspect is explained well in Hans-Jürgen Lüsebrink, "'Tirailleurs Sénégalais' und 'Schwarze Schande' – Verlaufsformen und Konsequenzen einer deutsch-französischen Auseinandersetzung (1910–1926)," in *"Tirailleurs sénégalais": zur bildlichen und literarischen Darstellung afrikanischer Soldaten im Dienste Frankreichs*, eds. János Riesz and Joachim Schultz (Frankfurt am Main: Peter Lang, 1989). See also Koller, *"Von Wilden aller Rassen niedergemetzelt,"* 30–1.

[32] Bakary Diallo, *Force-Bonté* (Paris: Rieder, 1926), 113.

[33] Koller, *"Von Wilden aller Rassen niedergemetzelt,"* 139–44, 270–4; Balesi, *From Adversaries to Comrades-in-Arms*, 99.

deployment of African troops in Europe a subject of the war of words between the opposing camps. In his memoirs, German Field Marshal Paul von Hindenburg argued that non-European soldiers had contributed to the German defeat; his observations mixed accusations of war crimes with the cannon fodder thesis: "Where he had no tanks, the enemy drove black waves against us, waves consisting of African bodies. Woe to us if these waves broke into our lines and murdered, or worse, tortured, the defenseless. Human outrage and accusation, however, should be directed not against the blacks who committed these atrocities but rather against those who drafted such hordes under the pretense of fighting for honor, freedom, and law on European soil. Thousands of blacks were led to the slaughter."[34] Hindenburg's stance was by no means unique; swayed by war hysteria, leading intellectuals such as Thomas Mann and Max Weber had expressed even sharper outrage at the use of non-European troops by Germany's enemies.[35]

No study focusing on the interactions between Germans and Tirailleurs Sénégalais during the First World War exists. Initially, the Germans at the front seem to have attached little importance to the colonial troops and respected them for their fighting spirit; some generals found that they could motivate their troops to fight harder and hold out longer under attack if they explained that colonial troops fought on the opposing side.[36] Later in the war, however, fear of black troops was widespread among the Germans after some bitter battles between Germans

---

[34] Paul von Hindenburg, *Aus meinem Leben* (Leipzig: S. Hirzel, 1920), 352.

[35] Christian Koller, "Der 'dunkle Verrat an Europa': Afrikanische Soldaten im Krieg 1914–1918 in der deutschen Wahrnehmung," in *Zwischen Charleston und Stechschritt. Schwarze im Nationalsozialismus*, eds. Peter Martin and Christine Alonzo (Hamburg: Dölling und Galitz, 2004), 111–12.

[36] Jean-Luc Susini, "La perception des 'troupes noires' par les allemands," in *Les troupes coloniales dans la Grande Guerre*, eds. Claude Carlier and Guy Pedroncini (Paris: Economica, 1997).

and West Africans occurred during which both sides appear to have mistreated and killed prisoners.[37] After sifting through the German documents and finding French reports of colonial soldiers displaying heads and ears of their enemies, historian Christian Koller concluded that the mutilation of German POWs by West African soldiers, as depicted by German propaganda, might occasionally have happened but that the German charges appear vastly exaggerated.[38] More important than the actual experience of German frontline troops may have been the fact that German soldiers and civilians in the First World War were increasingly exposed to propaganda casting the black African soldiers as cruel and barbaric, as illegitimate warriors in the footsteps of the anticolonial rebels. Even the charge of cannibalism belonged to the German propaganda arsenal.[39] Because Allied propaganda declared the fight against Germany a struggle of civilization against barbarism, German propagandists considered the French deployment of supposedly "barbarian" troops an ideal opportunity for a countercharge.[40] Many German officers of 1940 had fought in the First World War and considered it their shaping experience. It is hard to imagine that they had forgotten this propaganda even if they had not participated in combat with West African troops.

Ironically, German recrimination against the use of black soldiers in Europe coincided with widespread German use of black soldiers in one of the most celebrated success stories of World War I, the tenacious resistance of the protection force

[37] Marc Michel, *L'appel à l'Afrique: contributions et réactions à l'effort de guerre en A.O.F. (1914–1919)* (Paris: Publications de la Sorbonne, 1982), 291, 293; Koller, "Der 'dunkle Verrat an Europa,'" 113.

[38] Koller, *"Von Wilden aller Rassen niedergemetzelt,"* 101–2. See also Michel, *L'appel à l'Afrique,* 344–8.

[39] For a summary of the most common allegations, published in 1940, see Dammert, *Der Verrat an Europa.*

[40] Balesi, *From Adversaries to Comrades-in-Arms,* 109–11.

(*Schutztruppe*) in German East Africa under the command of General Paul von Lettow-Vorbeck against far superior British armies. As Lettow-Vorbeck admitted in his popular memoirs, the German military effort in eastern Africa relied on native soldiers, askaris, who outnumbered Germans by ten to one. In many phases of the campaign, moreover, the *Schutztruppe* required the services of thousands of porters drawn from the local population.[41] Although the *Schutztruppe* initially fought mostly against British units recruited in India and Central Africa, a large South African offensive in 1916 pitted white Boers against the black askaris under German command. Whether Lettow-Vorbeck and his many admirers were aware of the irony of this situation is not clear. Their primary interest after 1918 was to defend Germany's right to colonies, and they used the loyalty and support of the native population in German East Africa to demonstrate that German colonialism had been beneficial to the local population.[42] The claim to the loyalty of the natives was misleading, however, because many askaris were mercenaries without connection to the local population and because coercion played a larger role than Lettow-Vorbeck admitted.[43]

In France, the First World War led – after trials and tribulations – to an increased reliance on West African troops. Initially, the reports about the performance of the black soldiers were contradictory. Examples of exceptional heroism contrasted with cases of mass flight.[44] Poorly deployed and weakened by

---

[41] Paul von Lettow-Vorbeck, *Meine Erinnerungen aus Ostafrika* (Leipzig: Koehler, 1920), 9, 17, 21–2.

[42] Lettow-Vorbeck, *Meine Erinnerungen aus Ostafrika*, 9; Klaus Helbig, "Die deutsche Kriegführung in Ostafrika 1914–1918," *Militärgeschichte* 28, no. 2 (1989): 136.

[43] Helbig, "Die deutsche Kriegführung in Ostafrika 1914–1918," 140. Desertion also was high during some phases of the campaign.

[44] Echenberg, *Colonial Conscripts*, 32–8. For an example of a heroic feat accomplished by black East African soldiers from the French army, see Antoine Champeaux, "Les traditions du 1er battallion de tirailleurs somalis. De

disease, the Tirailleurs Sénégalais often fought heroically but ineffectively. By 1917 recruitment in West Africa almost collapsed because of doubts regarding the fighting virtues of colonial troops in France and because of African resistance to recruitment. It took a major reorganization of recruitment and deployment to revitalize Mangin's cause. This reorganization, however, brought a record number of Tirailleurs Sénégalais to France in 1918. Here, they were often used as shock troops in close connection with white units.[45] Although the overall casualty rate of black African troops in World War I was equal to the casualty rate of European French troops, historian Joe Lunn argues that the Tirailleurs Sénégalais suffered much higher casualties in the last two years of the war, as they were deliberately deployed in the most dangerous places to minimize French casualties. That the overall casualty rate of Tirailleurs Sénégalais is not higher stems from the fact that these troops were withdrawn from the front during the winter and had had lower casualty rates in the first two years of the war.[46]

After the First World War, France was even more committed to using West African troops in Europe. These troops had shown that they could fight effectively particularly when mixed with white units. Moreover, the demographic disadvantage of France, due to the low French birthrate, had increased because the losses of the French army were proportionally even higher than the German losses. Therefore conscription was introduced in French West Africa in 1919.[47] Responding to the war-weariness of white troops at the end of the war, the French army demobilized many

Donaumont à Djibouti," in *Les troupes coloniales dans la Grande Guerre*, eds. Claude Carlier and Guy Pedroncini (Paris: Economica, 1997).

45 Michel, *L'appel à l'Afrique*, 311–37.

46 Lunn, *Memoirs of the Maelstrom*, 120. Koller agrees with Lunn: Koller, "*Von Wilden aller Rassen niedergemetzelt*," 100. For the contrasting argument, see Michel, *L'appel à l'Afrique*, 337.

47 Echenberg, *Colonial Conscripts*, 43; Michel, *L'appel à l'Afrique*, 419–23.

white units while keeping colonial units ready for occupation duties. This led directly to the next, and most bitter, controversy over the deployment of colonial troops in Europe.

THE "BLACK HORROR" ON THE RHINE

The armistice of 11 November 1918 gave France and its allies the right to occupy the German Rhineland. The Treaty of Versailles later limited that right to fifteen years from the date on which the treaty took effect. France was assigned an occupation zone in the southern part of the Rhineland and moved some of its colonial units into this zone and later into other areas occupied after alleged German treaty violations. The presence of colonial soldiers in the French occupation force triggered a vicious media hype in Germany and elsewhere, although all evidence suggests that the relations between these troops and the local population were mostly friendly, sometimes *too* friendly for the critics.[48] In much of the German press, the colonial soldiers, particularly the black Africans, were stigmatized as sex-crazed perverts performing outrages against German women, men, and children. Inspired by the title of a pamphlet by Englishman E. D. Morel, the French occupation came to be known as the "Black Horror on the Rhine" (the German term was *Schwarze Schmach*, which denotes "disgrace" or "shame" and is closer to the French term *honte noire*).[49] Many Germans considered it humiliating and

---

[48] Joachim Schultz, "Die 'Utschebebbes' am Rhein – Zur Darstellung schwarzer Soldaten während der französischen Rheinlandbesetzung (1918–1930)," in *'Tirailleurs sénégalais' und 'Schwarze Schande' – Verlaufsformen und Konsequenzen einer deutsch-französischen Auseinandersetzung (1910–1926)*, eds. János Riesz and Joachim Schultz (Frankfurt am Main: Peter Lang, 1989), 79–80; Rainer Pommerin, *Sterilisierung der Rheinlandbastarde. Das Schicksal einer farbigen deutschen Minderheit 1918–1937* (Düsseldorf: Droste, 1979), 23.

[49] Robert C. Reinders, "Racialism on the Left: E. D. Morel and the 'Black Horror on the Rhine,'" *International Review of Social History* 13 (1968). The most comprehensive and up-to-date treatment of the subject, although based mostly

outrageous that colonial subjects possessed a position of power and authority over white Europeans in the Rhineland.[50] The presence of black Africans, in particular, triggered a widespread fear of epidemics and racial degeneration.[51] The German propaganda campaign, which vastly exaggerated and generalized a few incidents, found a receptive audience in some other countries and helped to delegitimize the foreign occupation of German territory. France kept refuting the more fantastic allegations and pointed out that actual crimes by colonial soldiers had been severely punished, but the international response to the Black Horror campaign persuaded the French to reduce their colonial

on French archival sources, is Le Naour, *La honte noire*. For older literature highlighting important aspects, see Th. J. Hooning, "De 'Zwarte Smaad' en zijn gevolgen," *Spiegel Historiael* 17, no. 1 (1982); Doris Kaufmann, "Die Ehre des Vaterlandes und die Ehre der Frauen oder der Kampf an der äusseren und inneren Front. Der Deutsch-Evangelische Frauenbund im Übergang vom Kaiserreich zur Weimarer Republik," *Evangelische Theologie* 46 (1986); Gisela Lebzelter, "Die 'Schwarze Schmach': Vorurteile – Propaganda – Mythos," *Geschichte und Gesellschaft* 11, no. 1 (1985); Sally Marks, "Black Watch on the Rhine: A Study in Propaganda, Prejudice and Prurience," *European Studies Review* 13 (1983); Maß, "Das Trauma des weißen Mannes"; Keith Nelson, "'The Black Horror on the Rhine.' Race as a Factor in Post-World War I Diplomacy," *Journal of Modern History* 42, no. 4 (1970); Ruth Harris, "The 'Child of the Barbarian': Rape, Race and Nationalism in France During the First World War." *Past and Present* 123, no. 141 (1993); Iris Wigger, "'Wenn 'Wilde wie Herren im Herzen Europas hausen.' Das Dogma weißer Überlegenheit in der Kampagne gegen die 'Schwarze Schmach,'" in *Zwischen Charleston und Stechschritt. Schwarze im Nationalsozialismus*, eds. Peter Martin and Christine Alonzo (Hamburg: Dölling und Galitz, 2004).

[50] Fears of race mixture ("Mulattoization") and of racial equality played a profound role. See Tina Campt, Pascal Grosse, and Yara-Colette Lemke-Muñiz de Faria, "Blacks, Germans, and the Politics of Imperial Imagination, 1920–60," in *The Imperialist Imagination: German Colonialism and Its Legacy*, eds. Sara Friedrichsmeyer, Sara Lennox, and Susanne Zantop (Ann Arbor: University of Michigan Press, 1998), 210–13.

[51] Martin, "'Schwarze Pest,'" 73–7. For the campaign of German right-wing women against the presence of colored soldiers in Germany, see Raffael Scheck, *Mothers of the Nation: Right-Wing Women in Weimar Politics* (Oxford and New York: Berg Publishers, 2004), 121–4.

troop contingents in Germany.[52] Interestingly, the Black Horror campaign did not always blame the black soldiers stationed in Europe for the alleged outrages. Frequently, blacks were seen as uncontrolled and wild by nature; if they committed crimes, it was not their responsibility but rather the responsibility of those who deployed them in Europe.[53]

Although North Africans predominated among the colonial units of France's occupation army, the propaganda focused particularly on the black African soldiers, who were a small minority in the French occupation forces.[54] It may have been easier to conjure up an image of "savage" soldiers by referring to the more distant civilization of West Africa rather than the North African civilizations, which enjoyed more prestige in Germany. The demagogic name for the occupation, *Black* Horror on the Rhine, evoked the image of black African rather than North African soldiers. Although the stereotypes were slightly different from the time of the colonial wars and World War I – they focused more on an imagined "wild" sexual desire of black men than on mutilations – the Black Horror campaign reinforced the negative image of the black African soldier.

As with the campaign against the use of colonial soldiers in Europe before World War I, utilitarian motives played a role in the Black Horror campaign of the 1920s. Protesting the alleged abuses of black French troops was meant to drive a wedge between France and its wartime allies and to undermine the legitimacy of the occupation and the Treaty of Versailles in general. Regardless of the motives, the hateful, irrational, and anxiety-provoking depiction of colonial troops in both cases attached a severe stigma to colonial soldiers, particularly to blacks

---

[52] The Tirailleurs Sénégalais were withdrawn already in 1920, and by 1923 other units with black soldiers had also left. See Le Naour, *La honte noire*, 8.

[53] Reinders, "Racialism on the Left," 4–5.

[54] There were some black soldiers in the North African units, but they certainly were not a majority.

recruited by France. The Black Horror campaign was supported by a broader public spectrum in Germany than the army's atrocity propaganda during the colonial wars; only the radical left opposed it. Luise Zietz, deputy of the Independent Social Democratic Party, provoked a storm of abuse in the German National Assembly when she denounced the racist character of the Black Horror campaign.[55]

THE NAZI PROPAGANDA OFFENSIVE AGAINST FRANCE

Given that the belief in a hierarchy of races belonged to the central tenets of National Socialism, it comes as no surprise that the Nazis participated enthusiastically in the Black Horror campaign and kept alive its memory after taking power in 1933. In secret, the Nazi regime also established a program to track down and sterilize the mixed-race children of German women from the Rhineland. Some of these children were abducted at night and sterilized after their mother or stepfather had been pressured to sign a declaration of consent, sometimes under the threat of being deported to a concentration camp.[56] In *Mein Kampf,* Hitler had attacked the stationing of African soldiers in Germany as a Jewish conspiracy and claimed that France, through racial mixing, was already "negroized" to the extent that one could speak of "an African state on European soil."[57] Racist arguments

---

55 *Verhandlungen des Reichstages, Deutsche Nationalversammlung* (Berlin: Reichsdruckerei, 1920), 5695.

56 Pommerin, *Sterilisierung der Rheinlandbastarde.*

57 Adolf Hitler, *Mein Kampf. Zwei Bände in einem Band,* 9 ed. (Munich: Zentralverlag der NSDAP, 1941), 206 and 730, quoted after Koller, "*Von Wilden aller Rassen niedergemetzelt,*" 330. See also Alfred Rosenberg, *Der Mythus des 20. Jahrhunderts. Eine Wertung der seelisch-geistigen Gestaltenkämpfe unserer Zeit,* 5 ed. (Munich: Hoheneichen-Verlag, 1933), 639; Koller, "*Von Wilden aller Rassen niedergemetzelt,*" 330–1.

against France were frequently presented by the SS newspaper *Das Schwarze Korps*. Articles and caricatures in *Das Schwarze Korps* suggested that France was a dying nation that could maintain its power only by intermingling with people from its colonies and thus creating a negroized, degenerate population.[58] Occasionally, Nazi commentators argued that this process was masterminded by Jews, who allegedly thrived on weakened populations.[59] Some popular treatises, such as Hans K. F. Günther's *Rassenkunde des jüdischen Volkes* (1930), even argued that Jews and blacks were genetically related.[60] Outside of *Das Schwarze Korps*, however, Nazi propaganda against France was subdued and inconsistent until the first weeks of the Western campaign in 1940 because Nazi Germany wanted to complete its rearmament without alienating France too much and hoped to drive a wedge into the Franco-British alliance.[61]

A drastic change happened in the days preceding the German offensive on the Somme, launched on 5 June. Nazi propaganda suddenly went into high gear against France and specifically targeted the black Africans in the French army. On 29 May 1940, in one of his customary staff conferences during which he formulated propaganda guidelines, Minister for Propaganda Joseph

---

[58] Koller, "*Von Wilden aller Rassen niedergemetzelt,*" 347–50; Klaus-Jürgen Müller, "Die deutsche öffentliche Meinung und Frankreich 1933–1939," in *Deutschland und Frankreich 1936–1939,* eds. Klaus Hildebrand and Karl Ferdinand Werner (Munich: Artemis-Verlag, 1981), 28–9, 37; Mario Zeck, *Das Schwarze Korps: Geschichte und Gestalt des Organs der Reichsführung SS* (Tübingen: Niemeyer, 2002), 310–11. For an early example of a tirade against "negroized France" by right-wing women's activist Käthe Schirmacher, see Scheck, *Mothers of the Nation,* 124.

[59] Koller, "Von Wilden aller Rassen niedergemetzelt," 349–50.

[60] Hans K. F. Günther, *Rassenkunde des jüdischen Volkes* (München: J. F. Lehmann, 1930); Manfred Sell, *Die schwarze Völkerwanderung. Der Einbruch des Negers in die Kulturwelt* (Wien: Frick, 1940), 22–4. See also Robert Proctor, *Racial Hygiene: Medicine under the Nazis* (Cambridge: Harvard University Press, 1988), 114.

[61] Wolfgang Geiger, *L'image de la France dans l'Allemagne nazie 1933–1945* (Rennes: Presses Universitaires de Rennes, 1999), 41–53.

Goebbels ordered a sharper media campaign against France.[62] In particular, the French deployment of black soldiers was to be attacked by pointing out the irony of the French using African soldiers to save European civilization from the Germans. An official of Goebbels' ministry later pointed out to representatives of the German press, however, that they should make a distinction between black Africans ("Negroes or Niggers,...inhabitants of the jungle") and North Africans, particularly Moroccans. The latter, as the official mentioned, had played a laudable role on the side of Nazi ally Francisco Franco during the Spanish Civil War.[63] The following day, Goebbels held another conference during which he demanded an even more ruthless tone against France. He encouraged journalists to revive memories of the Black Horror campaign, claiming that it had been a "cultural and racial disgrace...to bring Negroes to the Rhine." He called the French a people of "niggerized sadists" and requested that the German people become full of anger and hate against France within a fortnight.[64]

The essence of the propaganda campaign launched by Goebbels was not new, but it meant a significant change of focus from the initial weeks of the campaign. Although occasional stories of "crimes" committed by colored troops had appeared before, such as the charge made on 25 May 1940 that black soldiers had demolished a Belgian village that had housed them, the primary target of German wartime propaganda until May 1940

---

[62] On the character of these conferences, see Ralph Georg Reuth, *Goebbels*, trans. Krishna Winston (New York: Harcourt Brace & Company, 1993), 258; Willi A. Boelcke, ed., *Kriegspropaganda 1939–1941: Geheime Ministerkonferenzen im Reichspropagandaministerium* (Stuttgart: Deutsche Verlags-Anstalt, 1966), Chapter II. Already on 23 May, the propaganda division of the Wehrmacht High Command (OKW) had requested pictures contrasting well-built German soldiers with "animalized Senegal Negroes and other colored prisoners." Boelcke, *Kriegspropaganda*, 130, n. 21.

[63] Boelcke, *Kriegspropaganda*, 368.

[64] Ibid., 369–70.

was Britain. The British were accused of wanting to fight "to the last Frenchman," while the French appeared more as naïve victims of British manipulation than as the villain deserving the anger and hate Goebbels hoped to unleash.[65] By the end of May, however, most British troops were leaving the continent, and the German army, while still fighting to eliminate the Dunkirk pocket, was preparing for the final blow against the center of France. Thus, for the purposes of psychological warfare, it must have seemed important to Goebbels to disgrace France.[66] Moreover, Goebbels received encouragement from a powerful source: As he noted in a recently found version of his diary, he received a call from Hitler on 30 May demanding a sharper propaganda against France. Hitler appears to have been enraged over some French abuses of German POWs. Goebbels summarized the phone call as follows: "The French commit the wildest atrocities against our prisoners. They are the same as they have always been. Therefore we need to draw our conclusions. This will happen within a few days."[67] Although Goebbels had already ordered a more severe propaganda against France on the preceding day, Hitler's phone call may have inspired the even harsher tone Goebbels chose at the staff conference of 30 May.

A look at the *Völkischer Beobachter*, the official newspaper of the Nazi Party, reveals that Goebbels' directives were immediately

---

[65] Ibid., 349. See also Geiger, *L'image de la France dans l'Allemagne nazie 1933– 1945*, 129–36.

[66] Already during the German sickle cut maneuver in Belgium and northern France, Goebbels commissioned a song of hatred against France, assuming that it would be needed soon. Elke Fröhlich, ed., *Die Tagebücher von Joseph Goebbels: Teil I, Aufzeichnungen 1923–1941. Band 8: April–November 1940* (Munich: K. G. Saur, 1998), 115, 123 (entries of 17 and 19 May 1940). For a short reference to the press campaign, see Reuth, *Goebbels*, 271; Jay Baird, *The Mythical World of Nazi War Propaganda, 1939–1945* (Minneapolis: University of Minnesota Press, 1974), 103–5.

[67] Fröhlich, *Die Tagebücher von Joseph Goebbels: Teil I, Aufzeichnungen 1923–1941. Band 8: April–November 1940*, 144.

put into action – though not always with the called-for distinction between North African and black troops.[68] On 30 May the *Völkischer Beobachter* published a lengthy article that set the tone for the press campaign. The headline charged that the French had murdered defenseless German prisoners and would suffer harsh retribution as a consequence. The main text first related the story of a German pilot who had been mistreated by Moroccan troops and French civilians after parachuting from his damaged plane. The article culminated in the warning: "We will no longer tolerate that German soldiers have their throats cut by colored soldiers, that captured Germans are sent *en masse* toward German machine gun positions, and that our wounded are murdered in bestial ways. The charges that our war reporters level against the French government are so terrible that Paris ought not to have any illusions regarding German reprisals.... These murderous beasts will find no pardon." To provide evidence for the charges, several stories of alleged French violations followed, but only one involved colonial soldiers: It reported that Tirailleurs Sénégalais, "black animals clothed in khaki by the French," jumped from trees on unsuspecting Germans to cut off a hand or a head.[69] In characteristic fashion, the article used a true incident – the injuring or killing of grounded German airmen by the French occurred repeatedly – to incriminate the French army in general and the colonial soldiers in particular.[70]

---

[68] Still, Goebbels noted the success of his press campaign with much self-flattery in his diary: Fröhlich, *Die Tagebücher von Joseph Goebbels: Teil I, Aufzeichnungen 1923–1941. Band 8: April–November 1940*, 145–7 (entries for 31 May and 1 June 1940).

[69] "So führt das 'ritterliche' Frankreich Krieg. Augenzeugen berichten: Französische Morde an Wehrlosen. Harte Vergeltung ist diesem Abschaum der 'Grande Nation' gewiß!" *Völkischer Beobachter* 53, no. 151, 30 May 1940, p. 4. All references are to the northern German edition of the newspaper.

[70] On this tactic, see Willi A. Boelcke, *Wollt ihr den totalen Krieg? Die geheimen Goebbels-Konferenzen 1939–43* (Stuttgart: Deutsche Verlags-Anstalt, 1967), 15–16.

Although there were at this time no official reports on war crimes by black troops – jumping from trees or fighting with knives or bayonets is not illegal – the article evoked the notions of illegitimate ferocity and brutality of black soldiers inherited from the colonial wars, World War I, and the Rhineland occupation. The call for brutal treatment of French, particularly black, POWs was unmistakable.[71] Moreover, as during the Black Horror campaign, the negative stereotype was shifted from North African to black troops.

A string of articles that systematically revived the memory of the Black Horror followed; they charged all French troops, but particularly the black soldiers, with atrocities, and portrayed France as a negroized and degenerate nation. An article of 31 May 1940, for example, stated under a photo of colonial regiments (most likely North Africans, not black Africans) marching into the Rhineland in 1918: "The black representatives of French civilization march into the Rhineland. Several hours later they throw themselves like wild beasts on German women and girls. They rape, plunder, murder, and commit arson wherever they can." Another photo on the same page shows some black French soldiers in 1940. The caption establishes the connection between 1918 and 1940: "Today France has again let loose the cruel black beasts from the jungle against us, and again they have given free rein to their animalistic instincts. One part of these subhumans [*Untermenschen*] is already in German POW camps."[72]

To enhance the credibility of war crimes charges against the black units of the French army, these soldiers were depicted in the most revolting terms. One article describes in great detail how black POWs skinned a cow and ate its raw meat and barely washed entrails, a practice depicted as typical for their

---

[71] Zayas, *The Wehrmacht War Crimes Bureau 1939–45*, 147–51.
[72] "1918 und 1940. So führt das verkommene Frankreich Krieg!" *Völkischer Beobachter* 53, no. 152, 31 May 1940, p. 4.

culture.[73] A war report from the lower Somme called the Tirailleurs Sénégalais "black beasts" and claimed: "Their animalistic thirst for blood expresses itself in bestial atrocities. With long, rusty knives [*coupe-coupes*] they try to defend themselves desperately. Grinding their teeth, they grab their guns, even when they have been left behind wounded. They have to be shot down one by one from the trees and bushes."[74] Another war report accused a black soldier of having bitten to death a German.[75]

This propaganda sought to bring into disrepute the entire French nation by claiming that it was negroized, degenerate, and therefore cruel but weak. The *Völkischer Beobachter* published photos of black soldiers at Napoleon's grave, claimed that the French were drafting white women to tend to the various "needs" of the black soldiers, and spoke of a blood transfusion from Africa that the dying French people needed in order to maintain the appearance of power.[76] One article drew attention to the three colored deputies in the French parliament to advance its claim that "France has become a haven of mulattoism in which Americans who refuse to sit next to Negroes in Parisian cafés are arrested and expelled."[77] Several articles pointed out that leading French politicians and generals, including Pétain, had joined a support organization for black soldiers headed by a

---

[73] Werner Storz, "Die Hilfsvölker unserer Feinde: Unter den Gefangenen 47 Völker und Rassen! Besuch in einem Gefangenen-Durchgangslager," *Völkischer Beobachter* 53, no. 157, 5 June 1940.

[74] Friedrich Schultz, "Durch die Weygand-Linie," *Völkischer Beobachter* 53, no. 159, 7 June 1940, p. 1.

[75] Kriegsberichter Frowein, "Das sind Frankreichs 'Kulturverteidiger.' Schwarze Bestien morden an der Somme. Offener Brief eines deutschen Kriegsberichters an Reynaud," *Völkischer Beobachter* 53, no. 160, 8 June 1940, p. 4.

[76] See, for example, "Würdeloses Frankreich. Weibliche Hilfskräfte zur 'Aufmunterung' der Farbigen," *Völkischer Beobachter* 53, no. 166, 14 June 1940, p. 4.

[77] "Schwarze geben den Ton im verniggerten Frankreich an," *Völkischer Beobachter* 53, no. 157, 5 June 1940, p. 3.

black man. This was meant to demonstrate the willingness of the
French elite to submit themselves to an African as president.[78]
The bottom line was, as the self-appointed Nazi party ideologue
Alfred Rosenberg explained in a lengthy article, that France had
lost its healthy racial instincts and turned "mulattoization" into
its national idea.[79] But this argument was not meant to absolve
France from responsibility for the alleged cruelties committed
by colored soldiers in fighting the Germans. Rosenberg found it
a scandal that France had allowed Africans to take over a state
founded by the Germanic Franks, and several reports on atrocities demanded that French leaders be punished for conjuring
up the worst instincts of colonial peoples against the Germans.[80]

Occasionally, Nazi propaganda insinuated that Jews were
responsible for the decline of France. The fact that Georges
Mandel, a Jew who had been minister of the colonies, had
become French interior minister on 18 May offered Nazi propagandists a welcome link between alleged Jewish machina-
tions and the deployment of black troops. In a commentary
on Mandel's appointment, the *Völkischer Beobachter* argued that
Mandel, as minister of the colonies, had known only one goal:
"to recruit a lot of black cannon fodder."[81] Several articles in the
same newspaper claimed that Mandel was erecting a bloody dic-
tatorship in France, and one photo showed him in the company

---

[78] "Ein Neger Präsident über Pétain, Reynaud, Daladier," *Völkischer Beobachter* 53,
no. 156, 4 June 1940, p. 2.

[79] Alfred Rosenberg, "Der Zusammenbruch des französischen Nationalismus,"
Völkischer Beobachter 53, no. 154, 2 June 1940, pp. 1–2.

[80] Most clearly in Kriegsberichter Frowein, "Das sind Frankreichs 'Kulturverteidiger.' Schwarze Bestien morden an der Somme. Offener Brief eines deutschen
Kriegsberichters an Reynaud," *Völkischer Beobachter* 53, no. 160, 8 June 1940,
p. 4.

[81] "Der Pariser Sklavenhändler," *Völkischer Beobachter* 53, no. 143, 22 May 1940,
p. 4; see also Alfred Rosenberg, "Der Zusammenbruch des französischen
Nationalismus," *Völkischer Beobachter* 53, no. 154, 2 June 1940, pp. 1–2, and
Dammert, *Der Verrat an Europa*, 39.

of black African chiefs in their tribal outfits. The article to which this photo belonged claimed that the Jews, particularly Mandel, had an interest in the "negroization" of France because it made it easier for them to rule the country.[82] These insinuations notwithstanding, anti-Semitism was not the dominant theme of this propaganda campaign. The main thrust of the argument was that the French had allowed themselves to become a degenerate people by enlisting, and mixing with, cruel savages. According to Rosenberg, there were no black and white Frenchmen in France, but only "black or white Negroes." Although these arguments incriminated France as a whole, they stigmatized in particular the black soldiers serving in the French army.[83]

What were the effects of this propaganda, which was presented in similar fashion on the radio and on the weekly newsreels (*Wochenschauen*) shown in cinemas before the feature film? The biweekly statements on public opinion compiled by the SS Security Service (SD) suggest that it met with overwhelming and immediate success. By 3 June, the SD concluded on the basis of reports from the preceding three days: "The hatred of the population, which so far has targeted primarily England, begins to turn with full force on France, too. This is because of the news about the atrocities committed by French colonial troops." A local report from East Prussia quoted by the SD says: "The repeated news on the radio about the murder and abuse of German prisoners by the French, particularly by colored troops, have infused

---

[82] "Jud Mandels Blutregiment," *Völkischer Beobachter* 53, no. 156, 4 June 1940, p. 2; "Schwarze geben den Ton im verniggerten Frankreich an," *Völkischer Beobachter* 53, no. 157, 5 June 1940, p. 3. See also Dienke Hondius, "Ein Vergleich der Feindbilder 'Schwarze' und 'Juden' in Nazi-Deutschland," in *Zwischen Charleston und Stechschritt. Schwarze im Nationalsozialismus*, eds. Peter Martin and Christine Alonzo (Hamburg: Dölling und Galitz, 2004).

[83] For a broader discussion of Nazi images of France, see Geiger, *L'image de la France dans l'Allemagne nazie 1933–1945*; Eberhard Jäckel, *Frankreich in Hitlers Europa. Die deutsche Frankreichpolitik im 2. Weltkrieg* (Stuttgart: Deutsche Verlags-Anstalt, 1966).

the entire population with amazing anger and boundless hate." A report from the Austrian city Innsbruck detected overwhelming popular desire for "the most ruthless revenge for these crimes." One characteristic comment on the French colonial troops was: "One should gas this whole rabble."[84]

In its next report, written three days later, the SD assessed the reaction to the most recent *Wochenschau*, which had repeated the war crimes accusations and featured pictures of French colonial soldiers blamed for the crimes. The conclusion was that the newsreel had stirred up hatred and outrage among audiences all over the Reich exactly along the lines Goebbels had proposed in his conference of 30 May. To many viewers, the war now appeared to be a racial struggle against a negroized people that let loose wild "animals" on heroic, pure Germans. The SD correspondents suggested that propaganda material would be most effective if it contrasted white German soldiers with colored French troops. Goebbels accepted this suggestion at a conference two days later, and many photos of confident, good-looking Germans juxtaposed against black soldiers in the most unflattering poses did indeed appear in the wake of the campaign.[85]

The SD reports continued in a similar vein over the next few days. They pointed out that Germans were demanding reprisals against Allied POWs, particularly the black soldiers. Every reference in the media to the kind treatment of Allied POWs seems to have triggered outrage. One typical reaction was: "These black beasts should be shot after being captured."[86] On 10 June, the

---

[84] Heinz Boberach, ed., *Meldungen aus dem Reich 1938–1945: Die geheimen Lageberichte des Sicherheitsdienstes der SS. Band 4: Meldungen aus dem Reich Nr. 66 vom 15. März 1940–Nr. 101 vom 1. Juli 1940* (Herrsching: Pawlak, 1984), 1207.

[85] Boelcke, *Kriegspropaganda 1939–1941*, 382; Boberach, *Meldungen aus dem Reich 1938–1945. Band 4*, 1221–2. For an example contrasting a photo of depressed Africans, "France's fighters for civilization," with smiling German "Fighters for a new Europe": *Der Feldzug in Frankreich. 10. Mai–23. Juni 1940*, (n.p.: n.d.), 26–7.

[86] Boberach, *Meldungen aus dem Reich 1938–1945. Band 4*, 1222, 1238–9.

SD reported: "The descriptions of the acts of the blacks, in particular, have left a strong impression. Generally, people go very far when imagining the reprisals they want to be implemented, both in terms of the nature and extent of the measures."[87] Even the news about the good treatment of captured French officers provoked anger; one typical commentary was that these officers should be executed because they shared responsibility for the crimes of colored troops. This is significant in the context of the frequent threats against captured French officers commanding Tirailleurs Sénégalais in 1940.[88]

It is of course possible that the SD dispatches exaggerated the success of the propaganda campaign. They did mention occasional critical voices but dismissed them as too rare to be significant.[89] They also registered a little later, after the antiblack propaganda had died down, that some Germans had begun wondering whether the abuses had been as bad as the media had suggested.[90] But even if the public reaction was more varied than the SD reports suggest, the propaganda campaign against "negroized France" obviously triggered many calls for violent reprisals against black POWs.

After 8 June, the day on which it became clear that the German offensive on the Somme would succeed, the antiblack propaganda faded away, although similar news reports occasionally appeared after that date.[91] The war crimes accusations against the black French soldiers, however, became inseparable from the Nazi memory of the Western campaign. In a documentation on Allied war crimes published by the German Foreign Ministry a

[87] Ibid., 1240.
[88] Ibid., 1250.
[89] Ibid., 1238.
[90] Heinz Boberach, ed., *Meldungen aus dem Reich 1938–1945: Die geheimen Lageberichte des Sicherheitsdienstes der SS. Band 5: Meldungen aus dem Reich Nr. 102 vom 4. Juli 1940–Nr. 141 vom 14. November 1940* (Herrsching: Pawlak, 1984), 1338.
[91] On 4 July 1940, for example, Goebbels requested pictures of "the animalized meals of black POWs." Boelcke, *Kriegspropaganda 1939–1941*, 413.

few months after the campaign, allegations of widespread atrocities committed by French colored troops (North African and black) still figured prominently. Whatever the veracity of the actual incidents, which pale in comparison to the German massacres of black soldiers, the presentation of the documents and the witness reports were clouded by the propaganda offensive of early June 1940.[92] Many incidents allegedly perpetrated by blacks were no war crimes at all; often no distinction was made between Moroccan troops and Tirailleurs Sénégalais; and many accusations were based on the "bestial nature" of black soldiers.[93]

THE EFFECTS OF ANTIBLACK PROPAGANDA ON THE ARMY

How influential was this propaganda within the German army units preparing for their attack against the Weygand Line? Undoubtedly, many German soldiers read the *Völkischer Beobachter* and heard the radio programs that so impressed people at home. Because only small forces were fighting near Dunkirk after 1 June, many soldiers had the time to read and listen to the radio before new offensives were unleashed on 5 June on the lower Somme and on 9 June on the Aisne. Moreover, it was clear that the German army was aware of the war crimes charges circulating in the press at this time. On 31 May, for example, the *Völkischer Beobachter* published a photo of French ammunition with flattened explosive heads, claiming that the French were using illegal dum-dum ammunition.[94] This accusation was wrong and induced the German army, in an effort to prevent

---

[92] Auswärtiges Amt, ed., *Dokumente britisch-französischer Grausamkeit. Die britische und französische Kriegführung in den Niederlanden, Belgien und Nordfrankreich im Mai 1940* (Berlin: Verlag Volk und Reich, 1940).

[93] Ibid., 73–80.

[94] "1918 und 1940. So führt das verkommene Frankreich Krieg!" *Völkischer Beobachter* 53, no. 152, 31 May 1940.

reprisals, to distribute a disclaimer explaining that some French projectiles were produced with flattened heads, but that they were not dum-dum ammunition.[95] A corresponding disclaimer with respect to the "crimes" of colonial troops, however, was not issued. Did the propaganda offensive launched by Goebbels at the end of May influence the murder of black POWs in 1940? Military psychologists argue that hatred of the enemy is usually less strong among frontline troops than in more remote units and on the home front.[96] On the other hand, the degree of rage expressed by German civilians in calling for the execution of black POWs already in the first days of June suggests that many soldiers exposed to this propaganda would have had a similar reaction. Admittedly, the first massacres, the killings of wounded Tirailleurs in and near Aubigny, happened before the propaganda campaign started. But the vast majority of the abuses occurred later, and it appears plausible that many German soldiers, saturated with antiblack propaganda while waiting to attack the Weygand Line in early June, believed that they had a right to avenge the alleged atrocities committed by black troops. Given the tradition of stigmatizing black soldiers in much of German public discourse from the colonial wars on, Goebbels' propaganda offensive appealed to existing prejudices and derived greater credibility from them. Hence the "indescribable rage" a French officer observed among the Germans as soon as they emerged from the marshes and bushes on the southern shore of the Somme near Airaines on the morning of 5 June.[97]

The animalization of black soldiers present in the propaganda campaign was mirrored in many war diaries and reports

95 See "Meldung," 11 June 1940, in BA-MA, RH 26–12, vol. 12 (Anlagen zum KTB Nr. 2, Bd. V, 5.6.–8.6.1940).

96 See, for example, Ben Shalit, *The Psychology of Conflict and Combat* (New York: Praeger, 1988), 46–7.

97 Brugnet, SHAT 34 N 1081.

from frontline troops. Among the most revealing documents are the war diaries of the Infantry Regiment *Großdeutschland*, an elite unit that took part in the massacres of black POWs near Erquinvillers and Lyon. When the *Großdeutschland* started its attack near Amiens on 5 June, it encountered determined resistance from the 4th DIC. This resistance was repeatedly depicted as perfidious. As a diary entry for 7 June states with respect to combat south of Amiens: "There also are perfidious tank traps . . . where black 'bearers of culture' commanded by French officers have to fight to the last moment while the real French mostly avoid close combat and surrender."[98] One entry suggests that execution had to be considered as a just punishment for the alleged deviousness of the blacks. When a unit of the regiment *Großdeutschland* fell into an ambush of Tirailleurs Sénégalais on 10 June and lost many men, including an NCO, the war diary noted: "Our anger rose to an immeasurable level when we heard about this. It is the old story: a white officer at the head of the black 'bearers of culture.' An energetic soldier reacts to his outrage by making a firm decision – the only one that can be right for such beasts."[99] In one of the very rare cases of a German unit explicitly recording an execution of black POWs, a war diary from the *Großdeutschland* reported on 10 June near Erquinvillers: "Among our prisoners are twelve Negroes; we shot them because they had cut the throats of German soldiers."[100] Two days later, men of the regiment discovered some quarters left behind by black soldiers in a hurry. After describing the mess, the diarist concludes: "here lived no soldiers, but rather blacks – rabble and criminals."[101]

[98] Ibid., p. 43.
[99] Ibid., p. 46.
[100] Diary, BA-MA, RH 37/6328, 10 June 1940.
[101] Kriegschronik der 15. Kompanie des I. R. "Großdeutschland," BA-MA, RH 37/6335, p. 47.

These entries reflected the elements and language of the propaganda offensive launched by Goebbels. The ironic term "black
bearers of culture" (*schwarze Kulturträger*) frequently appeared in
the *Völkischer Beobachter*. The idea that the black soldiers were perfidious and were used as cannon fodder for otherwise cowardly
Frenchmen also belonged to the propaganda arsenal on display
in early June. It is notable that not once do the *Großdeutschland*
war diaries actually depict a war crime committed by black troops.
Establishing tank traps and fighting to the last man does not violate the international laws on warfare. Nor can the ambushing
of German troops be considered illegal. Cutting the throats of
enemy soldiers is not more inhumane than blowing them up with
a hand grenade, and it constitutes a war crime only if the killed
soldiers had surrendered.

It is possible that the men of the *Großdeutschland* regiment,
which had been formed out of the guard battalion in charge of
the government center in Berlin, were particularly receptive to
Nazi propaganda against blacks. Yet, elements of Goebbels' propaganda offensive also appear in documents from other units
both during and after the campaign. The idea that black soldiers were extremely dirty, for example, was widespread. A young
member of the German labor service (*Reichsarbeitsdienst*) who
entered a hospital in Alsace where colonial troops had been stationed wrote to his family: "the blacks made a terrible mess here.
The dirt in the rooms was meters high. . . . Consider that France
called this culture. . . . The soldiers say that it looked better in
Poland than here. We have received a nice picture of the civilization of the black men."[102] As historian Klaus Latzel explains,
many German soldiers of the Second World War described foreign places and people as "dirty," juxtaposing them against a

---

[102] Klaus Latzel, *Deutsche Soldaten – nationalsozialistischer Krieg? Kriegserlebnis –
Kriegserfahrung 1939–1945* (Paderborn: Schönigh, 1998), 43.

supposedly "clean" Germany and "clean" Germans.[103] Black soldiers were considered particularly unclean. In May and June 1940, horror stories circulated about colonial soldiers having destroyed an entire Belgian village through their filthiness.[104]

German documents from the campaign are replete with objections to the participation of black soldiers in the war on the basis of race and on the allegation that they were conducting war in a "savage" and "perfidious" manner, particularly by using *coupe-coupes*. The description of close combat from the 6th Infantry Division on the Somme on 5 June, as quoted above, depicts the black soldier as an animal trying to bite through the German's throat.[105] The finding of *coupe-coupes* was often recorded by German war diaries, and the animalization of the black soldier continued in documents and military publications after the campaign. Black soldiers were depicted as climbing trees like monkeys, sneaking up on their enemies like snakes, and biting their throats like beasts of prey.[106]

German soldiers attacking the Weygand Line in June 1940 thus had been exposed to a massive propaganda campaign aiming to dehumanize the black soldiers in the service of France. This propaganda harkened back to the atrocity stories spread during the anticolonial uprisings, World War I, and the Black Horror campaign. Notions of savage black warriors stood in close connection to an obsession with illegitimate, perfidious warfare, as expressed in the franc-tireur phobia of the German army in

[103] Ibid., 179.
[104] "Die Vorkämpfer für Freiheit und Zivilisation. Französische Kolonialtruppen demolieren belgische Wohnungseinrichtungen," *Völkischer Beobachter* 53, no. 146, 25 May 1940, p. 2. These stories were repeated in the Foreign Office's book on Allied "war crimes:" Auswärtiges Amt, *Dokumente britisch-französischer Grausamkeit*, 323–4.
[105] "Nahkampf mit Schwarzen," BA-MA, RH 26–6, vol. 108, pp. 15–16.
[106] *Die Wehrmacht*, 6 November 1940, pp. 21–22; in CHETOM 16 H 339. For some examples, see Geiger, *L'image de la France dans l'Allemagne nazie 1933–1945*, 198–99.

1914. This phobia had not been subjected to critical scrutiny in Germany, and the public resistance to the dehumanization of black soldiers, still manifest in 1904–07, had faded away after 1918. The Nazis made sure that it did not arise again. The stereotype of the black soldier as a mutilating savage was therefore thoroughly established by June 1940. The fact that the official party newspaper presented a systematic "dehumanization" of the black soldier and was explicitly calling for the killing of black POWs must have served as "authorization" in Kelman and Hamilton's sense.

3

Ideological and Situational Factors

It would be tempting to close the inquiry at this point, leading to the conclusion that the Germans killed black POWs because they were possessed by a hallucinatory racism that made them see black soldiers as illegitimate combatants. Yet this would not do justice to the complex circumstances of the 1940 campaign. Despite the widespread antiblack prejudice, the actions of German units toward black POWs were highly inconsistent. Some killed black POWs, while others did not, and often there was inconsistency even within the same unit. Despite the lack of precise numbers, we can plausibly say that the majority of black POWs were *not* killed after capture.[1]

In the absence of a general order pertaining to black POWs, it appears that each officer had to make his own decision about the treatment of these prisoners. This autonomy allowed captured French officers to influence the German commanders, and it produced a great deal of inconsistency. Sometimes a French appeal to the humane feelings of the Germans could help. We have seen how Dr. Hollecker averted a massacre of wounded

---

[1] Fargettas, "Le massacre des soldats du 25ème Régiment de Tirailleurs Sénégalais Région lyonnaise – 19 et 20 juin 1940," vol. 2, 126.

Tirailleurs near Erquinvillers by making such an appeal and enlisting the support of a German soldier who had been a missionary. Another example is the experience of an officer from the 44th RICMS who was captured together with a wounded Tirailleur on the lower Somme on 5 June, in an area where many executions of black POWs were occurring. He reported: "The Germans are ready to mishandle the Tirailleur. They seem furious. I intercede and humanize them by showing them his terrible wound."[2] In the bloody battles of the 25th RTS near Lyon, French army nurses deliberately wounded some Tirailleurs Sénégalais with their surgery knives because they believed that this would improve their chances for survival.[3]

Wounds did not always "humanize" German soldiers bent on killing black POWs, however. There are many reports on wounded Tirailleurs being murdered, for example in Aubigny, Erquinvillers, and during the final battles of the 26th RTS near Chartres. Many Tirailleurs, in turn, were saved without being wounded. Repeatedly, German officers stopped violence against black POWs or did not carry out a threatened execution. Amadée Fabre, the commander of the 24th RTS who witnessed the maltreatment of captured Tirailleurs, saw how a German officer stepped in to halt the abuses and to make sure the prisoners were led away in order. This happened in the immediate context of massacres, namely near Erquinvillers on 10 June.[4] When a German officer announced to captured French officers near Airaines on 7 June that "from noon on no Senegalese prisoners would be taken anymore," he may have spoken the truth for his own unit, but it is obvious from the documents that nearby

---

[2] Dejulliard, SHAT 34 N 1079.

[3] SHAT 34 N 5. The Red Cross gathered these soldiers on the following days and transported them to the military hospital in Lyon. The sources do not reveal, however, whether the Germans ever discovered them.

[4] Fabre, SHAT 34 N 1097.

German units continued to take black prisoners.[5] Sometimes French officers in hopeless situations negotiated with German emissaries and agreed to surrender only under the condition that black soldiers would not be executed. This happened, for example, to a battalion of the 12th RTS in Lorraine on 18 June. In captivity, the leading officer was threatened and had to hear the typical lectures about the atrocities committed by black troops, but in the end nothing happened to him. He noted that after eight days all black POWs were duly registered with Red Cross representatives and some initial restrictions on them lifted.[6] Another unit of the 12th RTS captured nearby was threatened with a massacre, but the Tirailleurs Sénégalais just stayed calm, and nothing happened to them.[7] In Lorraine in mid-June, the 6th RICMS fought bitter battles in forests and villages very much resembling the close combat in the region of Airaines, yet its officers reported no massacre of black POWs. The German units fighting the 6th RICMS behaved correctly during and after the battle. The West African sergeant Oumarou Alfa, for example, reported that a German major surprised him in his hideout and asked him to surrender, but Alfa quickly grabbed his gun and killed the German. In other places, the German might have shot an isolated black man instead of asking him to surrender.[8]

In some cases, French officers and physicians even praised the good treatment of black POWs. Captain Mathias of the 5th RICMS claimed that the Germans treated all their prisoners very well.[9] Mathias was captured before executions of black POWs became common, but similar evidence also comes from witnesses captured later and in the immediate vicinity of massacre sites. The

---

[5] Pottier, SHAT 34 N 1079.
[6] Graff, SHAT 34 N 1090.
[7] Blouch, SHAT 34 N 1090.
[8] "Histoire succincte du 6e RIC – 6e RICMS," CHETOM 15 H 146.
[9] Mathias, SHAT 34 N 1070.

regimental physician Dr. Vergez, for example, noted after being captured with many Tirailleurs of the 12th RTS near Neufchateau in Lorraine close to the end of the campaign: "The Tirailleurs are treated the same way as the Europeans – with great consider- . ation." Of the soldiers guarding the POWs, he wrote: "They are very correct; there is no incident with the Senegalese."[10]

This inconsistency begs two questions: First, is there evidence that some units were more "Nazified" than others and thus ready to implement the racial precepts of Nazi ideology with greater brutality? Second, was a certain type of combat or a specific situation particularly likely to trigger a massacre? We have to consider that many massacres happened immediately following battles. The combat situation with its omnipresent threat to life is known to produce a high degree of stress in soldiers, and this should not be discounted. It is necessary to identify situational factors – combat conditions at different stages of the campaign – and weigh them in comparison to ideological factors predisposing German units to kill black POWs. The two questions, of course, are not mutually exclusive: Situational factors could have played a role in triggering or preventing a massacre even in strongly Nazified units.

THE ROLE OF NAZI IDEOLOGY

Some strongly Nazified units were involved in larger massacres, in particular the SS Totenkopf Division and the Regiment *Großdeutschland.* The former belonged to the Waffen-SS, a group of units raised by the SS, the power conglomerate in Nazi Germany centered on police and security duties and considered the most ruthless executor of Nazi ideological precepts. Although not formally Wehrmacht units, the Waffen-SS divisions fought under the orders of the German Army Command. The SS

---

[10] Vergez, SHAT 34 N 1090.

Totenkopf Division was drafted in part from former concentration camp guards (particularly from Dachau) and soon acquired
a reputation for extreme boldness and cruelty in fighting.
Although scholars point out that the ideological schooling of SS
members was not consistent and well organized, there can be no
doubt that they were indoctrinated with racist images. While Jews
occupied center stage in the racist worldview of SS members, they
were also taught that black Africans were low-ranking people
unable to form a civilization on their own.[11] The SS journal *Das
Schwarze Korps*, published weekly, had pioneered the defamation
campaign against negroized France before the war and portrayed the black soldiers as marionettes in the hands of French,
British, and Jewish masters at the beginning of the war. When
Goebbels called for an anti-French propaganda campaign in late
May 1940, *Das Schwarze Korps* published the most inflammatory
rhetoric and the most dehumanizing pictures of black soldiers.
On 6 June, it stated: "In immense ignorance and denial of responsibility for the mission of the white race, in distasteful dishonor,
the men of France have drafted the animals of the jungle....
Beings who derive a cultic joy from murder and mutilation (as
authentic reports from the front prove), to whom the satisfaction
of drives means a service to God, and who stand on a level of
development not much higher than the gorilla: these beings are
driven in frivolous carelessness into the theaters of war."[12] On 13
June, the paper accused the black soldiers of cannibalism and

[11] Jürgen Matthäus, "Ausbildungsziel Judenmord? Zum Stellenwert der 'weltanschaulichen Erziehung' von SS und Polizei im Rahmen der 'Endlösung,'"
Zeitschrift für Geschichtswissenschaft 47, no. 8 (1999): 698–9, Bernd Wegner,
*Hitlers politische Soldaten. Die Waffen-SS 1933–1945: Studien zu Leitbild, Struktur
und Funktion einer nationalsozialistischen Elite*, 2 ed. (Paderborn: Schöningh,
1982), 71. See also Günther, *Rassenkunde des jüdischen Volkes*, and Sell, *Die
schwarze Völkerwanderung*, 22–4.

[12] "Die Garde der Zivilisation," *Das Schwarze Korps* 6, no. 23, 6 June 1940, p. 8. See
also Müller, "Die deutsche öffentliche Meinung und Frankreich 1933–1939,"
28–9, 37.

argued: "Hitlerism is to wish France for the French; it means to repeat the German thesis that the big black children from the jungle are no Frenchmen and that *la culture* is an inalienable characteristic only of the white, Aryan mankind."[13]

The SS Totenkopf Division, as mentioned, was guilty of the biggest war crime against white soldiers in the Western campaign of 1940, the murder of one hundred disarmed British soldiers in Le Paradis on 27 May. The unit later fought its way into the upper Seine valley and then south to the suburbs of Lyon, where it shared responsibility for the massacre of black soldiers. Moreover, on its way to Lyon, the division came through several places where massacres happened, although it is not clear whether its men were responsible.[14]

Given that the Waffen-SS believed that the example of a leader was better schooling than ideological instruction, we have to pay attention to the commander of the SS Totenkopf Division, Theodor Eicke.[15] Before the war, Eicke had made a career in the concentration camp network, leading to his appointment as the national concentration camp inspector. An order that Eicke passed two weeks after the end of the campaign, as his unit had taken over occupation duties in France, characterizes his state of mind. He chastised some of his soldiers for having become too informal and summoned them to offer the "fresh and tight" Hitler salute of 1929 rather than "the more comfortable, democratically-relaxed, so-called 'German salute' of 1936." He expressed outrage that some of his men had not returned

---

[13] "Vier haben sie aufgefressen," *Das Schwarze Korps* 6, no. 24, 13 June 1940, pp. 1–2.

[14] This is the case for the Côte d'Or (between Auxerre and Dijon) and the village of Lantignié in the Saône valley. See Table 1.

[15] Jürgen Förster, "Die weltanschauliche Erziehung in der Waffen-SS," in *Ausbildungsziel Judenmord? "Weltanschauliche Erziehung" von SS, Polizei und Waffen-SS im Rahmen der "Endlösung,"* eds. Jürgen Matthäus et al. (Frankfurt am Main: Fischer Taschenbuch Verlag, 2003), 106.

the Hitler salute and thus given "the impression that they wanted nothing to do with the greatest of all Germans." His special order culminated in the sentence: "The name of the Führer cannot be called often enough and loudly enough in the streets of France; everybody needs to remember that."[16] In short, Eicke was a Nazi of the most fanatical kind.

The few surviving period documents of the SS Totenkopf Division do not mention the killing of colonial soldiers, but this is hardly surprising. As historian George Stein writes, "it was not the habit of the SS to refer directly, especially in written communications, to atrocities."[17] But, as we have seen, it was common procedure in this division not to give quarter to black prisoners. Although the records occasionally list black POWs, the juxtaposition of white prisoners and "dead Negroes" is too frequent in battle reports from the SS Totenkopf Division to be incidental.[18] A postwar publication of veterans from the division treats the massacre of Le Paradis in detail, arguing that it was an unauthorized action by an officer of an otherwise extremely disciplined unit. The massacres near Lyon, however, do not figure in the detailed description of that battle.[19]

Another unit implicated in several massacres of black soldiers, the Infantry Regiment *Großdeutschland,* was also strongly Nazified. This regiment was guilty of some of the killings near Erquinvillers on 9 to 10 June and shared with the SS Totenkopf Division the responsibility for the murders of black soldiers northwest of Lyon. It had been formed out of the guard battalion in charge of protecting the government center in Berlin. Hitler is said to have called the *Großdeutschland* the bodyguard regiment of the

---

[16] "Sonderbefehl!" 5 July 1940, BA-MA, RS 3-3, vol. 10.

[17] Stein, *The Waffen SS,* 78.

[18] See "Gefechtsbericht vom 19./20.6.40" by SS-Hauptsturmführer Lönholdt, BA-MA, RS 3-3, vol. 8. One source, however, mentions 300 POWs, mostly Senegalese: "Gefechtsbericht 20.6.1940," BA-MA, RS 3-3, vol. 9.

[19] Vopersal, *Soldaten, Kämpfer, Kameraden,* 8–9, 189–92, 246–53.

German people (*Leibregiment des deutschen Volkes*). In addition to guard duty, the *Großdeutschland* had marched during ceremonies and parades in Berlin. It consisted largely of soldiers who had volunteered to serve longer than required. It is hard to imagine that these soldiers, given their guard duties at the power center of the Third Reich, would have been admitted had they not displayed a special devotion to the regime.[20] As mentioned, the documents of this unit from the French campaign reveal a great interest in black soldiers, who are depicted as barbarians and wild animals along the lines of the propaganda of the *Völkischer Beobachter*.[21] The records of the unit do not mention the massacres near Lyon although the fighting there receives much attention.

The heavy involvement of the SS Totenkopf Division and the Infantry Regiment *Großdeutschland* in the massacres suggests that exceptional devotion to Nazi ideology and loyalty to the regime lowered the inhibition to kill black POWs. But this was only one factor among others. Many divisions involved in the atrocities were not particularly Nazified. The fact that some of them repeatedly committed massacres could reflect the outcome of a routinization process rather than a high degree of Nazification. Moreover, we have to consider that even such fanatical units as the SS Totenkopf Division and the Infantry Regiment *Großdeutschland* did not murder *all* of their black POWs. Thus,

---

[20] See the materials collected in BA-MA, RH 37/6392. To be sure, the soldiers of the *Großdeutschland* were thirsting for revenge because they believed that the French had murdered seven of their comrades after capturing them in May. Although there was no indication that colonial units were responsible for this incident, which was never corroborated, the members of the regiment revealed their great receptivity for the racist propaganda by channeling all their rage against Africans. See Kriegschronik der 15. Kompanie des I. R. "Großdeutschland," BA-MA, RH 37/6335, p. 31.

[21] Durian, *Infanterie-Regiment Großdeutschland greift an*, 80, 164–5, and 177; Fritz Fillies, *Großdeutsche Grenadiere im Kampf. Kameraden aller Gaue in einem Regiment beim Feldzug durch Belgien und Frankreich* (Berlin: Zeitgeschichte-Verlag, 1941), 87–8, 98–101.

we must explore situational factors that may have worked as triggers for a massacre.

THE MUTILATION CHARGE

As shown previously, the Germans justified many massacres by claiming that Tirailleurs Sénégalais habitually mutilated German prisoners. German officers often threatened or ordered a massacre of black POWs after a dead German had been found with severed body parts or severe cuts. The fact that Tirailleurs Sénégalais carried *coupe-coupes* and used them in close combat added plausibility to the mutilation charge. Could the mutilation of German prisoners by black soldiers have been a trigger for a massacre?[22]

Typically, French officers denied the German allegations. Jean Coutures, a lieutenant from the 26th RTS, emphatically stated in a discussion with a German officer: "As to the alleged mutilations inflicted by our Tirailleurs on German prisoners – they belong to the realm of absurd legend."[23] There is no question that the officers of West African units would not have condoned the mutilation or mistreatment of German POWs. Some white French officers may have believed that West Africans would have been prone to mutilate prisoners had they not entered French military training, but most officers took pride in pointing out that France had "civilized" them.

Yet there are indications that not all accusations of mutilations were spurious. Occasionally, white French officers admitted in

---

[22] Consider what Alfred-Maurice de Zayas writes about German soldiers in the Soviet campaign: "Any discovery of mutilated corpses particularly increased the danger of indiscriminate revenge on enemy prisoners of war, though whether reprisals were indeed taken depended on the German officers involved; some permitted their troops to take revenge; others protected defenseless prisoners from being massacred." De Zayas, *The Wehrmacht War Crimes Bureau*, 106.

[23] Coutures, SHAT 34 N 1099.

their reports that they had needed to prevent the abuse of German POWs by black soldiers. On 6 June, for example, two severely wounded Germans were captured by the 53rd RICMS in Airaines. A French lieutenant reported: "I have to say that I had to intervene with vehemence in order to prevent a Tirailleur with a *coupe-coupe* in his hand from cutting off their heads."[24] In their interviews with Nancy Lawler, veterans from Ivory Coast vehemently rejected the accusations, but one of the testimonies denies only the mutilation of dead Germans while admitting that living Germans were sometimes mistreated: "It is a totem of war that you cannot take anything [from a dead soldier]. You could hurt the enemy while he is alive – put nails through his hand before he is dead. That I did see happen. *C'est la guerre* [That is war]. The Germans took our men and killed many of them. The French didn't let us kill Germans when we captured them. We had to keep them alive."[25]

If French officers had to intervene occasionally to prevent the torture, mutilation, or murder of German prisoners, we must assume that these acts could have happened when no officer was present. Indeed, a careful reading of French reports from some of the battles, particularly those in Aubigny, Airaines, and Erquinvillers, shows that groups of Tirailleurs Sénégalais occasionally lost their officers and were on their own for a while until another officer gathered them and took command.[26] Some Tirailleurs Sénégalais, moreover, were drafted from areas where the ritual decapitation of enemies belonged to the traditions of warfare and was reported even after 1940.[27]

Given the frequent German abuses, however, it would not be a surprise if Tirailleurs Sénégalais saw violence against German

[24] Bouzou, SHAT 34 N 1081.
[25] Lawler, *Soldiers of Misfortune*, 96.
[26] See, for example, Lapasse, SHAT 34 N 1079 (pp. 19–20), and Fabre, SHAT 34 N 1097.
[27] Claude Sterckx, *La tête et les seins: La mutilation rituelle des ennemis et le concept de l'âme* (Saarbrücken: Homo et Religio, 1981), 79–82.

POWs as an act of revenge. Although retaliation was forbidden by the Geneva Convention, violations of international accords by one side have often been used to legitimate reprisals by the other, although it is usually impossible to determine which side actually started with the violations. There is no doubt that the Tirailleurs Sénégalais expected to be handled in a cruel way by the Germans after being captured. Memories from the First World War as well as the French propaganda stressing the racial hatred of Nazi Germany toward blacks contributed to this feeling.[28] Once the first massacres of black POWs happened, the news of these acts spread with lightning speed from one West African unit to the other. Rumors circulated that the Germans took no black prisoners and that Hitler had ordered that all West Africans be executed.[29] Even in the 25th RTS, which had not been in combat before the battles northwest of Lyon, the African soldiers had heard rumors and expected the worst, although it seems that some white French officers of this unit were unaware of the danger to black POWs.[30]

While the available documentation makes it impossible to refute completely the German accusations, there is reason to believe that they were inflated. We must consider that many encounters between Germans and Tirailleurs Sénégalais involved close combat in houses, bushes, or forests. The bayonet and, naturally, the *coupe-coupe* were best suited for this. Killing the enemy with these weapons made no noise that might have betrayed the defender and his holdout. It is reported that black units, having run out of ammunition, repeatedly made suicidal charges with *coupe-coupes* and used this weapon in one-on-one combat with German soldiers, often in remote places without

[28] Echenberg, *Colonial Conscripts*, 95.
[29] "Le massacre des sénégalais de la 4ème DIC," CHETOM 15 H 144.
[30] Fargettas, "Le massacre des soldats du 25ème Régiment de Tirailleurs Sénégalais Région lyonnaise – 19 et 20 juin 1940," vol. 2, 80–1.

witnesses.[31] A long knife, wielded by a man fighting for his life, will inflict wounds on the enemy that, in retrospect, may look like deliberate mutilations. German soldiers might later discover their comrade with an arm or his head cut off. Convinced that black soldiers always mutilate their prisoners, they would then call for retribution. Many cases of claimed mutilations could actually have been the outcome of close combat that did not violate any international accords.

The prejudice toward black soldiers could be so pervasive among German soldiers that they sometimes mistook wounds caused by firearms for deliberate mutilations. On the evening of 16 June, for example, an advance party of German cyclists from the 1st Cavalry Division found the corpse of an officer on a road intersection north of Chartres. The officer, who belonged to a neighboring division, had an open stomach and severe eye wounds. Knowing that the 26th RTS had recently defended this area, the cyclists reported to their commander that they had found an officer killed and mutilated by black soldiers. The commander believed this interpretation and ordered the shooting of black prisoners from the 26th RTS as a reprisal. An inquiry about the identity of the dead officer revealed a different story, however. The officer, riding at the head of a motorcycle patrol, had been killed in an ambush by white French soldiers. As survivors testified, his wounds were inflicted by regular fire. This news came too late to stop the massacres of black prisoners. In search of an alternative justification for these murders, the commander of the 1st Cavalry Division, as mentioned previously, tried to induce Jean Moulin to sign a declaration blaming Tirailleurs Sénégalais for the death of French civilians.[32]

---

[31] See, for example, SHAT 34 N 1099: "Relation succincte des combats auxquels a pris part le régiment du 11 au 22 juin 1940."

[32] François, *La guerre de 1939-1940 en Eure-et-Loir* IV, 65–84, as quoted in Charles Onana, *La France et ses tirailleurs: Enquête sur les combattants de la République* (Paris: Duboiris, 2003), 166–76.

That the mutilation charge allowed a massacre of black POWs to count as a reprisal must have eased the decision of German officers to order such massacres. Reprisals against captured enemy soldiers were not explicitly forbidden until the Geneva Convention of 1929. In fact, the Lieber Code justified reprisals as a means to make the enemy change unlawful behavior (Articles 27 and 28). The Hague conventions on land warfare of 1899 and 1907 did not mention reprisals, but the fact that they did happen during the First World War induced the authors of the Geneva Convention to outlaw them explicitly.[33] The guidelines on the treatment of POWs printed in the pay book of Wehrmacht soldiers, however, still stated that reprisals were permissible on the orders of an officer.[34] This contradiction may have gone unnoticed because it appealed to the older notion that officers could order reprisals.

Yet, even if Tirailleurs Sénégalais occasionally mistreated German prisoners, this mistreatment would not suffice to justify the massacres and abuses that happened to many of these soldiers after being captured by the Germans. When German officers gave specifics on the alleged mutilations, they usually referred to one, two, or three victims. Yet the "retribution" was indiscriminate, amounting to the murder of dozens or hundreds of black POWs. Moreover, these executions usually happened without any investigation, which even the Lieber Code had required. Not once does a document indicate that a German officer tried to find out whether a dead soldier with severe cuts had surrendered before being "mutilated." Only in this case would the Tirailleur Sénégalais have committed a war crime. The use of the *coupe-coupe*, however, was not illegal. The mutilation of dead enemy soldiers, which the Germans also believed to have taken place, does

---

[33] For the relevant documents, see *http://www.yale.edu/lawweb/avalon/lawofwar/lawwar.htm* (last visited 12 August 2004).

[34] Liverpool, *The Scourge of the Swastika*, 253–4.

contradict article 76 of the Geneva Convention, which states that dead POWs have to be buried honorably, but here, too, an investigation into the allegations was never made.[35] The Germans, firmly believing that mutilations of POWs and dead enemies belonged to the way of fighting of Tirailleurs Sénégalais, saw what they wanted to see. An inquiry seemed unnecessary.

CLOSE COMBAT AND HEDGEHOG POSITIONS

Many massacres of black POWs happened after intense close combat, frequently at night. This was true in Aubigny on 24 May and later in Airaines, Erquinvillers, and many places in Lorraine. Close combat against an often invisible enemy is likely to induce battle stress at its most extreme. German soldiers would roam through a forest, expecting a Tirailleur with a *coupe-coupe* standing behind every tree. Or they would search dark corners of a house, ready to be assaulted at any moment. The Tirailleur, in turn, would wait anxiously behind or in a tree, in a little cave, or in the nook of a house to be discovered and, quite possibly, killed by a hand grenade or the thrust of a bayonet. These conditions make the surrender of a soldier particularly difficult.[36] A frenzied soldier may get scared and kill the person willing to surrender when he reveals himself. The anxiety-driven state of mind experienced by soldiers in close combat also makes fantastic allegations more believable and can provoke the call for reprisals.

Close combat between Germans and Tirailleurs Sénégalais had happened on several occasions before 5 June, although it

[35] "Belligerents shall see that prisoners of war dying in captivity are honorably buried and that the graves bear all due information, are respected and properly maintained." The Avalon Project at Yale Law School: *http://www.yale.edu/lawweb/avalon/lawofwar/geneva02.htm* (last visited 10 February 2004). See also Rey, "Violations du droit international commises par les allemands en France dans la guerre de 1939," 29.

[36] Barker, *Prisoners of War*, 43.

was not usually followed by massacres, except in Aubigny. When the Germans stormed across the Somme on 5 June, however, they found the French army pursuing a defensive strategy that magnified the occurrence of close combat. Rather than striving to hold a continuous line, which had proven disastrous in the first weeks of the campaign, the French now pursued a defense "in depth." Wherever French soldiers faced superior German forces, particularly motorized units, they dug in and formed "hedgehogs" in villages, remote castles, and forests. German tanks and infantry often overlooked these positions and bypassed them, believing that the enemy had withdrawn. The remaining French troops, however, harassed the Germans from the side and the rear, engaged them in close combat, and held out until the Germans overwhelmed them one by one.[37]

The determined French resistance from their hedgehogs on the Somme and later the Aisne frustrated and surprised the Wehrmacht, although some of its units had received warnings about the hedgehog tactic.[38] The Germans enjoyed a clear numerical superiority after the Allied defeat in Belgium but initially made little headway. Soldiers passing a village seemingly abandoned by the French were furious to discover that people shot at them from the rear. Divisional diaries described the hedgehog tactic as extremely annoying and disruptive. A battle report of the German 46th Infantry Division, for example, stated on the evening of 5 June 1940: "During the rapid advance of our infantry south of the Somme [near Airaines] it became distressingly obvious that we were often threatened from the side or rear because the colonial troops let our attack roll over them but afterwards re-appeared and fought tenaciously."[39]

---

[37] For a description of this tactic, see Horne, *To Lose a Battle*, 489.

[38] See, for example, "Weisungen für die Kampfführung" (6th Army, von Reichenau, 3 June 1940), BA-MA, RH 26–44, vol. 8.

[39] "Abendmeldung am 5.6.," BA-MA, RH 26–46, vol. 47. See also the description of the anger provoked by hidden French shooters in a diary of a soldier from

As historian Klaus Latzel observed after examining soldiers' letters written in both world wars, German soldiers appear to have shared an implicit code of conduct stating that combat should happen with an enemy whose location was certain and who shot from the front, not the rear. Enemy soldiers violating this code were quickly marked as franc-tireurs or partisans, thus as illegitimate combatants, and collective reprisals against them appeared justified.[40] Obviously, the resistance of soldiers from the French army in the hedgehog positions violated this code of conduct. The very concept of hedgehogs defied the idea of an unambiguous frontline. French soldiers on the Somme were often invisible, their location uncertain, and they did shoot into the backs of Germans. That many Tirailleurs Sénégalais are reported to have shot from trees not only helped to reinforce the notion of animalistic soldiers but also smacked of franc-tireur resistance in the collective memory of the Germans. The German word for snipers hidden in trees, *Baumschützen*, was often used as a synonym to franc-tireur.[41] A battle memoir from the German 6th Infantry Division fighting near Airaines, for example, spoke of "the blacks' perfidious way of fighting – soldiers shot out of trees and used hidden machine gun nests."[42]

Close combat and hedgehog resistance helped to trigger some massacres, but they would likely have been ineffective as catalysts without the racist prejudice so powerfully reaffirmed by Goebbels during the campaign. The hedgehog tactic was not just practiced

the 45th Infantry Division: "Die 45. Division im Feldzug von Frankreich 10.5.–20.7.1940," BA-MA, RH 26–45, vol. 9. This report does not mention the race of the defenders, however.

[40] Latzel, *Deutsche Soldaten – nationalsozialistischer Krieg? Kriegserlebnis – Kriegserfahrung 1939–1945*, 195.

[41] For an example of outrage at soldiers shooting at German troops from trees in 1914, see ibid., 194.

[42] "'Der Stoßtrupp' von Kriegsberichterstatter Friedrich Schultz, Ende Juni 1940," in BA-MA, RH 26–6, vol. 108.

by black units. British and white French soldiers defending the Weygand Line also shot from trees, built hidden machine gun nests, and opened fire on advancing Germans from the rear. But when black troops were involved, this kind of defense was perceived as illegitimate warfare.[43] Infantry Regiment 63, for example, fought as part of the 27th Infantry Division shoulder to shoulder with the 46th Infantry Division near Airaines on 5 June. The combat reports of this regiment describe in great detail the very same hedgehog tactic that the 46th Infantry Division found so perfidious that it killed many black POWs from the opposing units. But the reports of Infantry Regiment 63, fighting against predominantly white troops of the 13th French Infantry Division, reveal no objection to this tactic.[44] Later on, during its campaign in the Soviet Union, even the German army adopted the hedgehog tactic, which proved very effective in slowing down Soviet counterattacks.[45]

THE TENACITY OF TIRAILLEURS SÉNÉGALAIS

Most Tirailleurs Sénégalais fought hard throughout the campaign of 1940. Although there were some incidents of panic, particularly when Tirailleurs found themselves under air attack or under bombardment by mortars, they were less likely to surrender than white French troops even in hopeless situations.[46]

---

[43] BA-MA, RH 37/6335: "Kriegschronik," clipping from "Der Stoßtrupp" by war reporter Friedrich Schultz. One French report even mentions that the Germans discussed the Tirailleurs Sénégalais in the same breath as the franc-tireurs: Dhoste, SHAT 34 N 1097.

[44] Gefechtsberichte Frankreich, in BA-MA, RH 37/1340.

[45] Tim Ripley, *The Wehrmacht: The German Army in World War II 1939–1945*, *The Great Armies* (New York: Fitzroy Dearborn, 2003), 170–1.

[46] Serge Barcellini, "Les monuments en homage aux combatants de la 'Grande France' (Armée d'Afrique et Armée coloniale)," in *Les troupes coloniales dans la Grande Guerre*, eds. Claude Carlier and Guy Pedroncini (Paris: Economica, 1997), 131; Lawler, *Soldiers of Misfortune*, 88; Echenberg, *Colonial Conscripts*, 95; Bruge, *Juin 1940*, 118.

Some RTS units were elite troops and proudly looked back on a reputation of outstanding heroism acquired in the First World War or the counterinsurgency operations in the Rif Mountains of French Morocco in the 1920s. The fact that many West Africans expected to be killed if caught by the Germans, moreover, induced them to fight particularly hard. This became clear for example during the battles near Erquinvillers. After encountering a group of several hundred Tirailleurs who had lost their officer, Amadée Fabre, the commander of the 24th RTS, reported: "I told them that I intended to stay with them and to defend us to the end. I argued that the Germans took no black prisoners and that, in any case, we were predestined to die. After these words, all the men felt renewed energy and demanded only to fight."[47] A German war diary confirmed the link between the expectations of Tirailleurs and their reluctance to surrender: "The local resistance, in particular of the Negroes, was so hard because they had been told that the Germans would torture them to death after capturing them."[48]

Black soldiers found it nearly impossible, moreover, to disengage themselves from the frontline in the last days of the campaign. White Frenchmen could slip into civilian clothes and try to disappear from the front or pose as civilians long enough to get out of the danger zone and, if they wanted, to rejoin the French forces. Skin color prevented blacks from doing the same thing: They might have been caught as deserters by the French or taken prisoner by the Germans – in both cases risking execution. As one hopeless French commander remarked after ordering his white soldiers to change into civilian clothing while abandoning his black soldiers in a deserted farm: "Putting civilian clothes on them will not make them white."[49] Moreover, many

---

[47] Fabre, SHAT 34 N 1097.
[48] War diary of 1st Panzer Division, BA-MA, RH 27–1, vol. 15, entry of 14 June 1940.
[49] Maury, SHAT 34 N 1081.

Tirailleurs having lost their white officers had no idea where to go. Most of them knew very little French and were ignorant of the local geography and the position of friendly troops.[50] These factors combined to make the Tirailleur Sénégalais a soldier who usually put up a determined defense, holding out in hopeless positions while inflicting heavy casualties on the opposing Germans. French commanders sometimes appealed to this reputation of black troops when asked to surrender by the Germans. In Lorraine on 15 June, for example, an officer commanding a group of Tirailleurs from the 12th RTS had fortified a farm with his men. When the Germans asked him to surrender, he replied, "There is a Senegalese battalion here. Come and take us!" and opened fire.[51]

Although surrender without a struggle was no guarantee of survival, Tirailleurs Sénégalais who chose not to fight to the last were sometimes spared. A group of forty West Africans from the 16th RTS, for example, lay down their arms near Chateauneuf on the Loire on 19 June. For undisclosed reasons, the Germans killed one West African and wounded another one, but the rest went into captivity unharmed.[52] As we have seen, a group of fifty soldiers from the 26th RTS commanded by Lieutenant Rendinger surrendered without a fight near Chartres and were taken prisoner alive, unlike so many other members of this unit.[53]

The tenacity and exceptional courage of Tirailleurs Sénégalais in combat provoked much anxiety among the Germans. Already in World War I, charging Tirailleur regiments had sometimes triggered a panic among German soldiers, and the same happened during the attacks of the 12th RTS between Beaumont

---

[50] Lawler, *Soldiers of Misfortune*, 81, 86.
[51] Barberot, SHAT 34 N 1090.
[52] Sicaud, SHAT 34 N 1095.
[53] Coutures, SHAT 34 N 1099.

and Stenay on 18 and 19 May 1940.[54] Many French officers noted with astonishment the fear of Tirailleurs Sénégalais among the Germans, who did not have the experience of working together with black soldiers on their own side. Doctor Hollecker, the physician who saved twelve wounded Tirailleurs near Erquinvillers, believed that the treatment of Tirailleurs Sénégalais by the Germans "betrayed less savagery than instinctive fear that they felt when seeing the indigenous."[55] The fear must be placed within the context of the racist image of black soldiers, however. Although German units engaging Tirailleurs Sénégalais had to expect a hard and costly battle, the stereotype of mutilating savages propagated since the colonial wars and revived so vividly by Goebbels's propaganda campaign was apt to magnify the battle fear of German soldiers and to increase their desire for revenge during and after the battle.

UNEXPECTED RESISTANCE

After the Germans had breached the Weygand Line (5 to 10 June), they concluded that France was beaten, and Pétain's call for armistice conditions on 17 June appeared to them as a recognition of this fact. Many German soldiers now expected that the French would surrender or withdraw, although Hitler had ordered a relentless pursuit of the collapsing French army until the armistice took effect on 25 June. In some units, soldiers twice celebrated the end of the campaign prematurely: once on 14 June, when the fall of Paris triggered rumors of a French capitulation, and then on 17 June, following Pétain's

---

54 Rives and Dietrich, *Héros méconnus*, 155–6. See also CHETOM 15 H 141, dossier 1.
55 Hollecker, SHAT 34 N 1097.

announcement.[56] Indeed, French morale had collapsed in many places. A number of French soldiers and officers "disappeared" from the front by mixing in with the streams of civilian refugees, local officials hampered the setting up of positions for last-ditch defense, and Pétain's call for an armistice met with overwhelming popular approval.[57] German soldiers after 14 June commented on the low morale of captured French soldiers, who often expressed relief that the war was over for them. Abandoned by their officers, many of them had plundered the wine cellars of deserted houses and were intoxicated when they surrendered.[58] Not surprisingly, German advance patrols after 17 June sometimes approached French positions without the usual precautions, assuming that the French would no longer fire. Yet in some places the French army did mount resistance and inflicted heavy casualties on overconfident Wehrmacht units. Black troops were often involved in these battles. The determined resistance of Tirailleurs Sénégalais in the last days of the campaign dashed German hopes of seeing a painless end to the fighting and triggered outrage and calls for revenge.

Near Brillon in Lorraine, for example, the first battalion of the 12th RTS found itself in a hopeless situation during the night of 15 to 16 June. But, as we have seen, the French commander opened fire on German emissaries asking him to surrender. After soldiers from the 6th Panzer Division had stormed the position, they killed the black soldiers, including many severely wounded men. The

---

[56] A report from the 2nd Panzer Division notes that its soldiers celebrated the end of the war by firing signal rockets on 14 June, once the fall of Paris became known: "Die 2. Panzer-Brigade im Krieg an der Westfront," BA-MA, RH 27-2, vol. 11.

[57] Burrin, *La France à l'heure allemande*, 28–9.

[58] See, for example, the war diary of the 2nd Panzer Division, which also records that in some places French civilians greeted German troops with the Hitler salute: BA-MA, RH 27-2, vol. 45. For similar reports, see BA-MA, RH 27-4, vol. 6 (entries of 15 and 16 June 1940).

war diary from the 6th Panzer Division does not record the massacre but points out that the unit had spent a night filled with horror in a nearby forest (dubbed the "Negro forest"). Tirailleurs had attacked nervous German soldiers trying to sleep with their weapons in hand, and some Germans had allegedly been mutilated.[59] Further south, the massacre of soldiers from the 14th RTS in Bourmont on 19 June also followed desperate resistance after a withdrawal order issued by the French High Command had failed to reach the Tirailleurs. The two German regiments that murdered at least thirty black POWs had conquered the town at the price of over three hundred killed.[60]

Unexpected resistance triggered the massacres northwest of Lyon on 19 and 20 June as well. In the previous days, the SS Totenkopf Division and the Infantry Regiment *Großdeutschland* had advanced hundreds of kilometers encountering only token resistance. When an officer from the *Großdeutschland* regiment, at the head of a group of soldiers on motorcycles, approached a French roadblock with a white flag and announced (erroneously) that the armistice had been signed, the Tirailleurs opened fire and killed many Germans.[61] The attack on the French stronghold in the monastery of Montluzin proved particularly bloody for the Germans. As a French report on this battle stated: "This encounter had been deadly for the Wehrmacht, which lost close to one hundred men killed as well as

---

[59] BA-MA, RH 27–6, vol. 1 (Kriegstagebuch); Rives and Dietrich, *Héros méconnus,* 179–81. No mention of a massacre is made in Dartigues, *Des coloniaux au combat,* 127.

[60] Montangerand and Voillemin, SHAT 34 N 1093; see also Archives départementales de la Haute-Marne, Chaumont, 15 W 74: "La bataille de Bourmont 18–19–20 juin 1940," and Archives de la Mairie de Bourmont, 33 Rev. 898: "Historique de la bataille de Bourmont."

[61] Fargettas, "Le massacre des soldats du 25ème Régiment de Tirailleurs Sénégalais Région lyonnaise – 19 et 20 juin 1940," vol. 2, 104–5. See also Fargettas, "Les tirailleurs sénégalais dans la campagne de mai–juin 1940," 141.

several tanks and machine-gun vehicles. The German commanders expressed their surprise and anger at such unforeseen resistance, which they classified as an ambush – given that it came
after the declaration of Lyon as an open city."[62]

It is understandable that German soldiers were angered by
determined, if erratic, resistance causing heavy casualties at a
time when the outcome of the campaign could no longer be
doubted. Yet, their anger was not free from racist preconceptions.
During the massacres in the area northwest of Lyon, for example,
German troops directed their rage primarily at the black soldiers.
Hence, we see the entries in the SS Totenkopf Division's war
diaries juxtaposing captured Frenchmen and dead "Negroes." If
white prisoners were executed, it was usually officers who had
commanded black units. One report from the defenders of the
monastery of Montluzin, for example, reveals that of three officers captured by the Germans, two were shot because they had
been in charge of black troops. The one officer who was spared
had commanded a white artillery unit, but he had participated in
the resistance no less than the other officers and no less than the
black soldiers.[63] One of the nuns from the monastery observed
how one white and one black soldier, both wounded, were captured by the Germans; the black man was shot, but the white man
brought to safety.[64]

Although many German officers considered last-ditch resistance a manifestation of perfidiousness if black soldiers were
involved, they regarded it as a legitimate fight for the sake of
honor if conducted by a predominantly white unit. While interrogating an officer of the 26th RTS captured after heavy combat on 16 June, for example, the Germans asked why France

---

[62] "Le groupe de subdivisions de Lyon en alerte et en campagne à la IIème armée
10 mai – 24 juin 1940," SHAT 34 N 5. See also Fargettas, "Le massacre des
soldats du 25ème Régiment de Tirailleurs Sénégalais Région lyonnaise – 19 et
20 juin 1940," vol. 2, 105–6.

[63] Pangaud, SHAT 34 N 5.

[64] "Montluzin. Journée tragique du 19 juin 1940," SHAT 34 N 5.

was still fighting at all. When the French officer replied, "*pour l'honneur*," the Germans nodded and accepted his answer.[65] The heroic resistance by the mostly white cadets of the officer school of Saumur on the Loire on 20 June, moreover, did not lead to a massacre once the resistance had been overcome. The records of the German 1st Infantry Division fighting in Saumur exude respect for the defenders, not outrage.[66]

In some cases, German commanders recognized even the determined resistance of Tirailleur Sénégalais as honorable. In the area of Erquinvillers, for example, one single well-armed Tirailleur defended a foxhole for two days. When he was finally killed, nearby German troops paraded in front of his corpse and saluted him. The French officer who reported this incident also heard many expressions of respect and admiration for the 4th DIC, to which he and the Tirailleur belonged, from his German captors.[67] In Chabris (Indre), one NCO and twelve Tirailleurs of the 16th RTS – belonging to the few survivors of Erquinvillers – held up vastly superior German forces with nothing but a cannon and a machine gun for an entire day at the end of the campaign, inflicting heavy casualties on the Germans. When the NCO finally surrendered, the commanding German officer complimented him on his fantastic defense and requested to see his soldiers, intending to march his unit past them as a sign of respect. Most of the Tirailleurs, however, had been killed in combat, and the few survivors had fled moments before the Germans arrived.[68]

[65] Parisot, SHAT 34 N 1099.
[66] BA-MA, RH 26–1, vol. 102: "Berichte über den Übergang über die Loire." There are other examples of chivalrous behavior of German troops having defeated determined adversaries toward the end of the campaign: Fargettas, "Le massacre des soldats du 25ème Régiment de Tirailleurs Sénégalais Région lyonnaise – 19 et 20 juin 1940," vol. 2, 108.
[67] Froissard-Broissia, SHAT 34 N 1095. According to this testimony, however, the heroic Tirailleur was left unburied. This could have been in obedience to a general order for the area. For a similar example, see "Journal des marches et opérations du 12ème RTS," SHAT 34 N 1099.
[68] Sicaud, SHAT 34 N 1095.

ASSESSING SITUATIONAL FACTORS VERSUS
RACIAL PREJUDICE

We have seen that the dehumanization of black soldiers in German public imagery was powerful and pervasive and that the whipping up of vicious images of black soldiers by Goebbels's propaganda provided "authorization" to German officers ordering executions. But the evidence from the Western campaign of 1940 further suggests that certain situational factors acted as triggers for massacres of black POWs. The encounter of strong resistance from black units, the character of close combat, particularly around the French hedgehog positions, the finding of "mutilated" German soldiers, and the last-ditch resistance mounted by black African troops in the last days of the campaign all contributed to the causation of massacres. At least one of these factors was present at almost all the recorded executions of May and June 1940. Heavily Nazified units such as the SS Totenkopf Division and the Infantry Regiment *Großdeutschland* resorted to violence against black POWs more easily than others, but even for them the situational factors were a necessary link in the chain of causation leading to a massacre. Without the interpretive background provided by racist prejudice, however, the situational factors would rarely have been effective. Black soldiers shooting from hedgehogs, wounding German soldiers with their *coupe-coupes* in close combat, and attacking Germans instead of surrendering seemed to confirm the image of perfidious savages that many Germans carried with them. Few Germans probably understood the racial bias that made them "punish" blacks for some acts while excusing the identical behavior of white troops. The reality of combat with black Africans thus tended to strengthen the prejudice of Wehrmacht members indoctrinated with a racist worldview. Consequently, any investigation into the alleged mutilations of German soldiers seemed unnecessary. Even the little empathy and imagination required to explain the cutting wounds of many dead Germans as a likely outcome of close combat was apparently never activated.

Not surprisingly, the German actions tended to reinforce certain behavioral patterns of black soldiers, and thus the antiblack prejudices almost became self-fulfilling prophecies in the course of the campaign. German cruelty hardened the determination of Tirailleurs Sénégalais to fight to the last man. The rapidly spreading rumors about German executions of black POWs must have evoked a desire for revenge and lessened the commitment of black troops to treating correctly the few German POWs falling into their hands.

At the end of the campaign, following several weeks of massive racist propaganda, the German prejudices were so firmly entrenched that minor transgressions by Africans in transit to POW camps or in the camps themselves could provoke extremely harsh reactions. This was the case in Clamecy, where forty-one African prisoners were shot after one POW attacked an SS officer, perhaps biting him (which would have evoked the bestial image of Africans). Later, the finding of a razor and a knife on two Tirailleurs Sénégalais, also in Clamecy, led to their executions. Obviously, sharp objects in the possession of black men triggered the German fear of mutilation.

An explanation of the massacres of black POWs needs to consider both the racist prejudice of many Germans and the triggering situational factors. Still, some inconsistencies remain even if we consider situational factors in conjunction with racist prejudice. Combat situations identified as likely triggers of massacres did not always "work" that way. Some German commanders did not order a mass execution after prolonged close combat with black troops, some German soldiers in close combat asked a black man to surrender rather than shooting him immediately, and some Germans respected last-ditch resistance mounted by Tirailleurs Sénégalais. Even in the immediate vicinity of massacres, some German troops did *not* murder black prisoners.

Occasionally, the racist prejudice was clearly present but did not lead to a massacre, as in those cases where a German officer threatened but refrained from ordering the execution of black POWs. In other cases, the triggers failed to work because the racial prejudice was either not present or not strong enough to override concerns for legality and humanity. As has become clear in the context of other Nazi atrocities, there were Germans who had preserved humane moral standards. Sometimes these "saviors in uniform" were able to prevent harm to potential victims.[69]

[69] Wolfram Wette, ed., *Retter in Uniform. Handlungsspielräume im Vernichtungskrieg der Wehrmacht* (Frankfurt am Main: Fischer Taschenbuch Verlag, 2002); Wolfram Wette, ed., *Zivilcourage: Empörte, Helfer und Retter aus Wehrmacht, Polizei und SS* (Frankfurt am Main: Fischer Taschenbuch Verlag, 2004).

4

Implications

THE THIRD REICH AND BLACK AFRICANS

Research on blacks in the Third Reich has recently expanded. The recollections of black and mixed-race people, as presented in the memoirs of Hans Massaquoi and in a volume of memoirs of Afro-German women, reveal that these people experienced massive discrimination and a permanent threat emanating from neighbors and state officials.[1] The Nazi regime expressed intense fear that the presence of black or mixed-race people in Germany would lead to racial mixture and thus "contaminate" the German genetic pool, as if the African genes would cause something comparable to an epidemic. It was this fear that led to the secret sterilization of the mixed-race children from the

---

[1] Hans J. Massaquoi, *Destined to Witness: Growing up Black in Nazi Germany* (New York: W. Morrow, 1999); May Opitz, Katharina Oguntoye, and Dagmar Schultz, *Showing Our Colors: Afro-German Women Speak Out*, trans. Anne V. Adams (Amherst: University of Massachusetts Press, 1992); Tina Campt, *Other Germans: Black Germans and the Politics of Race, Gender, and Memory in the Third Reich* (Ann Arbor: University of Michigan Press, 2004); Tina Campt, Pascal Grosse, and Yara-Colette Lemke-Muñiz de Faria, "Blacks, Germans, and the Politics of Imperial Imagination, 1920–60," in *The Imperialist Imagination: German Colonialism and Its Legacy*, eds. Sara Friedrichsmeyer, Sara Lennox, and Susanne Zantop (Ann Arbor: University of Michigan Press, 1998); Martin, "'Schwarze Pest.' Traditionen einer Diffamierung."

Rhineland. Some black people were interned and murdered in concentration camps, including some blacks who were stranded in Germany or German-occupied Europe during World War II. It has often been impossible, however, to determine precisely why a black or mixed-raced person was persecuted. In some cases, the political stands of the interned person, not skin color, may have been decisive, as in the murder of the communist Hilarius Gilges by Nazi paramilitaries in 1933.[2] Although there is no doubt that black Africans and people of mixed African and European descent were considered of a very low racial value by the Nazis, the danger emanating from them did not seem strong enough to justify the formulation of special state policies for them. Their number was far too small, and the Nazis considered the danger allegedly presented by Jews so much bigger and more immediate that anti-Semitism always occupied center stage in their policies.

We do know that for a while the Nazi regime considered establishing a colonial presence in Africa. The defeat of France and Belgium made it conceivable that Germany might one day control their vast African colonies. Anticipating a war with the United States, the Nazi regime planned to establish military bases in northwestern Africa in 1940–1.[3] Harking back to German war aims from World War I, some government officials also developed plans for a huge German empire in Central and West Africa. These plans, as indicated, sparked some German interest in black POWs and inspired research dealing with sub-Saharan Africa. Colonial cohabitation of Germans and black Africans would, however, reawaken the specter of racial mixing that the Nazis were trying so hard to exorcise from the European continent. The colonial planners therefore took pains to define guidelines

---

[2] Lusane, *Hitler's Black Victims*, 234–5; Kesting, "Blacks Under the Swastika," 92, 94; Kesting, "The Black Experience During the Holocaust," 361.

[3] The authoritative work on this is Norman Goda, *Tomorrow the World: Hitler, Northwest Africa, and the Path toward America* (College Station: Texas A & M University Press, 1998).

aimed at preventing racial mixing in the colonies. According to their racial ideas, black Africans were decent and hard-working people who could contribute much to the economy of a German empire in Africa, but racial mixing with whites would make them demanding, vicious, and decadent. This was the argument of Manfred Sell's influential book on the "black migration" (*Die Schwarze Völkerwanderung*), published in 1940. Sell vehemently attacked the slave trade, but his occasional humanitarian musings served merely as a glaze for a hard-core racist line of thought: He considered the racial mixing following the deportation of black African slaves to the new world a cardinal sin against the white race. Predictably, Sell interpreted the French recruitment of black Africans along the lines of Nazi propaganda during the 1940 campaign, namely as a blood transfusion for a weakened people and as the opening of the floodgates allowing the "black migration" to flow into Europe.[4]

The Nazi vision of a colonial empire in sub-Saharan Africa resembled the state of slavery Hitler sought to impose on most of the Slavic peoples in Eastern Europe. In blatant ignorance of African history, Sell himself argued that the black man had never built up anything of cultural or economic value except under foreign coercion.[5] This implied, of course, that only a system of bonded labor similar to slavery would make a German empire in sub-Saharan Africa feasible. To be sure, the conquest of living space in Eastern Europe always was the highest Nazi priority, and none of the Nazis' African plans ever came to fruition. But occasionally soldiers fighting against black regiments in 1940

---

[4] Sell, *Die schwarze Völkerwanderung*, 294–301. For a detailed analysis of Nazi colonial schemes, see Alexandre Kum'a N'dumbé III, *Hitler voulait l'Afrique: Les plans secrets pour une Afrique fasciste, 1933–1945* (Paris: L'Harmattan, 1980); Chantal Metzger, *L'empire colonial français dans la stratégie du Troisième Reich (1936-1945)* (Frankfurt: Lang, 2002). Metzger argues plausibly that the Nazis' African colonial plans never received a high priority.

[5] Sell, *Die schwarze Völkerwanderung*, 11–12.

developed colonial fantasies. A soldier from the 10th Panzer Division, for example, noted as his unit was advancing toward southern France at the end of the campaign: "We are already imagining ourselves over there in the black continent distributing colonial possessions."[6]

The most striking feature of German perceptions of black soldiers in 1940 is that the black African civilizations were profoundly foreign and anxiety provoking to many German soldiers and officers. Whereas the Tirailleurs Sénégalais tended to see the Germans as evil brothers of their colonial "masters," the French, the Germans perceived the black Africans as extremely foreign. With other racially targeted groups, be it Poles, Jews, or Russians, the Germans had direct experience; they were more likely to feel contempt and hatred toward them than fear (although this changed with respect to the Russians when the Germans encountered fierce resistance after the invasion of the Soviet Union). French officers often noted with amazement the fear of blacks shown by the Germans. Cultural contacts between Germans and black Africans had been episodic and conflictual. Much of the contact that had occurred, moreover, was massively distorted by propaganda, as was the case with the "Black Horror on the Rhine." Unlike France, Germany had an empire only for a short time (1884–1918). No Germanized local elites that could have mediated between German and African civilization had emerged, as they did in some British and French colonies. Moreover, the end of Germany's colonial venture was inextricably linked to the humiliation of the Treaty of Versailles, which took the colonies away from Germany by arguing that Germany's brutal treatment of the natives had proven it unfit as a colonial power. German counterpropaganda dubbed this charge the "colonial guilt lie" in analogy to the "war guilt lie," the claim that Germany

---

[6] "Von Stonne – Calais," BA-MA, RH 37/1910.

had started World War I.[7] By contrast, black Africa had received much more positive attention in France, not least because of its military contribution in the two world wars. Although some French civilians and soldiers shared the feelings toward black Africans widespread among the Germans, these prejudices were always balanced by recognition of the fact that the Tirailleurs Sénégalais, along with thousands of West African auxiliary workers, twice came to the defense of France and helped to save French lives.

THE NAZIFICATION AND BARBARIZATION OF THE WEHRMACHT

For the first decades after the Second World War, the prevailing image of the Wehrmacht in West Germany, as presented in the memoirs of generals and the popular press, drew a strict line between atrocities committed by the SS and the alleged professionalism and fairness of the Wehrmacht.[8] Although there were always doubters in Germany and elsewhere, the paradigm of the "clean" Wehrmacht has vanished in scholarship only recently, and it may still be quite strong among a minority of Germans, as some angry reactions to the exhibit "The Crimes of the Wehrmacht" (launched in 1995) suggest.[9] In recent years, the pathbreaking works on the German army's complicity in racial crimes have understandably focused on the Soviet Union, where the greatest

---

[7] Riesz, "L'Afrique dans les lettres allemandes entre les deux guerres (1919–1939)," 110.

[8] Jean Solchany, "La lente dissipation d'une légende: La 'Wehrmacht' sous le regard de l'histoire," *Revue d'Histoire Moderne et Contemporaine* 47, no. 2 (2000); Wolfram Wette, *Die Wehrmacht. Feindbilder, Vernichtungskrieg, Legenden,* 2 ed. (Frankfurt am Main: Fischer, 2002), Chapters V and VI. Both are excellent surveys of the debate on the crimes of the Wehrmacht.

[9] Ulrich Herbert, ed., *Nationalsozialistische Vernichtungspolitik 1939–1945. Neue Forschungen und Kontroversen* (Frankfurt am Main: Fischer Taschenbuch Verlag, 1998).

atrocities happened and where the German army can be linked to the implementation of the Holocaust. Even the Wehrmacht exhibit, covering 1941–5, excludes the 1940 campaign in France (while giving short shrift to Wehrmacht crimes in Poland in 1939).[10]

In comparison to the German campaigns in Eastern Europe, mostly against Poland, Yugoslavia, and the Soviet Union, the Western campaign of 1940 is usually described as a traditional political and military conflict, rather than as an ideological or racial war. Certainly, the German army's behavior toward civilians was less abusive in Western Europe than it was in the East, although it deteriorated during the occupation of 1940–4. Yet, drawing conclusions from his study of the massacres outside of Lyon, historian Julien Fargettas suggests that the murders of black POWs reveal elements of a race war under the veneer of an otherwise mostly "correct" German behavior.[11]

This idea deserves to be pushed farther. The Nazi propaganda offensive during the campaign of 1940, like earlier arguments presented in some newspapers such as *Das Schwarze Korps*, depicted the French as a degenerate people that had been spoiled by its hedonistic and democratic tendencies and was weakened by the mixing with non-European races that had become necessary because of the decline of the French birthrate. That white soldiers and civilians were generally not mistreated in the Western campaign testifies not to the absence of racism in this war but rather to the higher status the white Western Europeans occupied on the Nazi racial hierarchy in comparison to black Africans. The war reports of many German soldiers and journalists reflected a great interest in the racial makeup of French

[10] Hannes Heer and Klaus Naumann, eds., *Vernichtungskrieg. Verbrechen der Wehrmacht 1941 bis 1944* (Hamburg: Hamburger Edition, 1995); Wette, *Die Wehrmacht*, 262–7.

[11] Fargettas, "Le massacre des soldats du 25ème Régiment de Tirailleurs Sénégalais Région lyonnaise – 19 et 20 juin 1940," vol. 2, 107.

POWs. "Germanic" Alsatians were considered as having the highest racial value; Bretons and Normans were also respected because many Germans believed that their ancestors were related to the Germanic tribes. North Africans were seen as more valuable than sub-Saharan (black) Africans. While many Alsatian POWs from the French army were quickly liberated and some Bretons were sent to separate camps with an eye to accelerated repatriation, Jews were separated from non-Jews and confined to a special camp in Germany.[12] The Western campaign of 1940 therefore was *not* a hiatus in an otherwise progressive Nazification and hence barbarization of the Wehrmacht.[13] Rather, the massacres of black French soldiers and the influence of racist precepts in Nazi propaganda against France, as well as in army policies regarding POWs, show that the Western campaign was an integral part of this process.

How do the massacres of black soldiers in 1940 compare to the Wehrmacht crimes in Eastern Europe? In the Polish campaign, the Wehrmacht was particularly worried about hostile actions of civilians against rapidly advancing German troops and attacks by Poles on the ethnic Germans living in Poland. The highest military commanders therefore agreed with the SS leadership that SS and police units should play an aggressive policing role in the rear areas. Although it was initially understood that army commanders had the last word on retaliation carried out by the SS, the commanders increasingly refrained from interfering with the SS, and army units sometimes even took retaliation into their own hands. Hence, the Wehrmacht did get involved in atrocities. Its units burned villages and rows of houses from which civilians or dispersed soldiers had shot at German troops, and some Polish POWs were mistreated and

---

[12] Scapini, *Mission sans gloire*, 129, 193, 195–7. For the separate treatment of North Africans, see Durand, *La captivité*, 59–60.

[13] See, for example, Rossino, *Hitler Strikes Poland*, xiv, 216.

killed. Like the SS, the army sometimes took civilians as hostages and killed them in retaliation for Polish attacks on German troops or ethnic Germans. This significant Wehrmacht involvement in atrocities has led Alexander Rossino to define the Polish campaign as a "dress rehearsal" for the campaign against the Soviet Union.[14]

The killing of innocent civilians and POWs in Poland was important in the process of "routinization" as described by Kelman and Hamilton. Most German soldiers fighting in France had also fought in Poland, and that some of them had experienced mass killings there must have facilitated their participation in the massacres of Tirailleurs Sénégalais in 1940. For example, Rossino offers a detailed description of the murders carried out by Infantry Regiment 41 of the 10th Infantry Division, which was one of the two units implicated in the massacre of Bourmont on 19 June 1940.[15]

The Wehrmacht participation in atrocities in Poland, however, was not consistent. German officers often prevented massacres their soldiers were planning to carry out. In some cases, German commanders protested against SS atrocities or even intervened energetically to prevent them. There were numerous instances of friction between army and SS. General Georg von Küchler, for example, ordered a halt to a pending massacre of partly Jewish civilians and had the responsible unit of the security police, a branch of the SS, disarmed and sent home.[16] Many other Wehrmacht commanders started disciplinary procedures, including court martials, against members of the SS

---

[14] Ibid., xiv–xv, 191–2.

[15] Ibid., 154–69.

[16] Ibid., 103–9. After counteracting criminal orders in Poland, Küchler was head of the 18th army in France, which committed a series of crimes against black soldiers from the 26th RTS southwest of Paris; on the eve of the German invasion of the Soviet Union, he defended the order to execute political commissars – while conceding that the average Soviet soldier was "probably decent." Förster, "'Verbrecherische Befehle,'" 145.

and Wehrmacht guilty of infractions against civilians and Polish soldiers. Hitler, however, made sure that the accused were acquitted or received only minimal sentences. In early October 1939, he even issued a general amnesty for all Germans accused of atrocities in Poland. Although Küchler and other commanders involved in similar actions claimed to have been angered mostly by the SS infringing on army responsibilities and by threats of indiscipline, these examples show that the Wehrmacht was by no means uniformly ready to follow the Nazi path toward ruthless race war in 1939.

One similarity between the massacres in Poland and those against black soldiers in France was the role of Nazi propaganda. Goebbels had launched a massive propaganda campaign against the Poles and Polish Jews before the start of the war.[17] The conflict between Poles and the German minority in Poland, of course, provided a special aspect to this campaign that was absent in France in 1940. But the dehumanization of Poles and Jews happened along similar lines as the dehumanization of black soldiers in 1940. Both were depicted as perfidious, primitive, and similar to animals. Before the Polish campaign, German soldiers even heard lectures promulgating these stereotypes.[18]

Situational factors appear to have played a less significant or at least less obvious role in triggering German army atrocities in Poland. Rossino stresses the inexperience, nervousness, and anxiety of German soldiers, whose concern with irregular warfare, in particular franc-tireurs, often sparked overreactions to civilian resistance.[19] The descriptions of Poles firing at German soldiers passing through seemingly abandoned villages read very much like descriptions of black soldiers ambushing advancing Germans from hedgehog positions.[20] One difference is, however,

[17] Jerzy W. Borejsza, "Racisme et antislavisme chez Hitler," in *La politique nazie d'extermination*, ed. François Bédarida (Paris: Albin Michel, 1989), 59.

[18] Rossino, *Hitler Strikes Poland*, 137–8, 191–2, 196–7, 205, 227, 231.

[19] Ibid., 153.

[20] For an example, see ibid., 123–4.

that in Poland individual soldiers appear to have taken the initiative for massacres, with their officers often restraining them. This cannot be said for the massacres of black POWs in France, which were usually ordered by the officers.

When Nazi Germany launched *Operation Barbarossa*, the invasion of the Soviet Union on 22 June 1941, Hitler made it clear at the outset that this was a crusade against the ideological and racial archenemy, Judeo-Bolshevism. Nazi propaganda had prepared this field extensively, albeit with an awkward interruption mandated by the conclusion of the nonaggression pact with the Soviet Union in August 1939. Orders by Hitler and the SS leadership, accepted by the Army Command, ensured that from the start this campaign would be waged in violation of all legal conventions. That the Soviet Union had not signed the Geneva Convention was no excuse because Germany in any case would have been obliged to observe the Hague conventions on land warfare, which also called for the humane treatment of POWs.[21] The *Kommissarbefehl* by Hitler required that political commissars be separated from the other POWs and shot on the spot. Other orders ensured that Jews would also be shot and that the rest of the Soviet POWs would be held under conditions that ensured mass starvation, freezing, and death through epidemics.[22] In

---

[21] Streit, *Keine Kameraden*, 68.

[22] Helmut Krausnick, "Kommissarbefehl und 'Gerichtsbarkeitserlaß Barbarossa' in neuer Sicht," *Vierteljahrshefte für Zeitgeschichte* 25 (1977); Alfred Streim, *Die Behandlung sowjetischer Kriegsgefangener im "Fall Barbarossa"* (Heidelberg: Juristischer Verlag, 1981); Förster, "The German Army and the Ideological War against the Soviet Union." See also Jörg Osterloh, "'Hier handelt es sich um die Vernichtung einer Weltanschauung...' – Die Wehrmacht und die Behandlung der sowjetischen Gefangenen in Deutschland," in *Die Wehrmacht. Mythos und Realität*, eds. Rolf-Dieter Müller and Erich Volkmann (Munich: Oldenbourg, 1999); Jörg Osterloh, *Sowjetische Kriegsgefangene 1941–1945 im Spiegel nationaler und internationaler Untersuchungen. Forschungsüberblick und Bibliographie*, 2 ed. (Dresden: Hannah-Arendt-Institut für Totalitarismusforschung, 1996).

agreement with Nazi racial theories, which assigned an increasingly lower racial status to groups of people the farther east they lived, POWs from the Asian parts of the Soviet Union were often separated from the rest and kept outside of Germany.[23] The mistreatment of Soviet POWs resulted in an absurdly high mortality, particularly at the beginning of the campaign: Nearly 95 percent of Soviet POWs captured in 1941 and early 1942 did not survive. The overall death rate of Soviet POWs in German captivity is still being debated, but it is plausible that it was over 60 percent. By comparison, the mortality of Western Allied POWs was well below 5 percent.[24]

Regarding the Wehrmacht crimes in the Soviet Union, Omer Bartov also found a combination of ideological indoctrination and situational factors at work. Among the primary situational factors were the German soldiers' frustration at facing a technologically better equipped enemy and the very high casualty rate from the start of the campaign. In units rapidly depleted and frequently refilled with reserve soldiers, the primary groups of soldiers that had provided cohesion and a supreme fighting morale in previous campaigns – and that might have provided some protection against the barbarization of the army – dissolved. A massive infusion of Nazi ideology and terror filled the gap, leading to further abuse and murder of Soviet POWs.[25] The role of Nazi propaganda was important, as it was during the French campaign. The situational factors, however, were very different. French units, least of all the Tirailleurs Sénégalais, were not better equipped than the Germans, and the Wehrmacht's casualties in France were never high enough to disrupt the primary groups.

---

[23] Streit, *Keine Kameraden*, 49–50, 91, 98.

[24] Manfred Zeidler and Ute Schmidt, eds., *Gefangene in deutschem und sowjetischem Gewahrsam 1941–1956: Dimensionen und Definitionen* (Dresden: Hannah-Arendt-Institut für Totalitarismusforschung e.V. an der Technischen Universität Dresden, 1999), 14, 29–38.

[25] Bartov, *Hitler's Army*.

Noteworthy are the increasing imposition of Nazi ideology on the army and the decreasing resistance of German officers and soldiers to the barbarization of warfare. If the Polish campaign was, as Rossino argues, a "dress rehearsal" for *Operation Barbarossa*, then it was a typical dress rehearsal during which many things went wrong – at least in the eyes of the stage managers. That a German general could disarm and send home a security police unit lining up to carry out an execution of Polish and Jewish civilians (what a humiliation!) would have been unthinkable in the campaign against the Soviet Union. That German generals court-martialled army soldiers and SS members because they had committed wrongdoings against civilians also would sound unreal in the context of *Barbarossa*. Obviously, the Nazi leadership learned from the difficulties they had encountered when trying to impose their racialized vision of warfare on the army in Poland. During *Operation Barbarossa*, the German army received assurances that abuses of civilians would not be prosecuted. The general amnesty that Hitler had given retrospectively in Poland was thus enshrined in the modus operandi for the Soviet Union from the beginning.

The presence of black soldiers in the French army was probably not seen as relevant enough to justify special orders for the Western campaign. Moreover, there was no black civilian population in the path of the Wehrmacht and hence no immediate plan for the enslavement of that population, as there was in Poland and the Soviet Union. Still, the propaganda offensive launched by Goebbels against the black soldiers amounted to an unofficial "authorization" from the regime. The strong racist elements in the campaign against France show, moreover, that this war was also perceived as a race war and thus forms an integral link in the incremental Nazification of the Wehrmacht. But as in Poland, the inconsistency of the German actions against black POWs shows that the Nazi regime still had to do much more to ensure that the Wehrmacht would consistently embrace the implications of Nazism's murderous racist precepts.

THE RESPONSIBILITY OF THE FRENCH
MILITARY LEADERSHIP

Did the French High Command and the predominantly white French officers who led black Africans into battle against the Wehrmacht not do enough to prevent the massacres? Historian David Killingray suggests that the Nazi regime and the German army were aware that abuses against black soldiers would hardly provoke the same reaction as abuses against white soldiers. By not protesting sharply enough against the murder of people who were considered second-class citizens or auxiliary peoples (most Tirailleurs Sénégalais did not have French citizenship), the French government (and later the U.S. government with respect to African-American POWs) signaled to the Germans that the mistreatment of black POWs would not trigger the retaliatory action that would have been likely in the case of abuses against white POWs.[26] Sometimes Free French forces participating in the liberation of France and the drive into southern Germany in 1944–5 killed German POWs and declared that they were retaliating for the massacres of Tirailleurs Sénégalais in 1940, but this was long after the fact.[27] An immediate reaction does not seem to have occurred. How should we assess the responsibility of French commanders for the massacres of black POWs?

First, we must consider the information available to French commanders of West African units. Fargettas has concluded that many officers were not aware of the danger black POWs faced. Although French propaganda claimed that the Germans would not take black prisoners, some commanders appear to have

[26] Killingray, "Africans and African Americans in Enemy Hands," 181–2. On the importance of potential retribution as a restraining factor for the mistreatment of POWs in World War II, see MacKenzie, "The Treatment of Prisoners of War in World War II," 491.

[27] Fargettas, "Les tirailleurs sénégalais dans la campagne de mai–juin 1940," 148. For the broader problem of the Free French and their POWs, see Bob Moore, "Unruly Allies: British Problems with the French Treatment of Axis Prisoners of War, 1943–1945," *War in History* 7, no. 2 (2000).

dismissed this assertion as a ploy to boost the fighting spirit of the black troops.[28] This was true of officers in the 25th RTS, engaged near Lyon. Their unit was recently formed, and the officers had not yet established closer connections to their men. In many other cases, however, the French officers knew very well what could happen to captured Tirailleurs, as did the commanders of the West African regiments defending the Weygand Line in early June. Although some officers may have used the threat of German atrocities merely to strengthen the will of Tirailleurs Sénégalais to hold out in battle, there is evidence that they often believed this threat to be real. That General Hube of the 16th Infantry Division issued instructions to his men on how to respond to French officers asking about the killings of black POWs suggests that captured French officers frequently raised this issue – at least toward the end of the campaign.[29]

The anticipation of massacres against black soldiers inspired many courageous actions by French officers. We have seen how Amadée Fabre, the commander of the 24th RTS, decided to stay with a group of dispersed Tirailleurs and tried to stop the abuses they suffered after capture. Fabre, who had been threatened with execution himself, reported the following scene with the German officer interrogating him: "When he asked me whether I was the one who commanded this regiment of savages, I answered that I commanded soldiers and not savages, and if there were savages nearby, they were not to be found among the Senegalese; this provoked a vehement reprimand."[30] Many other cases of French commanders committed to saving the Tirailleurs have been mentioned. The mere decision of a white officer to stay with the Tirailleurs in anticipation of surrender was important

---

[28] Fargettas, "Le massacre des soldats du 25ème Régiment de Tirailleurs Sénégalais Région lyonnaise – 19 et 20 juin 1940," vol. 2, 81, 88.

[29] "Richtlinien für das Verhalten gegenüber Gefangenen," BA-MA, RH 26–16, vol. 19.

[30] Fabre, SHAT 34 N 1097.

because most Tirailleurs, not knowing German or French, were unable to communicate with the Germans on their own. The presence of a French officer also helped to reassure frightened Tirailleurs, as becomes clear in a report written by a white French officer on the first day of the German Somme offensive. The officer, who had gathered dispersed soldiers of the 53rd RICMS, was asked by a colleague to withdraw without his men in order to avoid falling prisoner. He refused to leave: "The couple of Tirailleurs whom I had regrouped saw their salvation only in me. They feared being executed. I was unable to abandon them to their fate."[31] Clearly, many officers in command of black troops tried to persuade the Germans to stop a massacre, sought to protect black men in POW columns, and sometimes made legal treatment of black POWs a condition for surrender.[32] But there are also examples of a more callous attitude, not just in the 25th RTS. Some commanders who could have no illusions about the threat of massacres, for example, simply abandoned their black soldiers when the situation became hopeless.[33] Still, it is fair to say that many French officers who were aware of the danger did their utmost to save the Tirailleurs from abuse and execution, sometimes successfully.

What more could French officers of Tirailleur Sénégalais units have done? Perhaps they could have devoted more attention to communicating the abuses to the French High Command. It is not clear whether this happened at all.[34] Commanders of some

---

[31] Brugnet, SHAT 34 N 1081.
[32] For an example of a commander demanding correct treatment of Africans, see Dartigues, *Des coloniaux au combat*, 149. See also Fargettas, "Le massacre des soldats du 25ème Régiment de Tirailleurs Sénégalais Région lyonnaise – 19 et 20 juin 1940," vol. 2, 80.
[33] See, for example, Maury, SHAT 34 N 1081.
[34] Fargettas has found no evidence for this: Fargettas, "Le massacre des soldats du 25ème Régiment de Tirailleurs Sénégalais Région lyonnaise – 19 et 20 juin 1940", vol. 2, 81.

frontline units, such as the 24th RTS, had knowledge of massacres at an early date and could have requested that the High Command issue a threat of retaliatory executions of German POWs. Two factors, however, made such a course of action unlikely: First, the documented or anticipated killings of some POWs must have figured very low on the list of priorities of an army trying to avert a national catastrophe. After all, most massacres happened in quick succession during a period that was characterized by chaos and dissolution on the French side. Second, it is possible that French commanders doubted that such a protest would have been an entirely just cause. They may have understood that the Tirailleurs sometimes took revenge into their own hands. In some battles, both sides took no prisoners. Some French officers, moreover, may have believed that the German allegations of mutilation were not entirely spurious.

As for the French High Command, it did remove some troops from the frontline whose soldiers faced a high risk of murder upon capture by the Germans. This was true for émigrés from Germany and recently annexed or occupied territories (including Austria and Czechoslovakia); toward the end of the campaign, the German Army Command issued an order that these people, if serving in the French army, were to be court-martialled and shot. Aware of the threat, the French High Command sent many of them to the Italian front.[35] Removing black

---

[35] Fargettas, "Le massacre des soldats du 25ème Régiment de Tirailleurs Sénégalais Région lyonnaise – 19 et 20 juin 1940", vol. 2, 81. Jürgen Förster argues that this order, issued on 17 June, came too late to be enforced (Förster, "'Verbrecherische Befehle,'" 139). For the text of this order, see "Armee-oberkommando 12. Lagebericht West Nr. 35 vom 17. Juni," BA-MA, RH 27–2, vol. 45; "Vorläufige Lagerordnung für die Armee-Gefangenensammelstellen," 27.6.1940 (Befehl Nr. 3 für Gefangenen- und Flüchtlingswesen)," BA-MA, RH 20–1, vol. 161. Walther Nehring, Guderian's Chief of Staff, asked to suspend this order until more specific instructions had arrived – interestingly in the same message that called for the rigorous treatment of black POWs (BA-MA, RH 27–2, vol. 45, 21 June 1940). Veterans from the Republican forces of the

units from the frontlines opposing the Germans, however, would have deprived the French High Command of a more substantial force and of some of its best troops in places where it needed them most. It did not want to take that step at a time of national emergency. Moreover, many massacres that happened toward the end of the campaign, when it could be argued that the High Command must have heard about the executions, occurred after black units made a last stand not having received a withdrawal order or after having taken a conscious decision to fight to the last. This was true for the massacres near Brillon, Bourmont, and Lyon. Altogether, there seems to be little that French officers of colonial units or the French High Command could have done differently, except to communicate and publish the information about the massacres more actively, possibly coupled with the threat of reprisals. Whether this would have stopped the German abuses is doubtful, however.

MEMORY

The belated and marginal scholarly treatment of the executions of 1940 is surprising considering that they were well known at the time. A French radio broadcast shortly after the liberation of France stated that killings of African prisoners had been "common currency" during the German campaign of 1940.[36] Belgian artist Frans Masereel depicted downtrodden and exhausted Tirailleurs Sénégalais in his collection of black-and-white drawings called *Juin 40* (1941). German wartime publications,

---

Spanish Civil War also fought in the French army; when captured, they were sent to concentration camps, where most of them perished. See Szymon Datner, *Crimes against POWs. Responsibility of the Wehrmacht* (Warsaw: Zachodnia Agencja Prasowa, 1964), 307.

[36] "Notice sur le capitaine indigène Charles N'Tchoréré," SHAT 34 N 1081: "It has become known since then [1940] that these killings were common currency on the French front."

without openly admitting the atrocities, made unmistakable allusions.[37] But it seems that this knowledge soon went below the radar of public and scholarly perception due to the repression processes in France and Germany during the Cold War. French scholarship on the traumatic defeat of 1940 and the Vichy period was slow in coming, and the prevailing image of the Wehrmacht in West Germany, as mentioned, was heavily idealized.[38] The state and accessibility of archival resources may also have discouraged scholarly research into the matter: The incomplete and damaged German divisional records became available to the public only in the late 1960s, and it took until the early 1980s before France opened its military documents for 1940.[39]

At the local level, however, French citizens in many places protected the memory of murdered Tirailleurs Sénégalais. The largest initiative was taken during the war. In Chasselay, the departmental director of the service for veterans and war wounded, Jean Marchiani, built a cemetery for 188 Tirailleurs of the 25th RTS killed in combat or murdered on 19 and 20 June. This "Tata Sénégalais" was inaugurated in the presence of a Muslim Imam from Senegal on 8 November 1942, a few days before the Wehrmacht marched into the unoccupied zone of France. Marchiani had the full endorsement of Pétain, and the speeches at the inauguration were rather critical of Germany.[40]

---

[37] *Der Feldzug in Frankreich. 10. Mai–23. Juni 1940* (n.p.: n.d.), and *Mit dem Generalkommando XXXX. A.K. vom Rhein zum Atlantik,* (n.p.: n.d.). Both brochures are from the library of the Bundesarchiv-Militärarchiv, Freiburg im Breisgau.

[38] The classic work on the memory of Vichy is Henry Russo, *The Vichy Syndrome: History and Memory in France since 1944,* trans. Arthur Goldhammer (Cambridge: Harvard University Press, 1991).

[39] For the French documents, see Echenberg, *Colonial Conscripts,* 87.

[40] For the speeches, see Archives départmentales du Rhône, 437 W 173. See also Jean Marchiani, "Tata Sénégalais de Chasselay," in Archives départementales du Rhône, 437 W 173; Fargettas, "Le massacre des soldats du 25ème Régiment de Tirailleurs Sénégalais Région lyonnaise – 19 et 20 juin 1940", vol. 2, 134–49; Fargettas, "Les tirailleurs sénégalais dans la campagne de mai–juin 1940," 137.

Marchiani and his collaborators had gone to great lengths to identify every corpse and find out as much as possible about the dead soldiers. The cemetery was built in West African style and, according to Marchiani, was meant to symbolize a silent protest against the "abject German barbarism" that had manifested itself in the battles. The colonial minister of the Vichy government supported the project.[41] Other local initiatives also deserve mention. In Clamecy and La Machine, both in the department Nièvre, memorials to murdered colonial soldiers, mostly Tirailleurs Sénégalais, were inaugurated shortly after the liberation.[42] In 1965, the town of Airaines erected memorial stones for the 53rd RICMS and for Captain Charles N'Tchoréré, the latter with an expression of gratitude to all colonial troops having joined in the defense of France in 1940.[43] The town government of Sillé-le-Guillaume commissioned a memorial stone for the Tirailleurs murdered there and placed it in the communal cemetery. The inscription reads: "Here rest 14 Senegalese soldiers cowardly murdered by the Germans on 19 June 1940."[44]

In West Africa, returning veterans spread knowledge of the massacres and the conditions in German POW camps, but the dramatic events leading to the independence of all French West African territories in the late 1950s and early 1960s quickly relegated these memories to the background, not least because of the disillusioning experiences of West African veterans with the French authorities. Many veterans, after fighting so valiantly for France, were bitterly disappointed when they returned to a barely reformed colonial routine after 1944. The massive

---

[41] Fargettas, "Le massacre des soldats du 25ème Régiment de Tirailleurs Sénégalais Région lyonnaise – 19 et 20 juin 1940," vol. 2, 137, 142.

[42] Barcellini and Wieviorka, *Passant – souviens-toi*, 63.

[43] Echenberg, *Colonial Conscripts*, 166–8. See also Barcellini and Wieviorka, *Passant – souviens-toi*, 62–4.

[44] Archives départementales de la Sarthe, Le Mans, 2 R 88. Only six of the fourteen soldiers could be identified.

logistical problems associated with the repatriation of Tirailleurs
Sénégalais – including former POWs and members of units
drafted for the liberation of France – sparked unrest and rebellion. Frustration was compounded by the low pay and pension
rates assigned to West African veterans and by the failure of the
French authorities in many cases to hand out the money on time.
The most serious incident was an uprising of 1280 ex-POWs in
the camp of Thiaroye near Dakar on 1 December 1944. Members of the French colonial army shot thirty-five Tirailleur veterans and seriously wounded an equal number. Hundreds more
were injured. For a long time, the events of Thiaroye have occupied a much larger place in West African public memory than
the massacres of 1940.[45] The film *Camp de Thiaroye*, directed by
Ousmane Sembène (1987), drew much attention to these events
in an effort to portray the injustices of the colonial regime. Its
artistic qualities notwithstanding, the film's reflections on the
experience of captured Tirailleurs Sénégalais in Europe contain
many factual errors.[46] Only recently has the work of journalist Serge Bilé drawn wider attention in francophone Africa to
the plight of Tirailleurs Sénégalais and other blacks in German
camps. Based on interviews with survivors, Bilé has created a documentary film and published a book on blacks in Nazi camps.[47]

---

[45] Echenberg, *Colonial Conscripts*, 101 and 169.

[46] Papawongue Mbengue, Sembène Ousmane, and Thierno Faty Sow, "Camp de
Thiaroye" (Société nouvelle de promotion cinématographique, 1987). The
film is also misleading with respect to the events at Thiaroye. See Kenneth
W. Harrow, "*Camp de Thiaroye:* Who's That Hiding in Those Tanks and How
Come We Can't See Their Faces?" *Iris: A Journal of Theory on Image and Sound*
18 (1995).

[47] Serge Bilé, *Noirs dans les camps nazis* (Monaco: Éditions du Rocher: Le Serpent
à plumes, 2005), Serge Bilé, *Noirs dans les camps nazis* (video documentary)
(Secam, 2001).

Conclusion

The German army murdered at least 1,500 to 3,000 black African soldiers during its Blitzkrieg in Western Europe, mostly in the second phase of the campaign in France. An unknown number of black soldiers were also killed in operations during which no prisoners were taken and in German POW camps. These massacres happened in the context of widespread abuses, threats, and dehumanizing measures. Although several French towns have created memorial sites or plaques for the Africans murdered in 1940, these executions have been peripheral at best to the public memory of the war in France and to the historical narratives of the 1940 campaign. In Germany, knowledge of these massacres has been practically nonexistent.

In the absence of a formal order to kill black POWs, the massacres of black Africans were authorized by the traditional stigmatization of black men in arms in German public discourse and the massive racist propaganda of the Nazi media during the campaign. That the vast majority of abuses happened after this propaganda campaign was launched by Goebbels, with Hitler's approval, is certainly no coincidence. German soldiers read and heard repeatedly that black soldiers were savages who mutilated and killed German prisoners in bestial ways. The blacks were stamped as illegitimate combatants and thus deprived of the protection granted by the Geneva Convention. The racist background, however, was not sufficient to trigger massacres. Situational factors also played a role: The finding of mutilated German soldiers, the battle fear associated with fighting French hedgehog positions, or the frustration of having to overcome hard resistance at a time when France had obviously lost were relevant in almost all cases. Of course, the determined resistance of Tirailleurs Sénégalais was influenced by the ruthlessness of German fighting methods against them, and the mutilation charges were, though not always spurious, strongly exaggerated.

The inconsistency of the German actions toward black POWs, particularly the examples of correct and even friendly treatment, reveals that conclusions about the barbarization and Nazification of the Wehrmacht during the campaign of 1940 cannot be generalized. Some strongly Nazified units did show a propensity to commit massacres. Sometimes, however, commanders of other units who shared the racist prejudice against black African troops did not carry out massacres. In still other cases, there is no evidence at all that black troops were treated differently from whites. This is relevant in the context of the Wehrmacht's significant resistance to the brutalization of warfare expected by the Nazi leadership and the SS already in Poland and implemented with much greater verve – and Wehrmacht consent – later in Yugoslavia and the Soviet Union. After the friction between the Wehrmacht and the SS in Poland and after the inconsistent treatment of racially stigmatized soldiers in France, the Nazi regime understood that it needed to be more proactive and specific if it wanted to impose its racial views on Wehrmacht practices. Hence, the criminal orders for the treatment of POWs in the Soviet campaign were issued.

Sources

ARCHIVAL SOURCES

Archives du Comité international de la Croix-Rouge (CICR), Genève

CSC, Service des camps, France (Frontstalags)
B, G 3
B, G 7
B, G 10
B, G 17

Archives communales de Bourmont (Mairie de Bourmont)

33 Rev. 898

Archives communales de la ville de Clamecy (Mairie de Clamecy)

1 M 49
2 Z 1277
4 H 55
4 H 56
4 H 93
Soldats et civils morts, Guerre 39–45
Janette Colas, "A propos des 43 Tirailleurs"

Archives communales de Sillé-le-Guillaume (Mairie de Sillé-le-Guillaume)

4 H 99, 106, 107

Archives départementales de la Haute-Marne, Chaumont

15 W 74

Archives départementales de la Nièvre, Nevers

7 J (Fonds Bélile)
50 J 9
Niv. 1007
Niv. 2208
80 W 159/2
999 W 62/5

Archives départementales de l'Oise, Beauvais

33 W 8259

Archives départementales du Rhône (Section Moderne), Lyon

10 M 229
437 W 173
3808 W 879 (Chasselay)
3808 W 908 (Lyon)
3808 W 909 (Lyon)

Archives départementales de la Sarthe, Le Mans

2 R 88

Archives municipales de Lyon

0963 WP 103–1
1019 WP 04
1025 WP 045
1029 WP 026

Bundesarchiv-Militärarchiv (BA–MA), Freiburg im Breisgau

RH 10 OKH Generalinspekteur der Panzertruppen
RH 17 Schulen des Heeres
RH 20 Armeeoberkommandos
RH 24–14 XIV. Armeekorps
RH 24–38 XXXVIII. Armeekorps
RH 24–41 XLI. Armeekorps
RH 26 Infantry Divisions, most sections 1–87, and 208, 225, 227, 254.
RH 27 Panzer Divisions, sections 2–10
RH 37/130, 131 6. Schützenbrigade
RH 37/882, 883, 884, 885 Infanterieregiment 25
RH 37/1340, 1341, 1362, 1396 Infanterieregiment 63
RH 37/1909, 1910, 6517a Schützenregiment 69
RH 37/6327, 6328, 6332, 6335, 6392 Infanterieregiment *Großdeutschland*
RH 37/6420 Infanterieregiment 36
RH 39/348, 349 Aufklärungsregiment 9
RH 39/593, 594, 595 Aufklärungsabteilung 6
RH 49: Kriegsgefangenenlager
RHD 4/38, vol. 2
RS 3–3 SS-Panzer-Division Totenkopf
RS 4 Leibstandarte Adolf Hitler
RW 6/270–79 Kriegsgefangenenakten
RW 34, Deutsche Waffenstillstandskommission, vols. 45, 60, and 77

Centre historique d'études des troupes d'outre-mer (CHETOM), Fréjus

15 H 141, 144, 145, 146, 147
16 H 338, 339

Service historique de l'Armée de terre (SHAT), Vincennes

34 N 5: Groupement De Mesmay
34 N 111: 100th and 101st Infantry Regiment
34 N 130: 129e RIM
34 N 208: 40e DI/208e RALC
34 N 1070: 5e RICMS
34 N 1071: 6e RICMS
34 N 1074: 27e and 28e RICMS

34 N 1075: 33e RICMS
34 N 1076: Tirailleurs Malgaches
34 N 1079: 44e RIC
34 N 1081: 53e and 57e RICMS
34 N 1085: 4e RIC/4e RTS
34 N 1086: 5e RTS/1e Col.Mix
34 N 1088: 8e RTS
34 N 1089: 10e and 11e RTS
34 N 1090: 12e RTS
34 N 1092: 13e RTS
34 N 1093: 14e RTS
34 N 1095: 16e RTS
34 N 1097: 18e and 24e RTS
34 N 1098: 25e RTS
34 N 1099: 26e and 12e RTS
34 N 1102: Bataillon autonome de Tirailleurs Sénégalais
34 N 1104: Bataillon Malgache
34 N 1105
34 N 1112
34 N 1117

Société scientifique et artistique de Clamecy

Dossier Colas
Dossier "Les troupes coloniales"

PERIODICALS

–*Das Schwarze Korps*
–*Völkischer Beobachter* (Norddeutsche Ausgabe)
–*Die Wehrmacht*

PUBLISHED PRIMARY SOURCES, MEMOIRS, CONTEMPORARY WORKS

Albert-Sorel, Jean. *Le chemin de Croix, 1939–1940*. Paris: Julliard, 1943.
Auswärtiges Amt, ed. *Dokumente britisch-französischer Grausamkeit. Die britische und französische Kriegführung in den Niederlanden, Belgien und Nordfrankreich im Mai 1940*. Berlin: Verlag Volk und Reich, 1940.

Barlone, Daniel. *A French Officer's Diary*. Translated by Cass, L. V. Cambridge: Cambridge University Press, 1943.

Benoist-Méchin, Jacques. *De la défaite au désastre*. 2 vols. Pairs: Albin Michel, 1984–5.

Bloch, Marc. *Strange Defeat*. New York: Norton, 1968.

Boberach, Heinz, ed. *Meldungen aus dem Reich 1938–1945: Die geheimen Lageberichte des Sicherheitsdienstes der SS. Band 4: Meldungen aus dem Reich Nr. 66 vom 15. März 1940 – Nr. 101 vom 1. Juli 1940*. Herrsching: Pawlak, 1984.

———, ed. *Meldungen aus dem Reich 1938–1945: Die geheimen Lageberichte des Sicherheitsdienstes der SS. Band 5: Meldungen aus dem Reich Nr. 102 vom 4. Juli 1940 – Nr. 141 vom 14. November 1940*. Herrsching: Pawlak, 1984.

———, ed. *Meldungen aus dem Reich: Auswahl aus den geheimen Lageberichten des Sicherheitsdienstes der SS 1939–1944*. Neuwied and Berlin: Luchterhand, 1965.

Brehm, Werner. *Mein Kriegstagebuch 1939–1945: Mit der 7. Panzerdivision 5 Jahre in West und Ost*. Kassel: Selbstverlag, 1953.

Buchbender, Ortwin, and Reinhold Sterz, eds. *Das andere Gesicht des Krieges. Deutsche Feldpostbriefe 1939–1945*. Munich: Beck, 1982.

Comité International de la Croix-rouge, ed. *Rapport du Comité international de la Croix-Rouge sur son activité pendant la seconde guerre mondiale (1er septembre 1939–30 juin 1947): Volume II L'Agence centrale des prisonniers de guerre*. Geneva: CICR, 1948.

Conombo, Joseph Issoufou. *Souvenirs de guerre d'un Tirailleur sénégalais*. Paris: L'Harmattan, 1989.

Coutau-Bégarie, Hervé, and Claude Huan, eds. *Lettres et notes de l'amiral Darlan*. Paris: Economica, 1992.

Crémieux-Brilhac, Jean-Louis. *Les français de l'an 40*. 2 vols. Paris: Gallimard, 1990.

Dammert, Rudoph. *Der Verrat an Europa: Die Greueltaten der farbigen Truppen Frankreichs im Weltkrieg*. Stuttgart: Deutsche Verlags-Anstalt, 1940.

de Villelume, Paul. *Journal d'une défaite*. Paris: Fayard, 1976.

Delpla, F., ed. *Les papiers secrèts du Général Doumenc*. Paris: Orban, 1992.

Denuit, Désiré. *L'Eté ambigu de 1940*. Bruxelles: Louis Musin, 1978.

Der Feldzug in Frankreich. 10. Mai–23. Juni 1940. n.p., n.d.

Deutsches Institut für Außenpolitische Forschung, ed. *Europa. Handbuch der politischen, wirtschaftlichen und kulturellen Entwicklung des neuen Europa*. Leipzig: Helingsche Verlagsanstalt, 1943.

Diallo, Bakary. *Force-Bonté*. Paris: Rieder, 1926.

Dollinger, Hans, ed. *Kain, wo ist Dein Bruder? Was der Mensch im Zweiten Weltkrieg erleiden musste – dokumentiert in Tagebüchern und Briefen.* Frankfurt am Main: List, 1992.

Durian, Wolf. *Infanterie-Regiment Großdeutschland greift an. Die Geschichte eines Sieges.* Berlin: Scherl Verlag, 1942.

Eckert, Erhard. *Vom Rhein zu den Pyrenäen: Ein Luftwaffen-Kriegsberichter erzählt vom Krieg im Westen.* Stuttgart: Loewe, 1942.

Erbt, Wilhelm. *Weltgeschichte auf rassischer Grundlage. Urzeit, Morgenland, Mittelmeer, Abendland und Nordland.* 4 ed. Leipzig: Armanen-Verlag, 1936.

Fabre-Luce, Alfred. *Nach dem Waffenstillstand. Französisches Tagebuch 1940–1942.* Hamburg: Hanseatische Verlagsanstalt, 1943.

Fahrenkrog, Rolf Ludwig. *Europas Geschichte als Rassenschicksal. Vom Wesen und Wirken der Rassen im europäischen Schicksalsraum.* Leipzig: Hesse und Becker, 1937.

Fiala, Václav. *Das geschlagene Frankreich. Ein Tschechischer Journalist auf den Kriegsschauplätzen des Westens.* Prague: Orbis-Verlag, 1941.

Fillies, Fritz. *Großdeutsche Grenadiere im Kampf. Kameraden aller Gaue in einem Regiment beim Feldzug durch Belgien und Frankreich.* Berlin: Zeitgeschichte-Verlag, 1941.

Friedmann, Georges. *Journal de guerre, 1939–1940.* Paris: Gallimard, 1987.

Fröhlich, Elke, ed. *Die Tagebücher von Joseph Goebbels. Sämtliche Fragmente. Teil I: Aufzeichnungen 1924–1941, vol. 4 (1.1.1940–8.7.1941).* Munich, New York, London, and Paris: K. G. Saur, 1987.

————, ed. *Die Tagebücher von Joseph Goebbels: Teil I, Aufzeichnungen 1923–1941. Band 8: April–November 1940.* Munich: K. G. Saur, 1998.

Fuchs Richardson, Horst. *Sieg Heil! War Letters of Tank Gunner Karl Fuchs, 1937–1941.* Hamden, Connecticut: Archon, 1987.

Gide, André. *Pages de journal, 1939–1942.* New York: Pantheon, 1944.

Giese, Friedrich, and Eberhard Menzel, eds. *Deutsches Kriegführungsrecht. Sammlung der für die deutsche Kriegführung geltenden Rechtsvorschriften.* Berlin: Heymann, 1940.

Gobineau, Hélène de. *Noblesse d'Afrique.* Paris: Fasquelles Editeurs, 1946.

Goebbels, Joseph. *The Goebbels Diaries, 1939–1941.* Translated by Taylor, Fred. New York: G. P. Putnam's Sons, 1983.

Großmann, Horst. *Geschichte der rheinisch-westfälischen 6. Infanterie-Division 1939–1945, Divisionsgeschichten 1939–1945.* Bad Nauheim: Podzun-Verlag, 1958.

Guderian, Heinz. *Erinnerungen eines Soldaten.* Heidelberg: Vowinckel, 1951.

Günther, Hans K. F. *Rassenkunde des jüdischen Volkes.* München: J. F. Lehmann, 1930.

Gwassa, G. C. K., and John Iliffe. *Records of the Maji Maji Rising.* [Nairobi]: East African Publishing House, 1967.

Habe, Hans. "The Nazi Plan for Negroes." *The Nation* 152 (1941): 232–5.

———. *A Thousand Shall Fall.* New York: Harcourt, Brace, and Company, 1941.

Halder, Franz. *Kriegstagebuch. Tägliche Aufzeichnungen des Chefs des Generalstabes des Heeres 1939–1942.* 3 vols. Vol. 2. Stuttgart: Kohlhammer, 1962–4.

Hecht, Günther. *Die Bedeutung des Rassengedankens in der Kolonialpolitik.* Berlin: Rassenpolitisches Amt der NSDAP, 1937.

Hesse, Kurt, ed. *Über Schlachtfelder vorwärts! Mit dem siegreichen Heer durch Frankreich 1940.* Berlin: Wilhelm Limpert-Verlag, 1940.

Hindenburg, Paul von. *Aus meinem Leben.* Leipzig: S. Hirzel, 1920.

Hitler, Adolf. *Mein Kampf. Zwei Bände in einem Band.* 9 ed. Munich: Zentralverlag der NSDAP, 1941.

ICRC. *International Committee of the Red Cross: Report of Its Activities during the Second World War.* Geneva: International Committee of the Red Cross, 1948.

Kageneck, August von. *Examen de conscience. Nous étions vaincus mais nous nous croyions innocents.* Paris: Perrin, 1996.

Kesselring, Albert. *Soldat bis zum letzten Tag.* Bonn: Athenäum-Verlag, 1953.

Koestler, Arthur. *Scum of the Earth.* New York: Macmillan, 1941.

Léautaud, Paul. *Journal littéraire, février 1940-juin 1941.* Paris: Mercure de France, 1962.

Lefébure, Antoine. *Les conversations secrètes des Français sous l'Occupation.* Paris: Plon, 1993.

Les évènements survenus en France de 1933 à 1945. Témoignages. 9 vols. Paris: Presses universitaires de la France, 1951–2.

Lettow-Vorbeck, Paul von. *Meine Erinnerungen aus Ostafrika.* Leipzig: Koehler, 1920.

Mangin, Charles. *La Force noire.* Paris: Hachette, 1910.

Manteuffel, Hasso von. *Die 7. Panzer-Division 1935–1945. Die "Gespenster-Division."* Friedberg: Podzun-Pallas-Verlag, n.d.

Massaquoi, Hans J. *Destined to Witness: Growing up Black in Nazi Germany.* New York: W. Morrow, 1999.

Meifredy, Françoise, and Robert Hervet. *Missions sans frontières.* Paris: Editions France-Empire, 1966.

Mendès-France, Pierre. *Liberté, liberté chérie.* New York: Didier, 1943.

Mit dem Generalkommando XXXX. A.K. vom Rhein zum Atlantik. n.p., n.d.

Reh, Hans. *Vom großen Krieg zum großen Sieg: der Kampf im Westen.* Mühlhausen: Paul, 1941.

Rosenberg, Alfred. *Der Mythus des 20. Jahrhunderts. Eine Wertung der seelisch-geistigen Gestaltenkämpfe unserer Zeit.* 5 ed. Munich: Hoheneichen-Verlag, 1933.

Rückerl, Adalbert. *The Investigation of Nazi War Crimes 1945–1978: A Documentation.* Hamden, Connecticut: Archon Books, 1980.

Scapini, Georges. *Mission sans gloire.* Paris: Editions Morgan, 1960.

Schaefer, Hans. *Division Sintzenich. Erlebnisberichte aus dem Feldzuge in Frankreich 1940.* Frankfurt am Main: Hauserpresse, n.d.

Schick, Albert. *Die 10. Panzer-Division 1939–1943.* Köln: Pohle, 1993.

Séché, Alfred. *Les noirs.* Paris: Payot, 1919.

Sell, Manfred. *Die schwarze Völkerwanderung. Der Einbruch des Negers in die Kulturwelt.* Wien: Frick, 1940.

Société historique et archéologique de Bourmont, ed. *Témoignages recueillis à l'occasion du cinquantenaire de la bataille de Bourmont 18–19–20 juin 1940.* Neufchateau: Imprimerie du Progrès, 1990.

Spaeter, Helmut. *Die Geschichte des Panzerkorps Großdeutschland.* Duisburg-Ruhrort: Selbstverlag, 1958.

Tschimpke, Alfred. *Die Gespenster-Division. Mit der Panzerwaffe durch Belgien und Frankreich.* 3 ed. Munich: Zentralverlag der NSDAP, Franz Eher Nachf., 1941.

Veillon, Dominique. *Vivre et survivre en France 1939–1947.* Paris: Payot, 1995.

Verhandlungen des Reichstages, Deutsche Nationalversammlung. Berlin: Reichsdruckerei, 1920.

Vopersal, Wolfgang. *Soldaten, Kämpfer, Kameraden. Marsch und Kämpfe der SS-Totenkopf-Division.* 5 vols. Vol. 1. Bielefeld: Selbstverlag der Truppenkameradschaft der 3. SS-Panzer-Division e. V., 1983.

Weiss, Wilhelm, ed. *Der Krieg im Westen. Dargestellt nach den Berichten des "Völkischen Beobachters."* 5 ed. Munich: Franz Eher Nachf., 1942.

Werth, Léon. *33 jours.* Paris: Viviane Hamy, 1992.

———. *Déposition. Journal 1940–1944.* Paris: Grasset, 1946.

Wirth, Albrecht. *Völkische Weltgeschichte 1879–1933*. 6 ed. Braunschweig: Westermann, 1934.

Zschäckel, Friedrich. *Waffen-SS im Westen*. Munich: Franz Eher Nachf., 1941.

SECONDARY SOURCES

Adas, Michael. *Prophets of Rebellion: Millenarian Protest Movements against the European Colonial Order*. Chapel Hill and London: University of North Carolina Press, 1979.

Akpo-Vaché, Catherine. *L'AOF et la seconde guerre mondiale*. Paris: Karthala, 1996.

Amouroux, Henri. *Quarante millions de pétainistes; juin 1940–juin 1941, La grande histoire des français sous l'occupation*, 2. Paris: Laffont, 1977.

Anderson, Ross. "The Battle of Tanga, 2–5 November 1914." *War in History* 8, no. 3 (2001): 294–322.

Andrae, Friedrich. *Auch gegen Frauen und Kinder. Der Krieg der deutschen Wehrmacht gegen die Zivilbevölkerung in Italien 1943–1945*. Munich: Piper, 1995.

Auclert, Jean-Pierre. *La grande guerre des crayons. Les noirs dessins de la propagande en 1914–1918*. Paris: Laffont, 1981.

Azéma, Jean-Pierre. "Le choc armé et les débandades." In *La France des années noires. Tome 1. De la défaite à Vichy*, edited by Azéma, Jean-Pierre, and François Bédarida, 97–129. Paris: Seuil, 2000.

———. *1940, l'année terrible*. Paris: Editions du Seuil, 1990.

———. *From Munich to the Liberation, 1938–1944*. Translated by Lloyd, Janet. *The Cambridge History of Modern France*, 6. Cambridge: Cambridge University Press, 1984.

Azéma, Jean-Pierre, and François Bédarida. *La France des années noires. 1. De la défaite à Vichy, Points Histoire*. Paris: Seuil, 2000.

———. *La France des années noires. 2. De l'Occupation à la Libération, Points Histoire*. Paris: Seuil, 2000.

Baird, Jay. *The Mythical World of Nazi War Propaganda, 1939–1945*. Minneapolis: University of Minnesota Press, 1974.

Bald, Detlef. "Afrikanischer Kampf gegen koloniale Herrschaft. Der Maji-Maji Aufstand in Ost-Afrika." *Militärgeschichtliche Mitteilungen*, no. 1 (1976): 23–50.

Balesi, Charles John. *From Adversaries to Comrades-in-Arms: West Africans and the French Military 1885–1918*. Waltham: Crossroads Press, 1979.

Bancel, Nicolas, Pascal Blanchard, Gilles Boetsch, Eric Deroo, and Sandrine Lemaire, eds. *Zoos humains. De la vénus hottentote aux reality shows.* Paris: Editions la Découverte, 2002.

Bancel, Nicolas, Pascal Blanchard, and Laurent Gervereau. *Images et colonies. Iconographie et propagande coloniale sur l'Afrique française de 1880 à 1962.* Nanterre: BDIC-ACHAC, n.d.

Barcellini, Serge. "Les monuments en homage aux combatants de la 'Grande France' (Armée d'Afrique et Armée coloniale)." *In Les troupes coloniales dans la Grande Guerre,* edited by Carlier, Claude, and Guy Pedroncini, 113-53. Paris: Economica, 1997.

Barcellini, Serge, and Annette Wieviorka. *Passant – souviens-toi – Les lieux du souvenir de la Seconde Guerre mondiale en France.* Paris: Plon, 1995.

Barker, A. J. *Prisoners of War.* New York: Universe Books, 1975.

Bartov, Omer. *Hitler's Army.* Oxford and New York: Oxford University Press, 1992.

Bartov, Omer, Atina Grossmann, and Mary Nolan, eds. *Crimes of War: Guilt and Denial in the Twentieth Century.* New York: The New Press, 2002.

Becker, Annette. *Les oubliés de la Grande Guerre. Humanitaire et culture de guerre, 1914–1918: populations occupées, déportés civils, prisonniers de guerre.* Paris: Noesis, 1998.

Bergot, Erwan. *La Coloniale, du Rif au Tschad, 1925–1980.* Paris: Presses de la Cité, 1982.

Berman, Russell. *Enlightenment or Empire: Colonial Discourse in German Culture.* Lincoln: University of Nebraska Press, 1998.

Berner, Margrit. "Rassenforschung an kriegsgefangenen Schwarzen." In *Zwischen Charleston und Stechschritt. Schwarze im Nationalsozialismus,* edited by Martin, Peter, and Christine Alonzo, 605–13. Hamburg: Dölling and Galitz, 2004.

Best, Geoffrey. *Humanity in Warfare: The Modern History of the International Law of Armed Conflicts.* New York: Columbia University Press, 1980.

———. *War & Law since 1945.* Oxford and New York: Oxford University Press, 1994.

Bigmann, Louis. *Le capitaine Charles N'Tchoréré. Un officier gabonais dans la tourmente de la deuxième guerre mondiale.* Dakar and Libreville: NEA and Lion, 1983.

Bilé, Serge. *Noirs dans les camps nazis, Essais/Documents.* Monaco: Éditions du Rocher: Le Serpent à plumes, 2005.

———. *Noirs dans les camps nazis* (documentary film): Secam, 2001.

Blanchard, Pascal, Eric Deroo, and Gilles Manceron. *Le Paris Noir.* Paris: Éditions Hazan, 2001.

Blank, Rolf. *Politisierung, Vernichtung, Überleben: Das Deutsche Reich und der Zweite Weltkrieg, Band 9, 1. Halbband.* Munich: Deutsche Verlags-Anstalt, 2004.

Bley, Helmut. *Namibia under German Rule, Studien zur afrikanischen Geschichte 5.* Hamburg and Windhoek, Namibia: Lit-Verlag and Namibia Scientific Society, 1996.

⸻. *South-West Africa under German Rule, 1894–1914.* Translated by Ridley, Hugh. Evanston: Northwestern University Press, 1971.

Bloxham, Donald. *Genocide on Trial: War Crime Tribunals and the Formation of Holocaust History and Memory.* Oxford and New York: Oxford University Press, 2001.

Boelcke, Willi A., ed. *Wollt ihr den totalen Krieg? Die geheimen Goebbels-Konferenzen 1939–43.* Stuttgart: Deutsche Verlags-Anstalt, 1967.

⸻. *Kriegspropaganda 1939–1941: Geheime Ministerkonferenzen im Reichspropagandaministerium.* Stuttgart: Deutsche Verlags-Anstalt, 1966.

Böhme, Kurt. *Die deutschen Kriegsgefangenen in französischer Hand.* Bielefeld: Gieseking, 1971.

Boisbossel, Yves de. *Peaux noires, coeurs blancs. Centenaire des tirailleurs sénégalais (1854–1954).* Paris: J. Peyronnet, 1954.

Boisvert, Jean-Jacques. *Les relations franco-allemandes en 1920.* Montréal: Les Presses de l'Université du Québec, 1977.

Borejsza, Jerzy W. "Racisme et antislavisme chez Hitler." In *La politique nazie d'extermination,* edited by Bédarida, François, 57–74. Paris: Albin Michel, 1989.

Bridgman, Jon. *The Revolt of the Hereros.* Berkeley: University of California Press, 1981.

Bridgman, Jon, and Leslie J. Worley. "Genocide of the Hereros." In *Genocide in the Twentieth Century: Critical Essays and Eyewitness Accounts,* edited by Totten, Samuel, William S. Parsons, and Israel W. Charny, 3–48. New York and London: Garland, 1995.

Browning, Christopher R. *Ordinary Men: Reserve Police Battalion 101 and the Final Solution in Poland.* New York: Harper Row, 1992.

⸻. *Nazi Policy, Jewish Workers, German Killers.* Cambridge: Cambridge University Press, 2000.

⸻. *The Path to Genocide: Essays on Launching the Final Solution.* New York: Cambridge University Press, 1992.

Bruge, Roger. *Les combattants du 18 juin: Le sang versé.* Vol. 1. Paris: Fayard, 1982.

⸻. *Juin 1940: Le mois maudit.* Paris: Fayard, 1980.

Bucheton, Robert. *Un maquis dans la ville. Contribution à l'histoire de l'occupation allemande à Clamecy et dans la région (1940–1944).* n.p.: Private press, n.d.

Buchheim, Hans, ed. *Anatomie des SS-Staates. Gutachten des Instituts für Zeitgeschichte.* 5 ed. Vol. 2. Munich: Deutscher Taschenbuch-Verlag, 1989.

Bückendorf, Jutta. *"Schwarz-weiß-rot über Ostafrika!" Deutsche Kolonialpläne und afrikanische Realität.* Münster: Lit Verlag, 1997.

Burrin, Philippe. *La France à l'heure allemande: 1940–1944.* Paris: Seuil, 1995.

Buruma, Ian. *The Wages of Guilt: Memories of War in Germany and Japan.* New York: Farrar, Straus, and Giroux, 1994.

Calder, Angus. *The Myth of the Blitz.* London: J. Cape, 1991.

Campt, Tina. *Other Germans: Black Germans and the Politics of Race, Gender, and Memory in the Third Reich.* Ann Arbor: University of Michigan Press, 2004.

Campt, Tina, Pascal Grosse, and Yara-Colette Lemke-Muñiz de Faria. "Blacks, Germans, and the Politics of Imperial Imagination, 1920–60." In *The Imperialist Imagination: German Colonialism and Its Legacy,* edited by Friedrichsmeyer, Sara, Sara Lennox, and Susanne Zantop, 205–29. Ann Arbor: University of Michigan Press, 1998.

Carlier, Claude, and Guy Pedroncini, eds. *Les troupes coloniales dans la Grande Guerre.* Paris: Economica, 1997.

Castel, Albert. "The Fort Pillow Massacre: An Examination of the Evidence." In *Black Flag over Dixie: Racial Atrocities and Reprisals in the Civil War,* edited by Urwin, Gregory J. W., 89–103. Carbondale: Southern Illinois University Press, 2004.

Caucanas, Sylvie, Rémy Cazals, and Pascal Payen. *Les prisonniers de guerre dans l'histoire: contacts entre peuples et cultures.* Carcassonne and Toulouse: Les Audois and Editions Privat, 2003.

Centre d'études d'histoire de la défense. *Les troupes de marine dans l'Armée de terre. Un siècle d'histoire.* Panazol: Charles-Lavauzelle, 2001.

Champeaux, Antoine. "Les traditions du 1er battallion de tirailleurs somalis. De Donaumont à Djibouti." In *Les troupes coloniales dans la Grande Guerre,* edited by Carlier, Claude, and Guy Pedroncini, 23–51. Paris: Economica, 1997.

Clarke, Peter Bernard. *West Africans at War, 1914–18/1939–45: Colonial Propaganda and Its Cultural Aftermath.* London: Ethnographica, 1986.

Clayton, Anthony. *France, Soldiers, and Africa.* London: Brassey's Defense Publications, 1988.

Conte, Edouard, and Cornelia Essner. *La quête de la race – Une anthropologie du nazisme*. Paris: Hachette, 1995.

Coquery-Vidrovitch, Catherine. *Africa: Endurance and Change South of the Sahara*. Translated by Maisel, David. Berkeley: University of California Press, 1988.

Coquery-Vidrovitch, Catherine, and Charles-Robert Ageron. *Histoire de la France coloniale III: Le déclin*. Paris: Armand Colin, 1991.

Corum, James S. "Die Luftwaffe, ihre Führung und Doktrin und die Frage der Kriegsverbrechen." In *Kriegsverbrechen im 20. Jahrhundert*, edited by Wegner, Bernd, and Gerd R. Überschär, 288–302. Darmstadt: Primus Verlag, 2001.

Creveld, Martin van. "Die deutsche Wehrmacht: Eine militärische Beurteilung." In *Die Wehrmacht. Mythos und Realität*, edited by Müller, Rolf-Dieter, and Erich Volkmann, 331–45. Munich: Oldenbourg, 1999.

———. *Fighting Power. German and U.S. Army Performance, 1939–1945*. Westport: Greenwood Press, 1982.

Cucchi, Giuseppe. "Ascari: Storia delle truppe indigene delle colonie." *Rivista Militare*, no. 4 (1990): 90–101.

D'Almeida-Topor, Hélène, and János Riesz, eds. *Rencontres franco-allemandes sur l'Afrique. Lettres, sciences humaines et sociales, Groupe "Afrique Noire" 13*. Paris: L'Harmattan, 1992.

Dartigues, Louis. *Des coloniaux au combat: La 1re D.I.C. en 1939–40*. Bordeaux: Amicale des anciens de la 1re D. I. C. 1939–40, 1971.

Datner, Szymon. *Crimes against POWs. Responsibility of the Wehrmacht*. Warsaw: Zachodnia Agencja Prasowa, 1964.

———. *Crimes Committed by the Wehrmacht during the September Campaign and the Period of Military Government*. Poznan: Institute for Western Affairs, 1962.

de la Barre de Nanteuil, Hugues. "L'Armée d'Afrique dans la guerre 1939–1945." In *L'Armée d'Afrique 1830–1962*, edited by Huré, Robert, 321–420. Paris: Charles-Lavauzelle, 1977.

de la Barre de Nanteuil, Hugues. "L'Armée d'Afrique dans les campagnes du Second Empire (1854–1871)." In *L'Armée d'Afrique (1830–1962)*, edited by Huré, Robert, 79–150. Paris: Charles-Lavauzelle, 1977.

de Pradel de Lamaze, Jean, and Paul Devautour. "L'Armée d'Afrique dans la guerre 1914–1918 et les campagnes d'après-guerre (1918–1939)." In *L'Armée d'Afrique (1830–1962)*, edited by Huré, Robert, 263–307. Paris: Charles-Lavauzelle, 1977.

de Pradel de Lamaze, Jean, Paul Devautour, and Hugues de la Barre de Nanteuil. "L'Armée d'Afrique dans la guerre 1939–1945." In *L'Armée d'Afrique (1830–1962)*, edited by Huré, Robert, 321–420. Paris: Charles-Lavauzelle, 1977.

Dedering, Tilman. "'A Certain Rigorous Treatment of All Parts of the Nation': The Annihilation of the Herero in German South West Africa, 1904." In *The Massacre in History*, edited by Levene, Mark, and Penny Roberts, 205–22. New York and Oxford: Berghahn Books, 1999.

―――. "The German-Herero War of 1904: Revisionism of Genocide or Imaginary Historiography?" *Journal of Southern African Studies* 19, no. 1 (1993): 80–8.

Deschênes, Ch. "Les troupes coloniales dans la bataille de France (mai-juin 1940)." *L'Ancre d'Or*, no. 255 (1990): 27–39.

Dower, John. *War Without Mercy: Race and Power in the Pacific War*. New York: Pantheon Books, 1986.

Drechsler, Horst. *Let Us Die Fighting: The Struggle of the Herero and Nama against German Imperialism (1884–1915)*. Translated by Zöllner, Bernd. London: Zed Press, 1980.

Durand, André. *From Sarajevo to Hiroshima: History of the International Committee of the Red Cross*. Geneva: Institut Henri Dunant, 1984.

Durand, Yves. *La captivité: histoire des prisonniers de guerre français, 1939–1945*. Paris: Fédération nationale des combattants et prisonniers de guerre et combattants d'Algérie, de Tunisie et du Maroc, 1982.

Echenberg, Myron. *Colonial Conscripts: The Tirailleurs Sénégalais in French West Africa, 1857–1960, Social History of Africa*. Portsmouth, New Hampshire, and London: Heinemann and James Currey, 1991.

―――. "Morts pour la France; the African Soldier in France during the Second World War." *Journal of African History* 26, no. 4 (1985): 363–80.

Essner, Cornelia. "Zwischen Vernunft und Gefühl: Die Reichstagsdebatte von 1912 um koloniale 'Rassenmischehe' und 'Sexualität.'" *Zeitschrift für Geschichtswissenschaft* 45, no. 6 (1997): 503–19.

Evans, Andrew D. "Anthropology at War: Racial Studies of POWs during World War I." In *Worldly Provincialism: German Anthropology in the Age of Empire*, edited by Penny, H. Glenn, and Matti Bunzl, 198–229. Ann Arbor: University of Michigan Press, 2003.

Fall, Mar. *Des tirailleurs sénégalais aux . . . blacks. Les Africains noirs en France*. Paris: Editions L'Harmattan, 1986.

Fargettas, Julien. "Der andere Feldzug von 1940: Das Massaker an den schwarzen Soldaten." In *Zwischen Charleston und Stechschritt. Schwarze im Nationalsozialismus,* edited by Martin, Peter, and Christine Alonzo, 567–72. Hamburg: Dölling and Galitz, 2004.

————. "Les tirailleurs sénégalais dans la campagne de mai–juin 1940." In *Les troupes de marine dans l'Armée de terre. Un siècle d'histoire,* edited by Centre d'études d'histoire de la défense, 137–48. Panazol: Charles-Lavauzelle, 2001.

————. "Le massacre des soldats du 25ème Régiment de Tirailleurs Sénégalais Région lyonnaise – 19 et 20 juin 1940." 2 vols. Vol. 2. Mémoire de maîtrise, Université de Saint-Etienne, 2000.

Fishman, Sarah. *We Will Wait: Wives of French Prisoners of War, 1940–1945.* New Haven and London: Yale University Press, 1991.

Förster, Jürgen. "Die weltanschauliche Erziehung in der Waffen-SS." In *Ausbildungsziel Judenmord? "Weltanschauliche Erziehung" von SS, Polizei und Waffen-SS im Rahmen der "Endlösung,"* edited by Matthäus, Jürgen, Konrad Kwiet, Jürgen Förster, and Richard Breitman, 87–113. Frankfurt am Main: Fischer Taschenbuch Verlag, 2003.

————. "'Verbrecherische Befehle.'" In *Kriegsverbrechen im 20. Jahrhundert,* edited by Wette, Wolfram, and Gerd R. Überschär, 137–51. Darmstadt: Primus Verlag, 2001.

————. "Operation Barbarossa as a War of Conquest and Annihilation." In *Germany and the Second World War. Volume IV: The Attack on the Soviet Union,* edited by Militärgeschichtliches Forschungsamt, 481–521. Oxford: Clarendon Press, 1998.

————. "The German Army and the Ideological War against the Soviet Union." In *The Policies of Genocide: Jews and Soviet Prisoners of War in Nazi Germany,* edited by Hirschfeld, Gerhard, 15–29. London, Boston, and Sydney: Allen & Unwin, 1986.

Forwick, Helmut. "Zur Behandlung alliierter Kriegsgefangener im Zweiten Weltkrieg." *Militärgeschichtliche Mitteilungen* 2 (1967): 119–134.

France, Armée – Service historique. *Bibliographie des historiques des régiments de l'armée française: de 1914 à l'époque contemporaine.* Vincennes: Ministère des armées, Etat-major de l'armée de terre, Service historique, 1973.

François, Jean-Jacques. *La guerre de 1939–1945 en Eure-et-Loir.* Mainvilliers: Ed. La Parcheminière, n.d. 4 vols.

Friedeburg, Robert von. "Konservatismus und Reichskolonialrecht. Konservatives Weltbild und kolonialer Gedanke in England und

Deutschland vom späten 19. Jahrhundert bis zum Ersten Weltkrieg." *Historische Zeitschrift* 263 (1996): 345–93.

Friedrichsmeyer, Sara, Sara Lennox, and Susanne Zantop, eds. *The Imperialist Imagination: German Colonialism and Its Legacy.* Ann Arbor: University of Michigan Press, 1998.

Fritz, Stephen. *Endkampf: Soldiers, Civilians, and the Death of the Third Reich.* Lexington: University Press of Kentucky, 2004.

———. *Frontsoldaten. The German Soldier in World War II.* Lexington: The University Press of Kentucky, 1995.

Gann, Lewis H. *The Rulers of German Africa, 1884–1914.* Stanford: Stanford University Press, 1977.

Garrigues, Jean. *Banania. Histoire d'une passion française.* Paris: Editions du May, 1991.

Gascar, Pierre. *Histoire de la captivité des Français en Allemagne (1939–1945).* Paris: Gallimard, 1967.

Geiger, Wolfgang. *L'image de la France dans l'Allemagne nazie 1933–1945.* Rennes: Presses Universitaires de Rennes, 1999.

Gerlach, Christian. "Verbrechen deutscher Fronttruppen in Weißrußland 1941–1944. Eine Annäherung." In *Wehrmacht und Vernichtungspolitik. Militär im nationalsozialistischen System,* edited by Pohl, Karl Heinrich, 99–114. Göttingen: Vandenhoek & Ruprecht, 1999.

———. *Kalkulierte Morde: Die deutsche Wirtschafts- und Vernichtungspolitik in Weißrussland 1941 bis 1944.* Hamburg: HIS Verlagsgesellschaft, 1999.

Gewald, Jan-Bart. *Herero Heroes: A Socio-Political History of the Herero of Namibia 1890–1923.* Oxford, Cape Town, Athens: James Currey & Ohio University Press, 1999.

Ginio, Ruth. "La politique antijuive de Vichy en Afrique occidentale française." *Archives Juives* 36, no. 1 (2003): 109–18.

———. "French Colonial Reading of Ethnographic Research: The Case of the 'Desertion' of the Abron King and its Aftermath." *Cahiers d'Études africaines* 166, no. XLII-2 (2002): 337–57.

———. "Les enfants africains de la Révolution nationale: la politique vichyssoise de l'enfance et de la jeunesse dans les colonies de l'AOF (1940–1943)." *Revue d'Histoire Moderne et Contemporaine* 49, no. 4 (2002): 132–53.

———. "Marshall Pétain Spoke to Schoolchildren: Vichy Propaganda in French West Africa, 1940–1943." *The International Journal of African Historical Studies* 33, no. 2 (2000): 291–312.

Ginns, Margaret. "French North African Prisoners of War in Jersey." *Channel Islands Occupation Review* (1985): 50–70.

Goda, Norman. *Tomorrow the World: Hitler, Northwest Africa, and the Path toward America.* College Station: Texas A & M University Press, 1998.

Goralski, Robert. *World War II Almanac, 1931–1945: A Political and Military Record.* New York: Putnam, 1986.

Gordon, Bertram M., ed. *Historical Dictionary of World War II France: The Occupation, Vichy, and the Résistance, 1938–1946.* Westport: Greenwood Publishers, 1998.

Hamburg Institute for Social Research. *German Army and Genocide: Crimes against War Prisoners, Jews, and Other Civilians in the East, 1939–1944.* New York: New Press, 1999.

Harman, Nicholas. *Dunkirk: The Necessary Myth.* New York: Simon & Schuster, 1980.

Harris, Ruth. "The "Child of the Barbarian": Rape, Race and Nationalism in France During the First World War." *Past and Present* 123, no. 141 (1993): 170–206.

Harrow, Kenneth W. "*Camp de Thiaroye:* Who's That Hiding in Those Tanks and How Come We Can't See Their Faces?" *Iris: A Journal of Theory on Image and Sound* 18 (1995): 147–52.

Headrick, Rita. "African Soldiers in World War II." *Armed Forces and Society* 4 (1978): 502–26.

Heer, Hannes, and Klaus Naumann, eds. *Vernichtungskrieg. Verbrechen der Wehrmacht 1941 bis 1944.* Hamburg: Hamburger Edition, 1995.

Helbig, Klaus. "Die deutsche Kriegführung in Ostafrika 1914–1918." *Militärgeschichte* 28, no. 2 (1989): 136–45.

Henson, Jeffrey Allen. "The Role of *Das Schwarze Korps* in the SS's Campaign against the Catholic Church." M.A. thesis, Mississippi State University, 1997.

Herbert, Ulrich, ed. *Nationalsozialistische Vernichtungspolitik 1939–1945. Neue Forschungen und Kontroversen.* Frankfurt am Main: Fischer Taschenbuch Verlag, 1998.

Hildebrand, Klaus. *Vom Reich zum Weltreich. Hitler, NSDAP und koloniale Frage.* Munich: Wilhelm Fink, 1969.

Hildebrand, Klaus, and Karl Ferdinand Werner, eds. *Deutschland und Frankreich 1936–1939. 15. Deutsch-Französisches Historikerkolloquium des DHI in Paris.* Munich: Artemis-Verlag, 1981.

Hochstuhl, Kurt. *Zwischen Frieden und Krieg. Das Elsaß in den Jahren 1938–1940. Ein Beitrag zu den Problemen einer Grenzregion in Krisenzeiten.* Frankfurt am Main: Peter Lang, 1984.

Höhne, Heinz. *Der Orden unter dem Totenkopf. Die Geschichte der SS.* 2 vols. Frankfurt am Main: Fischer Bücherei, 1969.

Hollandsworth, James G., Jr. "The Execution of White Officers from Black Units by Confederate Forces during the Civil War." In *Black Flag over Dixie: Racial Atrocities and Reprisals in the Civil War*, edited by Urwin, Gregory J. W., 52–64. Carbondale: Southern Illinois University Press, 2004.

Hondius, Dienke. "Ein Vergleich der Feindbilder 'Schwarze' und 'Juden' in Nazi-Deutschland." In *Zwischen Charleston und Stechschritt. Schwarze im Nationalsozialismus*, edited by Martin, Peter, and Christine Alonzo, 383–91. Hamburg: Dölling und Galitz, 2004.

Hooning, Th. J. "De 'Zwarte Smaad' en zijn gevolgen." *Spiegel Historiael* 17, no. 1 (1982): 8–12.

Horne, Alistair. *To Lose a Battle: France 1940*. London: Macmillan, 1969.

Horne, John, and Alan Kramer. *German Atrocities, 1914: A History of Denial*. New Haven and London: Yale University Press, 2001.

Hubrich, Heinrich-Georg, and Henning Melber. *Namibia – Geschichte und Gegenwart. Zur Frage der Dekolonisation einer Siedlerkolonie*. Bonn: Informationsstelle südliches Afrika, 1995.

Huré, Robert, ed. *L'Armée d'Afrique 1830–1962*. Paris: Charles-Lavauzelle, 1977.

Hymans, Jacques L. *Léopold Sédar Senghor: An Intellectual Biography*. Edinburgh: Edinburgh University Press, 1971.

Iliffe, John. *A Modern History of Tanganyika, African Studies Series 25*. Cambridge and New York: Cambridge University Press, 1979.

———. *Tanganyika under German Rule, 1905–1912*. London: Cambridge University Press, 1969.

Jäckel, Eberhard. "Die Wehrmacht als Teil des NS-Unrechtsstaates: Einführende Bemerkungen." In *Die Wehrmacht. Mythos und Realität*, edited by Müller, Rolf-Dieter, and Erich Volkmann, 739–42. Munich: Oldenbourg, 1999.

———. *Frankreich in Hitlers Europa. Die deutsche Frankreichpolitik im 2. Weltkrieg, Quellen und Darstellungen zur Zeitgeschichte, 14*. Stuttgart: Deutsche Verlags-Anstalt, 1966.

Jackson, Julian. *The Fall of France: The Nazi Invasion of 1940*. Oxford and New York: Oxford University Press, 2003.

Jaffré, Yves Frédéric. *Les tribunaux d'exception, 1940–1962*. Paris: Nouvelles Editions Latines, 1963.

James, C. L. R., George Breitman, and Edgar Keemer. *Fighting Racism in World War II*. New York: Monad Press, 1980.

Jordan, Weymouth T., Jr., and Gerald W. Thomas. "Massacre at Plymouth: April 20, 1864." In *Black Flag over Dixie: Racial Atrocities and Reprisals in the Civil War,* edited by Urwin, Gregory J. W., 153–202. Carbondale: Southern Illinois University Press, 2004.

Julien, M. *La loi du 15 septembre 1948 sur les crimes de guerre.* Paris: Institut de criminologie, 1952.

Kaufmann, Doris. "Die Ehre des Vaterlandes und die Ehre der Frauen oder der Kampf an der äusseren und inneren Front. Der Deutsch-Evangelische Frauenbund im Übergang vom Kaiserreich zur Weimarer Republik." *Evangelische Theologie* 46 (1986): 277–92.

Keithly, David M. "Khaki Foxes: The East Afrika Korps." *Small Wars and Insurgencies* 12, no. 1 (2001): 166–85.

Kelman, Herbert C., and V. Lee Hamilton. *Crimes of Obedience: Toward a Social Psychology of Authority and Responsibility.* New Haven: Yale University Press, 1989.

Kesting, Robert W. "The Black Experience During the Holocaust." In *The Holocaust and History: The Known, the Unknown, the Disputed, and the Reexamined,* edited by Berenbaum, Michael, and Abraham J. Peck, 358–65. Bloomington and Indianapolis: Indiana University Press, 1998.

———. "Blacks Under the Swastika: A Research Note." *Journal of Negro History* 83 (1998): 84–99.

———. "Forgotten Victims: Blacks in the Holocaust." *Journal of Negro History* 77 (1992): 30–36.

Killingray, David. *Guardians of Empire: The Armed Forces of the Colonial Powers c. 1700–1964, Studies in Imperialism.* Manchester and New York: Manchester University Press, 1999.

———. "Africans and African Americans in Enemy Hands." In *Prisoners of War and Their Captors in World War II,* edited by Moore, Bob, and Kent Fedorowich, 181–204. Oxford and Washington, D.C.: Berg, 1996.

———. "Labour Exploitation for Military Campaigns in British Colonial Africa 1870–1945." *Journal of Contemporary History* 24, no. 3 (1989): 483–501.

Knigge, Volkhard. *"Triviales" Geschichtsbewußtsein und verstehender Geschichtsunterricht.* Pfaffenweiler: Centaurus-Verlagsgesellschaft, 1988.

Knoll, Arthur J., and Lewis H. Gann. *Germans in the Tropics: Essays in German Colonial History.* New York: Greenwood, 1987.

Kochavi, Arieh J. *Prelude to Nuremberg: Allied War Crimes Policy and the Question of Punishment.* Chapel Hill and London: University of North Carolina Press, 1998.

Koller, Christian. "Der 'dunkle Verrat an Europa': Afrikanische Soldaten im Krieg 1914–1918 in der deutschen Wahrnehmung." In *Zwischen Charleston und Stechschritt. Schwarze im Nationalsozialismus*, edited by Martin, Peter, and Christine Alonzo, 111–15. Hamburg: Dölling und Galitz, 2004.

_____. *"Von Wilden aller Rassen niedergemetzelt." Die Diskussion um die Verwendung von Kolonialtruppen in Europa zwischen Rassismus, Kolonial- und Militärpolitik (1914–1930)*. Stuttgart: Franz Steiner, 2001.

Koponen, Juhani. *Development for Exploitation: German Colonial Policies in Mainland Tanzania, 1884–1914*. 2 ed. Boulder: Westview, 1995.

Kramer, Alan. "Les 'atrocités allemandes': mythologie populaire, propagande et manipulation dans l'armée allemande." *Guerres mondiales et conflits contemporains*, no. 171 (1993): 47–67.

Krausnick, Helmut. "Kommissarbefehl und 'Gerichtsbarkeitserlaß Barbarossa' in neuer Sicht." *Vierteljahrshefte für Zeitgeschichte* 25 (1977): 682–738.

Krausnick, Helmut, and Hans-Heinrich Wilhelm. *Die Truppe des Weltanschauungskrieges. Die Einsatzgruppen der Sicherheitspolizei und des S.D. 1938–1942*. Stuttgart: Deutsche Verlags-Anstalt, 1981.

Krüger, Gesine. *Kriegsbewältigung und Geschichtsbewusstsein: Realität, Deutung und Verarbeitung des deutschen Kolonialkriegs in Namibia 1904 bis 1907, Kritische Studien zur Geschichtswissenschaft 133*. Göttingen: Vandenhoeck & Ruprecht, 1999.

Kum'a N'dumbé III, Alexandre. "Afrika in der NS-Planung eines großgermanischen Reiches." In *Zwischen Charleston und Stechschritt. Schwarze im Nationalsozialismus*, edited by Martin, Peter, and Christine Alonzo, 423–8. Hamburg: Dölling and Galitz, 2004.

_____. *Hitler voulait l'Afrique: Les plans secrets pour une Afrique fasciste, 1933–1945*. Paris: L'Harmattan, 1980.

Kursietis, Andris J. *The Wehrmacht at War 1939–1945. The Units and Commanders of the German Ground Forces during World War II*. Soesterberg: Aspekt, 1999.

Kutz, Martin. "Realitätsflucht – Krieg – Kriegsverbrechen." In *Kriegsverbrechen im 20. Jahrhundert*, edited by Wegner, Bernd, and Gerd R. Überschär, 507–18. Darmstadt: Primus Verlag, 2001.

Laboulet, André. *Les combats d'Airaines et environs. Juin 1940*. Abbéville: Lafosse, 1972.

Latzel, Klaus. *Deutsche Soldaten – nationalsozialistischer Krieg? Kriegserlebnis – Kriegserfahrung 1939–1945, Krieg in der Geschichte*. Paderborn: Schönigh, 1998.

_____. "Tourismus und Gewalt: Kriegswahrnehmungen in Feldpost-briefen." In *Vernichtungskrieg. Verbrechen der Wehrmacht 1941 bis 1944*, edited by Heer, Hannes, and Klaus Naumann, 447–59. Hamburg: HIS Verlagsgesellschaft, 1995.

Laurien, Ingrid. "Der Maji-Maji-Aufstand in Deutsch-Ostafrika 1905/06: Zum Forschungsstand." *1999. Zeitschrift für Sozialgeschichte des 20. und 21. Jahrhunderts* 9, no. 1 (1994): 85–109.

Lawler, Nancy Ellen. *Soldiers, Airmen, Spies, and Whisperers: The Gold Coast in World War II.* Athens, Ohio: Ohio University Press, 2002.

_____. *Soldiers of Misfortune: Ivoirien Tirailleurs of World War II.* Athens, Ohio: Ohio University Press, 1992.

Lebzelter, Gisela. "Die 'Schwarze Schmach': Vorurteile – Propaganda – Mythos." *Geschichte und Gesellschaft* 11, no. 1 (1985): 37–58.

Le Naour, Jean-Yves. *La honte noire. L'Allemagne et les troupes coloniales françaises 1914–1945.* Paris: Hachette Littérature, 2003.

"Les combats de Montluzin." *L'Ancre d'Or*, no. 96 (1968): 8–9.

Lewin, Christophe. *Le retour des prisonniers de guerre. Naissance et développement de la F.N.P.G. 1944–1958.* Paris: Publications de la Sorbonne, 1987.

Liverpool, Russell, Lord of. *The Scourge of the Swastika: A Short History of Nazi War Crimes.* New York: Philosophical Library, 1954.

Lukacs, John. *The Duel.* New Haven: Yale University Press, 2001.

_____. *The Last European War: September 1939–December 1941.* New Haven: Yale University Press, 2001.

_____. *Five Days in London: May 1940.* New Haven: Yale University Press, 1999.

Lunn, Joe. *Memoirs of the Maelstrom: A Senegalese Oral History of the First World War, Social History of Africa.* Portsmouth, New Hampshire: Heine-mann, 1999.

Lusane, Clarence. *Hitler's Black Victims: The Historical Experiences of Afro-Germans, European Blacks, Africans, and African Americans in the Nazi Era.* New York: Routledge, 2002.

Lüsebrink, Hans-Jürgen. "'Tirailleurs Sénégalais' und 'Schwarze Schande' – Verlaufsformen und Konsequenzen einer deutsch-französischen Auseinandersetzung (1910–1926)." In *"Tirailleurs sénégalais": zur bildlichen und literarischen Darstellung afrikanischer Soldaten im Dienste Frankreichs*, edited by Riesz, János, and Joachim Schultz, 57–71. Frankfurt am Main: Peter Lang, 1989.

Luther, Hans. "Zu den gegenwärtigen Kriegsverbrecherprozessen in Frankreich." *Neue Juristische Wochenschrift* 7 (1954): 376–7.

Mabire, Jean. *La Division "Tête de mort" (Totenkopf)*. Paris: J. Grancher, 1994.

————. *SS en France, mai–juin 1940*. Paris: J. Grancher, 1988.

Mabon, Armelle. "La tragédie de Thiaroye, symbole d'un déni d'égalité." *Hommes & migrations*, no. 1235 (2002): 86–95.

————. "Les prisonniers de guerre coloniaux durant l'occupation en France." *Hommes & migrations*, no. 1228 (2000): 15–28.

Mabon, Armelle, and Martine Cuttier. "La singulière captivité des prisonniers de guerre africains (1939–1945)." In *Les prisonniers de guerre dans l'histoire. Contacts entre peuples et cultures*, edited by Caucanas, Sylvie, Rémy Cazals, and Pascal Payen, 137–54. Carcassonne and Toulouse: Les Audois and Editions Privat, 2003.

MacKenzie, Simon Paul. "The Treatment of Prisoners of War in World War II." *The Journal of Modern History* 66, no. 3 (1994): 487–520.

Macmaster, Neil. *Racism in Europe, 1870–2000*. Basingstoke: Palgrave, 2001.

Maguire, Peter. *Law and War: An American Story*. New York: Columbia University Press, 2000.

Manceron, Gilles. *Marianne et les colonies. Une introduction à l'histoire coloniale de la France*. Paris: La Découverte/Ligue des Droits de l'Homme, 2003.

Mann, Erick. *Mikono ya Damu: "Hands of Blood." African Mercenaries and the Politics of Conflict in German East Africa, 1888–1904*. Frankfurt am Main: Peter Lang, 2002.

Manoschek, Walter, ed. *Die Wehrmacht im Rassenkrieg. Der Vernichtungskrieg hinter der Front*. Vienna: Picus Verlag, 1996.

————, ed. *"Es gibt nur eines für das Judentum: Vernichtung." Das Judenbild in deutschen Soldatenbriefen 1939–1944*. Hamburg: Hamburger Edition, 1995.

Marks, Sally. "Black Watch on the Rhine: A Study in Propaganda, Prejudice and Prurience." *European Studies Review* 13 (1983): 297–334.

Martin, Gregory. "German and French Perceptions of the French North and West African Contingents, 1910–1918." *Militärgeschichtliche Mitteilungen* 56 (1997): 31–68.

Martin, Peter. "'. . . auf jeden Fall zu erschießen.' Schwarze Kriegsgefangene in den Lagern der Nazis." *Mittelweg 36* 8, no. 5 (1999): 76–91.

————. "'Kulturpest.' Der Kampf der Nazis gegen die 'negerische Unkultur.'" *Mittelweg 36* 8, no. 1 (1999): 66–77.

————. "'Schwarze Pest.' Traditionen einer Diffamierung." *Mittelweg 36* 4, no. 3 (1995): 69–81.

_____. *Schwarze Teufel, edle Mohren*. Hamburg: Junius, 1993.

Martin, Peter, and Christine Alonzo, eds. *Zwischen Charleston und Stechschritt: Schwarze im Nationalsozialismus*. Hamburg: Dölling und Galitz, 2004.

Martinet, Jean-Claude. *Histoire de l'occupation et de la résistance dans la Nièvre 1940–1944*. La Charité-sur-Loire: Éditions Delayance, 1978.

Maß, Sandra. "Das Trauma des weißen Mannes. Afrikanische Kolonialsoldaten in propagandistischen Texten, 1914–1923." *L'Homme. Zeitschrift für feministische Geschichtswissenschaft* 12, no. 1 (2001): 11–33.

Masson, Philippe. *Histoire de l'armée allemande 1939–1945*. Paris: Perrin, 1994.

Matthäus, Jürgen. "Ausbildungsziel Judenmord? Zum Stellenwert der 'weltanschaulichen Erziehung' von SS und Polizei im Rahmen der 'Endlösung.'" *Zeitschrift für Geschichtswissenschaft* 47, no. 8 (1999): 673–99.

Matthäus, Jürgen, Konrad Kwiet, Jürgen Förster, and Richard Breitman. *Ausbildungsziel Judenmord? "Weltanschauliche Erziehung" von SS, Polizei und Waffen-SS im Rahmen der "Endlösung."* Frankfurt am Main: Fischer Taschenbuch Verlag, 2003.

May, Ernest R. *Strange Victory: Hitler's Conquest of France*. New York: Hill and Wang, 2000.

Mbengue, Papawongue, Sembène Ousmane, and Thierno Faty Sow. "Camp de Thiaroye." 152 min.: Société nouvelle de promotion cinématographique, 1987.

Mehner, Kurt, ed. *Die Waffen-SS und Polizei 1939–1945. Führung und Truppe. Aus den Akten des Bundesarchivs Koblenz*. Norderstedt: Militär-Verlag Patzwall, 1995.

Messenger, Charles. *The Chronological Atlas of World War II*. New York: Macmillan, 1989.

Messerschmidt, Manfred. "Die Wehrmacht als tragende Säule des NS-Staates (1933–1939)." In *Die Wehrmacht im Rassenkrieg. Der Vernichtungskrieg hinter der Front*, edited by Manoschek, Walter, 39–54. Vienna: Picus Verlag, 1996.

_____. "Völkerrecht und 'Kriegsnotwendigkeit' in der deutschen militärischen Tradition." In *Was damals Recht war... NS-Militär- und Strafjustiz im Vernichtungskrieg*, edited by Messerschmidt, Manfred, 191–229. Essen: Klartext, 1996.

_____. *Militärgeschichtliche Aspekte der Entwicklung des deutschen Nationalstaates*. Düsseldorf: Droste, 1988.

———. *Die Wehrmachtsjustiz im Dienste des Nationalsozialismus.* Baden-Baden: Nomos Verlagsgesellschaft, 1987.

———. "Völkerrecht und 'Kriegsnotwendigkeit' in der deutschen militärischen Tradition seit den Einigungskriegen." *German Studies Review* 6, no. 2 (1983): 237–69.

———. *Die Wehrmacht im N.S.-Staat. Zeit der Indoktrination.* Hamburg: Decker, 1969.

Metzger, Chantal. *L'empire colonial français dans la stratégie du Troisième Reich (1936–1945).* Frankfurt: Lang, 2002.

Meyer, Ahlrich. "Kriegs- und Besatzungsverbrechen in Frankreich 1940–1944." In *Kriegsverbrechen im 20. Jahrhundert,* edited by Wette, Wolfram, and Gerd R. Überschär, 274–87. Darmstadt: Primus Verlag, 2001.

Michel, Marc. "Colonisation et défense nationale. Le Général Mangin et la force noire." *Guerres mondiales et conflits contemporains* 37, no. 145 (1987): 27–44.

———. *L'appel à l'Afrique: contributions et réactions à l'effort de guerre en A.O.F. (1914–1919), Publications de la Sorbonne. Série "Afrique" 6.* Paris: Publications de la Sorbonne, 1982.

Militärgeschichtliches Forschungsamt, ed. *Das Deutsche Reich und der Zweite Weltkrieg.* Stuttgart and Munich: Deutsche Verlags-Anstalt, 1979.

Ministère de la Défense, ed. *Les Tirailleurs sénégalais dans la campagne de France 10 mai – 25 juin 1940, Collection "Mémoire et Citoyenneté" 10.* Paris: Ministère de la défense, 2001.

"'Missions sans frontières' Chasselay-Montluzin 19–20 juin 1940." *L'Ancre d'Or,* no. 178 (1977): 9–10.

Moir, Guthrie. *Beyond Hatred.* Philadelphia: Fortress Press, 1970.

Monson, Jamie. "Relocating Maji Maji: The Politics of Alliance and Authority in the Southern Highlands of Tanzania, 1870–1918." *Journal of African History* 39, no. 1 (1998): 95–120.

Moore, Bob. "Unruly Allies: British Problems with the French Treatment of Axis Prisoners of War, 1943–1945." *War in History* 7, no. 2 (2000): 180–98.

Moore, Bob, and Kent Fedorowich. *Prisoners of War and Their Captors in World War II.* Oxford and Washington, D.C.: Berg, 1996.

———. "Prisoners of War in the Second World War: An Overview." In *Prisoners of War and Their Captors in World War II,* edited by Moore, Bob, and Kent Fedorowich, 1–17. Oxford and Washington, D.C.: Berg, 1996.

Müller, Klaus-Dieter, Konstantin Nikischkin, and Günther Wagenlehner, eds. *Die Tragödie der Gefangenenschaft in Deutschland und der Sowjetunion 1941–1956.* Köln: Böhlau, 1998.

Müller, Klaus-Jürgen. "Die deutsche öffentliche Meinung und Frankreich 1933–1939." In *Deutschland und Frankreich 1936–1939. 15. Deutsch-Französisches Historikerkolloquium des DHI in Paris,* edited by Hildebrand, Klaus, and Karl Ferdinand Werner, 17–46. Munich: Artemis-Verlag, 1981.

Müller, Rolf-Dieter, and Gerd R. Überschär. *Hitlers Krieg im Osten 1941–1945: Ein Forschungsbericht.* Darmstadt: Wissenschaftliche Buchgesellschaft, 2000.

Müller, Rolf-Dieter, and Erich Volkmann, eds. *Die Wehrmacht. Mythos und Realität.* Munich: Oldenbourg Verlag, 1999.

Naranch, Bradley D. "'Colonized Body,' 'Oriental Machine': Debating Race, Railroads, and the Politics of Reconstruction in Germany and East Africa, 1906–1910." *Central European History* 33, no. 3 (2001): 299–338.

Nehring, Hubertus, ed. *90 Jahre – Fast ein Jahrhundert. Walter K. Nehring 15.8.1892–15.8.1982.* Siek: Selbstverlag, 1982.

Nelson, Keith. "'The Black Horror on the Rhine.' Race as a Factor in Post-World War I Diplomacy." *Journal of Modern History* 42, no. 4 (1970): 606–27.

Neulen, Hans Werner. *Europa und das Dritte Reich: Einigungsbestrebungen im deutschen Machtbereich.* Munich: Universitas-Verlag, 1987.

———. *Eurofaschismus und der Zweite Weltkrieg. Europas verratene Söhne.* Munich: Universitas-Verlag, 1980.

Nuhn, Walter. *Flammen über Deutschost: Der Maji-Maji-Aufstand in Deutsch-Ostafrika 1905–1906.* Bonn: Bernhard & Graefe, 1998.

Oliver, Roland. *The African Experience: Major Themes in African History from Earliest Times to the Present.* New York: Harper Collins, 1991.

Onana, Charles. *La France et ses tirailleurs. Enquête sur les combattants de la République.* Paris: Editions Duboiris, 2003.

Opitz, May, Katharina Oguntoye, and Dagmar Schultz. *Showing Our Colors: Afro-German Women Speak Out.* Translated by Adams, Anne V. Amherst: University of Massachusetts Press, 1992.

Osterloh, Jörg. "'Hier handelt es sich um die Vernichtung einer Weltanschauung . . .' – Die Wehrmacht und die Behandlung der sowjetischen Gefangenen in Deutschland." In *Die Wehrmacht. Mythos und Realität,* edited by Müller, Rolf-Dieter, and Erich Volkmann, 783–802. Munich: Oldenbourg, 1999.

————. *Sowjetische Kriegsgefangene 1941–1945 im Spiegel nationaler und internationaler Untersuchungen. Forschungsüberblick und Bibliographie.* 2 ed. Dresden: Hannah-Arendt-Institut für Totalitarismusforschung, 1996.

Paillat, Claude. *Le désastre de 1940. La guerre éclair, Dossiers secrets de la France contemporaine 5.* Paris: Robert Laffont, 1985.

Pannetier, Pierre. "Le quarante-quatrième tirailleur." *Bulletin de la Société Scientifique et Artistique de Clamecy* (2000): 65–83.

Patin, M. "La France et le jugement des crimes de guerre." *Revue de science criminelle et de droit pénal comparé* 6 (1951): 393–405.

Péan, Pierre. *Vies et morts de Jean Moulin.* Paris: Fayard, 1998.

Pendaries, Yveline. *Les procès de Rastatt (1946–1954): Le jugement des crimes de guerre en zone française d'occupation en Allemagne.* Bern: Lang, 1995.

Penny, H. Glenn, and Matti Bunzl. *Worldly Provincialism: German Anthropology in the Age of Empire, Social history, popular culture, and politics in Germany.* Ann Arbor: University of Michigan Press, 2003.

Pohl, Karl Heinrich, ed. *Wehrmacht und Vernichtungspolitik. Militär im nationalsozialistischen System.* Göttingen: Vandenhoeck & Ruprecht, 1999.

Pommerin, Rainer. *Sterilisierung der Rheinlandbastarde. Das Schicksal einer farbigen deutschen Minderheit 1918–1937.* Düsseldorf: Droste, 1979.

Proctor, Robert. *Racial Hygiene: Medicine under the Nazis.* Cambridge: Harvard University Press, 1988.

Reed-Anderson, Paulette. *Eine Geschichte von mehr als 100 Jahren. Die Anfänge der afrikanischen Diaspora in Berlin.* Berlin: Ausländerbeauftragte des Senats, 1995.

Reinders, Robert C. "Racialism on the Left: E. D. Morel and the 'Black Horror on the Rhine.'" *International Review of Social History* 13 (1968): 1–28.

Reuth, Ralph Georg. *Goebbels.* Translated by Winston, Krishna. New York: Harcourt Brace & Company, 1993.

Rey, Francis. "Violations du droit international commises par les allemands en France dans la guerre de 1939." *Revue générale de droit international public* 49, no. 2 (1945–6): 1–127.

Rieß, Volker. "Malmédy – Verbrechen, Justiz und Nachkriegspolitik." In *Kriegsverbrechen im 20. Jahrhundert,* edited by Wette, Wolfram, and Gerd R. Überschär, 247–58. Darmstadt: Primus Verlag, 2001.

Riesz, János. "Léopold Sédar Senghor in deutscher Kriegsgefangenschaft." In *Zwischen Charleston und Stechschritt. Schwarze im*

Nationalsozialismus, edited by Martin, Peter, and Christine Alonzo, 596–603. Hamburg: Dölling and Galitz, 2004.

———. "L'Afrique dans les lettres allemandes entre les deux guerres (1919–1939)." In *Rencontres franco-allemandes sur l'Afrique. Lettres, sciences humaines et sociales*, edited by D'Almeida-Topor, Hélène, and János Riesz, 103–16. Paris: L'Harmattan, 1992.

Riesz, János, and Joachim Schultz, eds. *"Tirailleurs sénégalais": zur bildlichen und literarischen Darstellung afrikanischer Soldaten im Dienste Frankreichs.* Frankfurt am Main: Peter Lang Verlag, 1989.

Ripley, Tim. *The Wehrmacht: The German Army in World War II, 1939–1945, The Great Armies.* New York: Fitzroy Dearborn, 2003.

Rives, Maurice. "Die Tirailleurs Sénégalais in der Résistance." In *Zwischen Charleston und Stechschritt. Schwarze im Nationalsozialismus*, edited by Martin, Peter, and Christine Alonzo, 675–95. Hamburg: Dölling and Galitz, 2004.

———. "Les combattants de l'honneur (1)." *L'Ancre d'Or*, no. 260 (1991): 27–38.

Rives, Maurice, and Robert Dietrich. *Héros méconnus 1914–1918, 1939–1945.* Paris: Association Frères d'Armes, 1990.

Rocolle, Pierre. *La guerre de 1940: La défaite, 10 mai–25 juin.* Paris: Armand Colin, 1990.

Rolf, David. *Prisoners of the Reich: Germany's Captives 1939–1945.* London: Cooper, 1988.

Rooney, David. "A German Guerilla Chief in Africa." *History Today* (1999): 28–34.

Rossino, Alexander. *Hitler Strikes Poland: Blitzkrieg, Ideology, and Atrocity, Modern War Studies.* Lawrence: University of Kansas Press, 2003.

Ruchniewicz, Malgorzata, and Krzysztof Ruchniewicz. "Die sowjetischen Kriegsverbrechen gegenüber Polen: Katyn 1940." In *Kriegsverbrechen im 20. Jahrhundert*, edited by Wette, Wolfram, and Gerd R. Überschär, 356–69. Darmstadt: Primus Verlag, 2001.

Russo, Henry. *The Vichy Syndrome: History and Memory in France since 1944.* Translated by Goldhammer, Arthur. Cambridge: Harvard University Press, 1991.

Scheck, Raffael. "The Killing of Black Soldiers from the French Army by the *Wehrmacht* in 1940: The Question of Authorization." *German Studies Review* 29 (2005): 595–606.

———. "'They Are Just Savages': German Massacres of Black Soldiers from the French Army in 1940." *Journal of Modern History* 77 (2005): 325–44.

————. *Mothers of the Nation: Right-Wing Women in Weimar Politics.* Oxford and New York: Berg Publishers, 2004.

Schmokel, Wolfe W. *Dream of Empire: German Colonialism 1919–1945.* New Haven: Yale University Press, 1964.

Schneider, Fernand Thiébaud. "Der Krieg in französischer Sicht." In *Entscheidung 1870. Der deutsch-französische Krieg,* edited by Groote, Wolfgang von, and Ursula von Gersdorff, 165–203. Stuttgart: Deutsche Verlags-Anstalt, 1970.

Schreiber, Gerhard. *Deutsche Kriegsverbrechen in Italien. Täter, Opfer, Strafverfolgung.* Munich: Beck, 1996.

Schultz, Joachim. "Die 'Utschebebbes' am Rhein – Zur Darstellung schwarzer Soldaten während der französischen Rheinlandbesetzung (1918–1930)." In *"Tirailleurs sénégalais" und "Schwarze Schande" – Verlaufsformen und Konsequenzen einer deutsch-französischen Auseinandersetzung (1910–1926),* edited by Riesz, János, and Joachim Schultz, 75–95. Frankfurt am Main: Peter Lang, 1989.

Shalit, Ben. *The Psychology of Conflict and Combat.* New York: Praeger, 1988.

Shennan, Andrew. *The Fall of France 1940, Turning Points.* New York: Longman, 2000.

Shils, Edward A., and Morris Janowitz. "Cohesion and Disintegration in the Wehrmacht in World War II." *Public Opinion Quarterly* 12 (1948): 161–75.

Showalter, Dennis. *The Wars of German Unification.* London: Arnold, 2004.

Smith, Helmut Walser. "The Talk of Genocide, the Rhetoric of Miscegenation: Notes on Debates in the German Reichstag Concerning Southwest Africa, 1904–1914." In *The Imperialist Imagination: German Colonialism and Its Legacy,* edited by Friedrichsmeyer, Sara, Sara Lennox, and Susanne Zantop, 107–23. Ann Arbor: Michigan University Press, 1998.

Smith, Woodruff D. *The German Colonial Empire.* Chapel Hill: University of North Carolina Press, 1978.

Solchany, Jean. "La lente dissipation d'une légende: La 'Wehrmacht' sous le regard de l'histoire." *Revue d'Histoire Moderne et Contemporaine* 47, no. 2 (2000): 323–53.

————. *Comprendre le nazisme dans l'Allemagne des années zéro (1945–1949).* Paris: Presses universitaires de France, 1997.

Speed, Richard B. *Prisoners, Diplomats, and the Great War: A Study in the Diplomacy of Captivity.* New York: Greenwood Press, 1990.

Staub, Ervin. *The Roots of Evil: The Origins of Genocide and Other Group Violence.* Cambridge and New York: Cambridge University Press, 1989.

Stein, George H. *The Waffen SS: Hitler's Elite Guard at War.* Ithaca: Cornell University Press, 1966.

Sterckx, Claude. *La tête et les seins: La mutilation rituelle des ennemis et le concept de l'âme, Forschungen zur Anthropologie und Religionsgeschichte 6.* Saarbrücken: Homo et Religio, 1981.

Stollowsky, Otto, and John W. East, trans. "On the Background to the Rebellion in German East Africa in 1905–1906." *International Journal of African Historical Studies* 21, no. 4 (1988): 677–96.

Streim, Alfred. *Die Behandlung sowjetischer Kriegsgefangener im "Fall Barbarossa."* Heidelberg: Juristischer Verlag, 1981.

Streit, Christian. "Deutsche und sowjetische Kriegsgefangene." In *Kriegsverbrechen im 20. Jahrhundert,* edited by Wette, Wolfram, and Gerd R. Überschär, 178–92. Darmstadt: Primus Verlag, 2001.

———. "Die sowjetischen Kriegsgefangenen in der Hand der Wehrmacht." In *Die Wehrmacht im Rassenkrieg. Der Vernichtungskrieg hinter der Front,* edited by Manoschek, Walter, 74–89. Vienna: Picus Verlag, 1996.

———. "Die Behandlung der verwundeten sowjetischen Kriegsgefangenen." In *Vernichtungskrieg. Verbrechen der Wehrmacht 1941–1944,* edited by Heer, Hannes, and Klaus Naumann, 78–91. Hamburg: Hamburger Edition, 1995.

———. *Keine Kameraden. Die Wehrmacht und die sowjetischen Kriegsgefangenen 1941–1945.* Stuttgart: Deutsche Verlags-Anstalt, 1978.

Suderow, Bruce A. "The Battle of the Crater: The Civil War's Worst Massacre." In *Black Flag over Dixie: Racial Atrocities and Reprisals in the Civil War,* edited by Urwin, Gregory J. W., 203–9. Carbondale: Southern Illinois University Press, 2004.

Sunseri, Thaddeus. "Majimaji and the Millennium: Abrahamic Sources and the Creation of a Tanzanian Resistance Tradition." *History in Africa* 26 (1999): 365–78.

———. "Famine and Wild Pigs: Gender Struggles and the Outbreak of the Majimaji War in Uzaramo (Tanzania)." *Journal of African History* 38, no. 2 (1997): 235–59.

Susini, Jean-Luc. "La perception des 'troupes noires' par les allemands." In *Les troupes coloniales dans la Grande Guerre,* 53–67. Paris: Economica, 1997.

Sydnor, Charles W. Jr. *Soldiers of Destruction: The SS Death's Head Division, 1933–1945.* Princeton: Princeton University Press, 1977.

Taylor, Barry. "Prussian Jungle Tactics." *Military History* 8, no. 2 (1991): 8–16.

Tessin, Georg. *Verbände und Truppen der deutschen Wehrmacht und Waffen-SS im Zweiten Weltkrieg 1939–1945.* 17 vols. Osnabrück: Biblio-Verlag, 1972–2002.

Thierry, Christophe. "Janette Colas: une employée des postes résistante à Clamecy." Mémoire de Maîtrise, Université de Bourgogne Dijon, 1996.

Thies, Klaus-Jürgen. *Der Westfeldzug: 10. Mai bis 25. Juni. Ein Lageatlas der Operationsabteilung des Generalstabs des Heeres, Der Zweite Weltkrieg im Kartenbild, 3.* Osnabrück: Biblio-Verlag, 1994.

Thomas, Martin. *The French Empire at War 1940–45.* Manchester and New York: Manchester University Press, 1998.

———. "Captives of Their Countrymen: Free French and Vichy French POWs in Africa and the Middle East, 1940–43." In *Prisoners of War and Their Captors in World War II,* edited by Moore, Bob, and Kent Fedorowich, 87–118. Oxford and Washington, D.C.: Berg, 1996.

Thornton, John Kelly. *Warfare in Atlantic Africa, 1500–1800, Warfare and History.* London and New York: UCL Press, 1999.

Totten, Samuel, William S. Parsons, and Israel W. Charny. *Genocide in the Twentieth Century: Critical Essays and Eyewitness Accounts.* New York: Garland Publishers, 1995.

"Troupes Coloniales en 1939–1940: La mobilisation et la période d'attente." *L'Ancre d'Or Bazeilles,* no. 256 (1990): 27–38.

Ulrich, Herbert. "Vergeltung, Zeitdruck, Sachzwang. Die deutsche Wehrmacht in Frankreich und der Ukraine." *Mittelweg 36* 11, no. 6 (2002): 25–42.

Umbreit, Hans. "Intervention." In *Deutschland und Frankreich 1936–1939. 15. Deutsch-Französisches Historikerkolloquium des DHI in Paris,* edited by Hildebrand, Klaus, and Karl Ferdinand Werner, 671–3. Munich: Artemis-Verlag, 1981.

———. *Der Militärbefehlshaber in Frankreich, 1940–1944.* Boppard: Boldt, 1968.

Urwin, Gregory J. W., ed. *Black Flag over Dixie: Racial Atrocities and Reprisals in the Civil War.* Carbondale: Southern Illinois University Press, 2004.

———. "'We *Cannot* Treat Negroes . . . as Prisoners of War': Racial Atrocities and Reprisals in Civil War Arkansas." In *Black Flag over Dixie: Racial Atrocities and Reprisals in the Civil War,* edited by Urwin, Gregory J. W., 132–52. Carbondale: Southern Illinois University Press, 2004.

Vaillant, Janet G. *Black, French, and African: A Life of Léopold Sédar Senghor.* Cambridge: Harvard University Press, 1990.

Vandervort, Bruce. *Wars of Imperial Conquest in Africa, 1830–1914.* Bloomington: Indiana University Press, 1998.

Vogel, Detlef. "Der Kriegsalltag im Spiegel von Feldpostbriefen (1939–1945)." In *Der Krieg des kleinen Mannes: Eine Militärgeschichte von unten,* edited by Wette, Wolfram, 199–212. Munich: Piper, 1992.

Waller, James. *Becoming Evil: How Ordinary People Commit Genocide and Mass Killing.* Oxford and New York: Oxford University Press, 2002.

Wegner, Bernd. *Hitlers politische Soldaten. Die Waffen-SS 1933–1945: Studien zu Leitbild, Struktur und Funktion einer nationalsozialistischen Elite.* 2 ed. Paderborn: Schöningh, 1982.

Weinberg, Gerhard L. "Total war: the global dimensions of conflict." In *A World at Total War: Global Conflict and the Politics of Destruction, 1937–1947,* edited by Chickering, Roger, Stig Förster, and Bernd Greiner, 19–32. Cambridge and New York: Cambridge University Press, 2005.

Westwood, Howard C. "Captured Black Union Soldiers in Charleston: What to Do?" In *Black Flag over Dixie: Racial Atrocities and Reprisals in the Civil War,* edited by Urwin, Gregory J. W., 34–51. Carbondale: Southern Illinois University Press, 2004.

Wette, Wolfram, ed. *Zivilcourage: Empörte, Helfer und Retter aus Wehrmacht, Polizei und SS.* Frankfurt am Main: Fischer Taschenbuch Verlag, 2004.

———. *Die Wehrmacht. Feindbilder, Vernichtungskrieg, Legenden.* 2 ed. Frankfurt am Main: Fischer, 2002.

———, ed. *Retter in Uniform. Handlungsspielräume im Vernichtungskrieg der Wehrmacht.* Frankfurt am Main: Fischer Taschenbuch Verlag, 2002.

———. "'Rassenfeind.' Antisemitismus und Antislawismus in der Wehrmachtpropaganda." In *Die Wehrmacht im Rassenkrieg. Der Vernichtungskrieg hinter der Front,* edited by Manoschek, Walter, 55–73. Vienna: Picus Verlag, 1996.

———, ed. *Der Krieg des kleinen Mannes: Eine Militärgeschichte von unten.* Munich: Piper, 1992.

Wette, Wolfram, and Gerd R. Überschär, eds. *Kriegsverbrechen im 20. Jahrhundert.* Darmstadt: Primus Verlag, 2001.

Wieland, Lothar. *Belgien 1914. Die Frage des belgischen "Franctireurkrieges" und die deutsche öffentliche Meinung 1914–1936, Studien zum Kontinuitätsproblem der deutschen Geschichte 2.* Frankfurt am Main: Peter Lang, 1984.

Wigger, Iris. "Wenn 'Wilde wie Herren im Herzen Europas hausen.' Das Dogma weißer Überlegenheit in der Kampagne gegen die 'Schwarze

Schmach.'" In *Zwischen Charleston und Stechschritt. Schwarze im Nationalsozialismus*, edited by Martin, Peter, and Christine Alonzo, 137–41. Hamburg: Dölling und Galitz, 2004.

Williams, John. *The Ides of May: The Defeat of France, May–June 1940.* London: Constable, 1968.

Wittendorfer, Frank. "Waffenstillstand, Rheinlandbesetzung, Versailler Vertrag und Ruhreinbruch: Nachlässe französischer Offiziere im Heeresarchiv Vincennes." *Militärgeschichtliche Mitteilungen* 49, no. 2 (1990): 143–6.

Wrochem, Oliver von. "Die Auseinandersetzung mit Wehrmachtsverbrechen im Prozeß gegen den Generalfeldmarschall von Manstein 1949." *Zeitschrift für Geschichtswissenschaft* 46, no. 4 (1998): 329–53.

Young, Robert. *France and the Origins of the Second World War.* New York: St. Martin's, 1996.

Zayas, Alfred-Maurice de. "The Wehrmacht Bureau on War Crimes." *The Historical Journal* 35, no. 2 (1992): 383–99.

———. *The Wehrmacht War Crimes Bureau 1939–45.* Lincoln: University of Nebraska Press, 1990.

Zeck, Mario. *Das Schwarze Korps: Geschichte und Gestalt des Organs der Reichsführung SS.* Tübingen: Niemeyer, 2002.

Zeidler, Manfred. "Die Tötungs- und Vergewaltigungsverbrechen der Roten Armee." In *Kriegsverbrechen im 20. Jahrhundert*, edited by Wette, Wolfram, and Gerd R. Überschär, 419–32. Darmstadt: Primus Verlag, 2001.

Zeidler, Manfred, and Ute Schmidt, eds. *Gefangene in deutschem und sowjetischem Gewahrsam 1941–1956: Dimensionen und Definitionen, Berichte und Studien. Hannah-Arendt-Institut für Totalitarismusforschung e.V. an der Technischen Universität Dresden, 23.* Dresden: Hannah-Arendt-Institut für Totalitarismusforschung e.V. an der Technischen Universität Dresden, 1999.

Zimmerer, Jürgen, and Joachim Zeller, eds. *Völkermord in Deutsch-Südwestafrika. Der Kolonialkrieg (1904–1908) in Namibia und seine Folgen.* Berlin: Christoph Links Verlag, 2003.

Zuckerman, Larry. *The Rape of Belgium: The Untold Story of World War I.* New York: New York University Press, 2004.

Index